Medieval
Clothing and Textiles

Volume 16

Medieval
Clothing and Textiles

ISSN 1744-5787

Medieval
Clothing and Textiles

Volume 16

edited by

MONICA L. WRIGHT

with the assistance of

ROBIN NETHERTON

and

GALE R. OWEN-CROCKER

THE BOYDELL PRESS

First published 2020
The Boydell Press, Woodbridge

ISBN 978-1-78327-515-1

The Boydell Press is an imprint of Boydell & Brewer Ltd
PO Box 9, Woodbridge, Suffolk IP12 3DF, UK
and of Boydell & Brewer Inc.
668 Mt Hope Avenue, Rochester, NY 14620–2731, USA
website: www.boydellandbrewer.com

A CIP catalogue record for this book is available
from the British Library

The publisher has no responsibility for the continued existence or accuracy of URLs for
external or third-party internet websites referred to in this book, and does not guarantee that
any content on such websites is, or will remain, accurate or appropriate

This publication is printed on acid-free paper

Typeset by Sparks Publishing Services Ltd—www.sparkspublishing.com

Printed and bound in Great Britain by TJ International Ltd, Padstow, Cornwall

Contents

Illustrations

The editor, contributors, and publishers are grateful to all the institutions and persons listed for permission to reproduce the materials in which they hold copyright. Every effort has been made to trace the copyright holders; apologies are offered for any omission, and the publishers will be pleased to add any necessary acknowledgement in subsequent editions.

Tables

Contributors

MONICA L. WRIGHT (Editor) is the Granger and Debaillon Professor of French and Medieval Studies at the University of Louisiana at Lafayette. Her publications include the book *Weaving Narrative: Clothing in Twelfth-Century Romance* (2009) and many articles on the use of clothing in medieval French literature. She wrote a chapter on literary representations of clothing in literature for the "Medieval Age" volume of the six-volume *Cultural History of Dress and Fashion* (2016). Her most recent article in *Medieval Clothing and Textiles* (in volume 14) examined the French literary sources for the term *bliaut*.

MELANIE SCHUESSLER BOND is Professor of Costume Design at Eastern Michigan University and author of *Dressing the Scottish Court, 1543–1553: Clothing in the Accounts of the Lord High Treasurer of Scotland* (2019). Her scholarly work focuses on clothing in England, Scotland, France, and the Low Countries in the mid- to late sixteenth century. In addition to research and writing, she designs costumes for both academic and professional theatre. Professional costume design credits include shows for the Michigan Shakespeare Festival, Williamston Theatre (Williamston, Michigan), Tipping Point Theatre (Northville, Michigan), Croswell Opera House (Adrian, Michigan), Skylight Opera Theatre (Milwaukee), and the Milwaukee Shakespeare Company.

JOHN BLOCK FRIEDMAN is a Visiting Scholar at the Center for Medieval and Renaissance Studies at Ohio State University and the author, editor, or associate editor of numerous books and articles. Recent scholarship includes (with Kristen Figg and Kathrin Giogoli) *Book of Wonders of the World: Secrets of Natural History, BNF MS fr.22971: Studies and Translation of the Facsimile Edition* (2018). His past articles in *Medieval Clothing and Textiles* have addressed such topics as medieval hair removal, fashions for animals, and dagged clothing. He is currently exploring the topic of the mirror, especially carved ivory cosmetic mirrors, and Chaucer's *Merchant's Tale*.

M. WENDY HENNEQUIN is Professor of English and Women's Studies at Tennessee State University, where she teaches writing, women's studies, and literature classes ranging from World Literature I to Medieval Literature to Shakespeare to *Harry Potter*. She has published frequently on Old English literature, particularly *Beowulf*, pedagogy, and medieval literature. Her current research projects include a pedagogical project on

Harry Potter and a study of Anglo-Norman power couple Earl Waltheof and Countess Judith, the last Anglo-Saxon earl and niece of William the Conqueror (collaborating with historian Elizabeth Dachowski). This is her first foray into textile studies.

CYNTHIA JACKSON is a professional embroiderer, international tutor, and independent researcher based in Ottawa, Canada. As a maker, her specialist interest is the investigation and reconstruction of sixteenth-century embroidery. Her research focuses on professional Tudor embroiderers and the impact of their craft on the material culture of early modern England.

MARK D. JOHNSTON is professor emeritus of Modern Languages at DePaul University in Chicago. His publications include numerous studies and translations of medieval conduct literature, the Catalan lay philosopher Ramon Llull, and the Spanish prelate Hernando de Talavera.

MAGGIE KNEEN is a professional illustrator with an M.A. in Graphic Design from the Central School of Art and Design (now Central St. Martin's) and an internationally known children's book illustrator and author. For her second Master's degree at the University of Manchester, she wrote her dissertation on the architectural structures of the Bayeux Tapestry. She now works principally as an illustrator for archaeologists and historians of art and architecture, reenvisaging earlier stages of Anglo-Saxon buildings such as Deerhurst Church and the structures at the seventh-century royal palace of Yeavering.

ROBIN NETHERTON (Book Reviews Editor) is a costume historian specializing in Western European clothing of the Middle Ages and its interpretation by artists and historians. Since 1982, she has given lectures and workshops on practical aspects of medieval dress and on costume as an approach to social history, art history, and literature. Her published articles have addressed such topics as fourteenth-century sleeve embellishments, the cut of Norman tunics, and medieval Greenlanders' interpretation of European female fashion. A journalist by training, she also works as a professional editor.

GALE R. OWEN-CROCKER is Professor Emerita of the University of Manchester. Her recent publications on dress and textiles include *Refashioning Medieval and Early Modern Dress: A Tribute to Robin Netherton*, with Maren Clegg Hyer (2019); *Clothing the Past: Surviving Garments from Early Medieval to Early Modern Western Europe*, with Elizabeth Coatsworth (2018); *Making Sense of the Bayeux Tapestry: Readings and Reworkings*, with Anna Henderson (2016); articles on "Dress" (2014) and "Textiles" (2012) in Oxford Bibliographies Online: Medieval Studies, both with Elizabeth Coatsworth; The Lexis of Cloth and Clothing in Britain ca. 700–1450, a database available at http://lexisproject.arts.manchester.ac.uk; *Medieval Dress and Textiles in Britain: A*

Multilingual Sourcebook, with Louise Sylvester and Mark Chambers (2014); *Encyclopedia of Dress and Textiles in the British Isles c. 450–1450*, with Elizabeth Coatsworth and Maria Hayward (2012); and *The Bayeux Tapestry: Collected Papers* (2012).

GIT SKOGLUND is a textile historian based in Gothenburg, Sweden. Her research focuses on ethnological and botanical aspects of textile production, with special depth on hemp and hops textiles. Her scholarship has been awarded funding from the Agnes Geijer Foundation for Nordic textile research.

JOHN SLEFINGER holds a Ph.D. in Medieval Literature and is a humanities teacher at the Derryfield School in Manchester, New Hampshire. After completing a dissertation on the relationship between material culture and allegory, he has focused on the ambiguity of Langland's representation of clothing in *Piers Plowman*. He is also interested in the theatricality of fifteenth-century mystery plays, focusing specifically on the tension between the moral valances attached to costume in the text and the audience members' dress.

Preface

Volume 16 continues this journal's tradition of publishing a wide range of studies from a variety of disciplines, and this particular volume boasts an unusually large number of images. The seven essays extend chronologically from the tenth through the sixteenth century and cover a wide geography: Scandinavia to Spain, with stops in England and the Low Countries.

M. Wendy Hennequin provides a detailed examination of lexical items for banners in the Old English *Beowulf* and argues that the prevalence of such terms in the poem attest to the cultural importance of banners for the society, as well as their poetic significance.

Maggie Kneen and Gale R. Owen-Crocker propose a fascinating new theory about the composition of the Bayeux Tapestry: They present evidence that multiple embroiderers used curved templates to draw the tapestry's design, which contributed to the uniform appearance.

Git Skoglund's essay opens a previously under-studied line of inquiry into the cultivation of hemp for textile production in medieval Scandinavia and provides an overview of conditions for and practices involved in growing hemp and its transformation into textiles.

By reading the character of Lady Mede (*Piers Plowman*) in the context of costume history, John Slefinger brings new depth to our understanding of her allegorical clothing and how fourteenth-century English authors used allegory generally.

By placing Spanish *verdugados* (farthingales) in their historical context and analyzing their use as political propaganda, Mark D. Johnston illustrates how Juana of Portugal's detractors used her clothing to demean her and turned their derision to the article of clothing itself.

John Bloch Friedman and Melanie Schuessler Bond provide an analysis of the sartorial imagery on a Dutch tabletop painting (attributed to Bosch) depicting the Seven Deadly Sins, arguing that the specific styles shown offer a complex message that conveys at once desirability and outmodedness, which comments upon fashion's fickleness.

In her article on her reconstruction of a sixteenth-century ceremonial crown from one of the London livery companies, Cynthia Jackson furnishes rich details about materials and techniques that the embroiderers used during the period to produce such ceremonial objects.

Professor Monica L. Wright became the sole editor for the current volume as founding editors Robin Netherton and Gale R. Owen-Crocker assumed an advisory role, for which Monica remains extremely grateful. Monica will be joined by a new collaborator in 2020. Robin and Gale joined the journal's editorial board and remain General Editors of the affiliated book series Medieval and Renaissance Clothing and Textiles (see below).

The editor thanks the board members and the many other scholars who have generously devoted their time and expertise to review article submissions and consult with authors.

We continue to consider for publication in this journal both independent submissions and papers read at sessions sponsored by DISTAFF (Discussion, Interpretation, and Study of Textile Arts, Fabrics, and Fashion) at the international congresses held annually in Kalamazoo, Michigan, and Leeds, England. Proposals from potential conference speakers should be sent to robin@netherton.net (for Kalamazoo) or gale.owencrocker@ntlworld.com (for Leeds). Potential authors for *Medieval Clothing and Textiles* should read our author guidelines at http://www.distaff.org/MCTguidelines. pdf, and send a 300-word synopsis to mlwright@louisiana.edu.

Authors of larger studies interested in submitting a monograph or collaborative book manuscript for our subsidia series, Medieval and Renaissance Clothing and Textiles, should apply using the publication proposal form on the website of our publisher, Boydell & Brewer, at http://www.boydellandbrewer.com/authors_submit_proposal. asp. We encourage potential authors to discuss their ideas with the General Editors, Robin Netherton (robin@netherton.net) and Gale Owen-Crocker (gale.owencrocker@ntlworld.com), before making a formal proposal.

꙼ ꙼ ꙼

It is with great sadness that we announce the death of Michelle (Shelly) Nordtorp-Madson on November 2, 2019, after a long illness. She was Professor Emerita and Chief Curator at the Department of Art History at the University of St. Thomas in St. Paul, Minnesota, where she taught in the Department of Art History. With a special interest in medieval Scandinavia, she worked on the medieval garments from Herjolfsnæs, Greenland, and on dress in Scandinavian literature and medieval art. She was a member of our Editorial Board since the inception of *Medieval Clothing and Textiles*, wrote book reviews for us, and was active in advising the editors on submissions to the journal. She worked valiantly through illness and medical treatment to complete and revise her chapter "Dress, Disguise, and Shapeshifting in *Nibelungenlied* and *Volsunga Saga*," which was published in *Refashioning Medieval and Early Modern Dress: A Tribute to Robin Netherton* (Boydell, 2019) just two weeks after her death.

Anglo-Saxon Banners and *Beowulf*

M. Wendy Hennequin

The poem *Beowulf* is obsessed with treasures. The poet describes hoards in Hrothgar's hall Heorot, in Grendel's mother's underground hall, and in the dragon's hall under the mountain. Many episodes of the poem concern treasure exchange: Hrothgar builds Heorot in order to give treasures; he rewards Beowulf with magnificent treasures; Beowulf gives a sword to a coast guard; Beowulf and his king Hygelac exchange treasures; and the dying Beowulf gives treasures to his loyal thane Wiglaf and his people. Only a few treasures are specifically described, however, generally heirloom swords, and these descriptions usually concern their martial quality rather than their appearance: Hrunting, for instance, is decorated, but more importantly, has never failed in battle and Beowulf judges it to be a good sword, though it could not cut Grendel's mother.[1] Yet the *Beowulf* poet gives pointed time and attention to *segnas*—banners or military standards.[2] The first of these *segnas* is raised above Scyld Scefing's body on his funeral ship (47b). Hrothgar gives an heirloom banner to Beowulf as a reward for defeating Grendel; Beowulf later re-gifts this banner to his own king, Hygelac (1020–22a and 2152). Wiglaf finds the third prominent banner in the dragon's hoard (2767–71a). The poet mentions banners elsewhere briefly in important episodes of the feud between the Swedes and Geats (1202–07b; 2957b–60; 2500–2508a). In a poem that values treasures, but specifies very few, banners, like swords, are meant to be noticed.

This article is an expanded version of a paper presented in May 2018 at a DISTAFF session at the International Congress on Medieval Studies at Kalamazoo, Michigan. The author wishes to thank Robin Netherton for the suggestion to submit to this session; Monica Wright for her interest, encouragement, and feedback; and Elizabeth Dachowski, Sara Burdorff, and Sarah Barott for their feedback and suggestions.

1 *Beowulf*, in *Klaeber's Beowulf and the Fight at Finnsburg*, ed. R. D. Fulk, Robert E. Bjork, and John D. Niles (Toronto: University of Toronto Press, 2008), lines 1455–64 and 807–12. Subsequent references to the poem will be made parenthetically by line number. Translations of Old English texts are my own, unless otherwise noted.

2 Joseph Bosworth and T. Northcote Toller, ed., *An Anglo-Saxon Dictionary Based on the Manuscript Collections of the Late Joseph Bosworth* (1898, repr. Oxford: Clarendon, 1976), 857.

The pointed and repeated mention of these banners, their association with royalty and gift-giving, and the detailed description of the dragon's banner argue that banners carried some cultural weight and textual importance. Yet, while *Beowulf*'s swords are often discussed in literary criticism, the banners have largely gone unstudied. Analyses of these banners, such as those by John Hill, Barbara Raw, and Cameron McNabb, consist of a few sentences in larger discussions of treasure.[3] I have found little analysis of Anglo-Saxon banners in archeological or textile research—again, a few sentences based on primary literary and historical sources. Derek Renn's discussion of flags in the Bayeux Tapestry and Robert W. Jones's studies of banners and pre-heraldic military identification offer more information, but these studies focus on post-Conquest sources.[4] Given their prominence, however, *Beowulf*'s banners deserve the same sort of detailed examination that scholars have given to the poem's swords, for banners serve a similar function. Just as the swords in *Beowulf* indicate royalty and succession[5] and warrior prowess,[6] the banners in *Beowulf*—and in Old English texts generally—signal royalty, military might, and conquest, and like the swords, the giving, receiving, and finding of these banners indicate not only the recognition of prowess but royal succession.

BANNERS IN ANGLO-SAXON DICTION, LITERATURE, AND MATERIAL CULTURE

Beowulf uses three words for banners: *segn*, *cumbol*, and *beacen*. *Segn* occurs most commonly, seven times, once in the kenning "eaforhēafodsegn" [boar's-head banner] (47b, 1021a, 1204a, 2767b, 2776b, 2958b, and 2152b). *Cumbol* occurs twice, once in

3 John M. Hill, "Beowulf and the Danish Succession: Gift Giving as an Occasion for Complex Gesture," *Medievalia et Humanistica: Studies in Medieval and Renaissance Culture* 11 (1982): 177–97, at 183–92; Barbara Raw, "Royal Power and Royal Symbols in *Beowulf*," *The Age of Sutton Hoo: The Seventh Century in North-Western Europe*, ed. M. O. H. Carter (Woodbridge, UK: Boydell, 1992), 167–74, at 172–73; Cameron Hunt McNabb, "'Eldum Unnyt': Treasure Spaces in *Beowulf*," *Neophilologus* 95, no. 1 (2011): 145–64, at 152–56.
4 Derek Renn, "Burhgeat and Gonfanon: Two Sidelights from the Bayeux Tapestry," in *Anglo-Norman Castles*, ed. Robert Liddiard (Woodbridge, UK: Boydell, 2003), 69–90; Robert W. Jones, "Identifying the Warrior on the Pre-Heraldic Battlefield," *Anglo-Norman Studies* XXX (2008), 154–67; Robert W. Jones, *Bloodied Banners: Martial Display on the Medieval Battlefield* (Woodbridge, UK: Boydell, 2015).
5 M. J. Swanton, *Crisis and Development in Germanic Society 700–800: Beowulf and the Burden of Kingship* (Göppingen, Germany: Kümmerle Verlag, 1982), 115; Hill, "Beowulf and the Danish Succession," 183–85, 192–93; Robert Payson Creed, "*Beowulf*'s Fourth Act," in *De Gustibus: Essays for Alain Renoir*, ed. John Miles Foley, J. Chris Womack, and Whitney A. Womack (New York: Garland, 1992), 85–109, at 194.
6 Swanton, *Crisis and Development*, 99; J. D. A. Ogilvy, "Unferth: Foil to Beowulf?" *PMLA* 79, no. 4 (1964): 370–75, at 372; Judy King, "Transforming the Hero: *Beowulf* and the Conversion of Hunferth," in *The Hero Recovered: Essays on Medieval Heroism in Honor of George Clark*, ed. Robin Waugh and James Weldon (Kalamazoo, MI: Medieval Institute, 2010), 47–64, at 50.

line 1022a in the kenning "hildecumbor" [war-banner], and once in 2505b, where the Frisian champion Dæghrefn is designated as the "cumbles hyrde" [banner's guardian]. *Beacen* occurs only once, in reference to the banner in the dragon's hoard (2777a). *Segn, cumbol*, and *beacen* also occur as variations, or poetic appositives, of each other. The "segn" that Hrothgar gives Beowulf (1021a) is called "hildecumbor" in the next line (1022a) and the "segn" that Wiglaf finds in the hoard (2767b) is the "beacna be-orhtost" [brightest of banners] a few lines later (2777a). The poet's use of these three words as variations shows that the words at least denote the same objects or class of objects and that the audience would have recognized these words as synonyms, probably bearing different connotations.

Segn, cumbol, and *beacen* denote banners elsewhere in Old English, but Anglo-Saxon writers also use several other words to signify banners: *þuf, fana* (also spelled *fane* and *fanu*), and *tacn*. All six of these words occur both alone and in kennings such as "eaforhēafodsegn," "hildecumbor," "sigeþuf" [victory-banner], "guðfana" [battle-banner], and "tacnberend" [banner-bearer or standard-bearer]. These banner words occur commonly: A search of *The Dictionary of Old English Web Corpus* for these words and their kennings initially yielded 238 pages of results.[7] These results were artificially inflated; duplicates were common, as a search for *segn* would also include its kennings, and several of the banner words have other meanings. *Segn, tacn*, and *beacen* can all mean "sign" or "token" or even "miracle" as well as "banner," and *beacen* can also denote "beacon" in the modern sense; in its kenning *herebeacen*, it may mean "signal fire" as well as "army-banner."[8] To further confuse the matter, *segn* and *tacn*, with appropriate verbal endings and/or in variant spellings (*segen* and *tacen*), form part of the conjugations of common verbs *seon* (to see), *tacan* (to take), and *tacnian* (to betoken). Still, after eliminating the duplicates and the irrelevant instances, we are left with enough occurrences of these six banner words and their kennings to draw some conclusions about the use of these words, the objects they signified, and the cultural importance of those objects.

The first conclusion that we can draw is that all six of these words—*segn, cumbol, beacen, þuf, tacn*, and *fana*—denote the same object and class of objects. We have seen that *segn, beacen*, and *cumbol* refer to the same objects in *Beowulf*, and this pattern is borne out elsewhere. In *Exodus*, for instance, *segn* and *beacen* both refer to the banner of the tribe of Judah: "Hæfdon him to segne, þa hie on sund stigon, / Ofer bordhreoðan beacen aræred" [They had as their banner, when they rose to the sea, / Over the shield-phalanx, a banner raised up].[9] Also in *Exodus*, *segn* and *cumbol* both refer to the Pharoah's banners:

7 Antonette diPaolo Healey, John Price Wilkin, and Xin Xiang, eds., *The Dictionary of Old English Web Corpus* (Toronto: Dictionary of Old English Project, 2009; hereafter *DOE Corpus*), http://tapor.library.utoronto.ca/doecorpus.

8 Bosworth and Toller, *Anglo-Saxon Dictionary*, 532.

9 *Exodus*, in *The Junius Manuscript*, ed. George Phillip Krapp, Anglo-Saxon Poetic Records 1 (New York: Columbia University Press, 1931), 91–107, at lines 319–20. Subsequent references will be made parenthetically by line number.

Him þær segncyning   wið þone segn foran,
manna þengel,   mearcþreate[10] rad;
guðweard gumena   grimhelm gespeon,
cyning cinberge,   (cumbol lixton),
wiges on wenum … (172–76a)

[There the banner-king, with the banner before him,
The prince of men, rode with the border-troop,
The battle-guardian of warriors fastened his helmet,
The king his chin-strap; the banners shone
In expectation of battle.]

Once again, we have these three words denoting the same objects; the vocabulary varies to fulfill the alliteration. Furthermore, *þuf, fana,* and *tacn* also refer to these objects. In *Exodus*, the Pharoah's banners signified by *segn* and *cumbol* in lines 172b and 175b are called *þufas* earlier: "þufas þunian" [Banners crashed] (159a). *Þuf* and *segn* are used in variation in Cynewulf's *Elene*: "þa þæs þuf hafen, / Seʒn for speotum, sigeleoð ʒalen"[11] [Then was the banner lifted, / The banner before the troops, the victory-song sung]. This variation shows clearly that *segn* and *þuf* refer to the same object—in this case, a representation of the cross, probably on a banner.[12] In the Old English *Judith*, the "sigeþufas" [victory-banners] which the Hebrews bear to battle are called "guðfanum" [battle-banners] less than ten lines later:

Stopon cynerofe,
secgas ond gesiðas,   bæron sigeþufas[13]

[The royally brave ones advanced,
Warriors and companions bore victory banners]
…

syððan Ebreas
under guðfanum   gegan hæfdon
to ðam fyrdwicum. (218b–20a)

[… after the Hebrews
Under battle-banners had gone forth
To the army-dwelling.]

10 Bosworth and Toller (*Anglo-Saxon Dictionary*, 673) gloss *mearc* not only as "limit," "boundary," and "territory," but also as "mark, ensign." Possibly "mearcþreate" here means "banner-troop," but I have not found other instances where "mearc" may mean banner.

11 Cynewulf, *Cynewulf's Elene*, ed. P. O. E. Gradon (Exeter, UK: University of Exeter Press, 1977), lines 124b–25. Subsequent references will be made parenthetically by line number.

12 In *Elene* (99–104), Constantine orders that a "tacen" be made of the "beacen" he saw in his dream of the cross. In other versions of the story, Constantine has the cross painted on shields, but Cynewulf does not specify in his version what form the "tacen" takes. Given the diction here, the implication may be that Constantine is not only *constructing* a banner (*tacen*), but that the cross in his dream was presented as a banner (*beacen*); in line 123b, this object with the cross is later called a "þuf."

13 *Judith*, ed. Mark Griffith (Exeter, UK: University of Exeter Press, 1997), lines 200b–201. Subsequent references will be made parenthetically by line number.

So *guðfana*, a compound of *fana* and *guð* [battle], evidently also denotes the same objects as *þuf, segn, cumbol,* and *beacen. Tacn,* too, can signify these objects, as we find in the Old English translation of Bede's *Ecclesiastical History of the English People*:

> It ðæt sægd, ðæt in ða tid swa micel sib wære in Breotone æghwyder ymb, swa Eadwines rice wære .... Swelce he hæfde swa micle heannisse in þæm cynerice, þætte nales þæt aan þæt heo segn fore him bæron æt gefeohte, ac eac swylce in sibbe tiide, þær he rad betweoh his hamum oðþe be tuunum mid his þegnum, ge þeah he eode, þæt him mon symle þæt tacn beforan bær.[14]

> [It is said that in those times, there was such great peace in Britain, anywhere Eadwine's rule was .... He had such great highness in the kingdom, that not only did they bear a banner before him in battle, but also in peacetime, wherever he rode, among his villages or towns with his thanes, and even if he walked, someone always bore the banner before him.]

Here, the *segn* becomes not a *cumbol* or a *fana* or *guðfana*, but a *tacn*, a word that can also mean "token" or "sign."[15] Oddly enough, the Anglo-Saxon translator of Bede uses the word *tacn* here to translate *tufa* from the original Latin text:

> … semper antecedere signifer consuesset; nec non et incedente illo ubilibet per plateas, illud genus uexilli, quod Romani tufam, Angli appellant thuuf, ante eum ferri solebat.[16]

> [… the royal standard was always borne before him. Even when he passed through the streets on foot, the standard known to the Romans as a *Tufa* and to the English as a *Tuf*, was carried in front of him.][17]

In Latin, the *signifer* of the first clause becomes a *uexilla* in the second, and then a *tufa*, which Bede specifically informs us, is called a *thuuf* (transliterating *þuf*) in English. Yet the Anglo-Saxon translator renders the *tufa* not as *þuf*, but as *tacn*. We can therefore add *tacn* to our list of Old English words referring to banners and standards. Table 1.1 shows the relationships between these Old English words, but to use mathematical shorthand, *segn = cumbol = þuf = fana = beacen = tacn*.

An examination of Latin glosses, as appears in table 1.2, confirms that these six Old English words indeed refer to the same objects or class of objects. *An Anglo-Saxon Dictionary* and the *DOE Corpus* both give multiple examples of *segn* glossing the Latin *vexilla* (also spelled *uexilla*) and *labarum*.[18] But these two sources and the Bosworth-Toller

14 Thomas Miller, ed., *Bede's Ecclesiastical History of the English People* (London: N. Trübner, 1890), 144–46; available online at the Internet Archive, https://archive.org/details/oldenglish-versioo1bede, accessed May 1, 2018.
15 Bosworth and Toller, *Anglo-Saxon Dictionary*, 966–67.
16 Bede, *Historiam Ecclesiasticam Gentis Anglorum*, ed. Charles Plummer (1898), book 2, chap. 16; available online at The Latin Library, www.thelatinlibrary.com/bede.html, accessed March 19, 2018.
17 Bede, *A History of the English Church and People*, trans. Leo Sherley-Price (New York: Penguin, 1968), 132.
18 Bosworth and Toller, *Anglo-Saxon Dictionary*, 857; *DOE Corpus*.

Table 1.1: Banner words and sample variations in Anglo-Saxon texts

This table represents a sampling of poetic variations and translations and is by no means comprehensive or complete. Poetic compounds are listed under the main word (e.g., *sigeþuf* is listed under *þuf*).

Word for banner	Occurrences, including kennings	Variations, including kennings
segn	Bede, *Ecclesiastical History* 144, 184 *Beowulf* 47b, 1021a, 1204a, 2152b, 2767b, 2776b, 2958b *Elene* 124a *Exodus* 172a, 172b, 302a, 585b *Poetical Dialogues of Salomon and Saturn* 444a	tacn (Bede, *Ecclesiastical History* 146) hildecumbor (*Beowulf* 1022a) hondwundra mæst (*Beowulf* 2768b) beacna beorhtost (*Beowulf* 2777a) þuf (*Elene* 123b)
cumbol	*Andreas* 4b, 1204a *Beowulf* 1022a, 2505b *Elene* 25a, 76a, 107a, 259a *Exodus* 175b *Judith* 332a	segn (*Beowulf* 1021a, *Exodus* 172b) beacen (*Elene* 109a)
þuf	*Elene* 123b *Exodus* 160a, 342a *Judith* 201b	segn (*Elene* 124a)
fana / fanu	*Exodus* 249b *Prose Dialogue of Salomon and Saturn* 170	beama (*Exodus* 250a)
guðfana	*Anglo-Saxon Chronicle* MS B 879 *Judith* 219a Orosius, *History* 84, 136	
beacen	*Beowulf* 2777a *Elene* 109a, 162b, 168b, 974a *Exodus* 320b	segn (*Beowulf* 2776b, *Exodus* 319a) tacn (*Elene* 164a)
tacn	Bede, *Ecclesiastical History* 146 *Elene* 164a	beacen (*Elene* 162b) segn (Bede, *Ecclesiastical History* 144)

Sources: Poetic works are cited by line number. Prose works (Bede, *Ecclesiastical History*; *Anglo-Saxon Chronicle*; Orosius, *History*; and *Prose Dialogue of Salomon and Saturn*) are cited by page number of the editions referenced in the accompanying article (see notes 14, 29, 30, and 34, respectively).

Supplement also tell us that *guðfana* and *fana* also translate these two Latin words.[19] *An Anglo-Saxon Dictionary* lists *vexilla* as a Latin gloss for *tacn*, *beacen*, and *þuf* as well.[20] Furthermore, the *DOE Corpus* gives multiple examples of *tacnberend*, *tacnbora(n)*, and *segnbora(n)* [banner-bearer or standard-bearer] glossing the Latin *uexillarii* and *signif-*

19 *DOE Corpus*; T. Northcote Toller, *An Anglo-Saxon Dictionary Based on the Manuscript Collections of Joseph Bosworth: A Supplement* (Oxford: Oxford University Press, 1972), 490.
20 Bosworth and Toller, *Anglo-Saxon Dictionary*, 69, 966, 1075.

Table 1.2: Latin glosses for banner words in Anglo-Saxon texts

These are examples of words used by Anglo-Saxon writers to gloss or translate Latin texts. This list is by no means comprehensive or complete.

Latin text	Old English glosses
labarum[a]	fana (*DOE* "fana") guðfana (*BT Supp* 490, *DOE* "guðfana") segn (*BT* 857, *DOE Corpus*)
signa	guðfana (*BT* 493)
signum militare	cumbol (*BT* 174)
tufa[b]	tacn (*Bede* 146)
uexilla, vexilla[c]	beacen (*BT* 69) fana (*BT* 270, *DOE* "fana") guðfana (*BT Supp* 490, *DOE* "guðfana") segn (*BT* 857, *DOE Corpus*) tacn (*BT* 966) þuf (*BT* 1075)

a The *Dictionary of Old English Web Corpus* entry for *guðfana* and *BT Supp* (490) note several instances where *labarum* glosses both *segn* and *guðfana*.

b The Latin version of the *Ecclesiastical History* says this is a kind of banner called *thuuf* in English.

c The *Dictionary of Old English Web Corpus* also gives examples of glosses of *tacnboran/tacnberend* and *segnboran/segnbora* for *uexillarii* and *signiferi*.

Sources:

Bede: Thomas Miller, ed., *Bede's Ecclesiastical History of the English People* (London: N. Trübner, 1890); available online at the Internet Archive, https://archive.org/details/oldenglishversioo1bede, accessed May 1, 2018.

BT: Joseph Bosworth and T. Northcote Toller, ed., *An Anglo-Saxon Dictionary Based on the Manuscript Collections of the Late Joseph Bosworth (1898, repr. Oxford: Clarendon, 1976).*

BT Supp: T. Northcote Toller, *An Anglo-Saxon Dictionary Based on the Manuscript Collections of Joseph Bosworth: A Supplement* (Oxford: Oxford University Press, 1972).

DOE: Angus Cameron et al., eds., *Dictionary of Old English: A to I*, online ed. (Toronto: Dictionary of Old English Project, 2018), http://tapor.library.utoronto.ca/doe.

DOE Corpus: Antonette diPaolo Healey, John Price Wilkin, and Xin Xiang, eds., *The Dictionary of Old English Web Corpus* (Toronto: Dictionary of Old English Project, 2009), http://tapor.library.utoronto.ca/doecorpus.

eri [standard-bearer].[21] *Cumbol* is glossed as *signum militare,*[22] another Latin synonym for a banner or standard. As these words are used interchangeably in Old English and render synonymous Latin words into Old English, it follows that *segn, beacen, cumbol, þuf, fana*, and *tacn* are referring to the same object or class of objects.

21 *DOE Corpus.*
22 Bosworth and Toller, *Anglo-Saxon Dictionary*, 174.

These words probably bore different connotations, but the nuances in meaning are difficult to determine. Despite the high number of results in the *DOE Corpus*, we generally do not have enough evidence to determine why one banner word is used instead of another. Often, the banner words used in poetry are determined by alliteration; in *Beowulf*, for instance, the banner words always alliterate, and in the cases of "eaforhēafodsegn" in line 2152b and "hildecumbor" in line 1022a, the poet forms kennings in order to include the banner words in the alliterative structure. Indeed, Anglo-Saxon poets often form kennings of the banner words, often combining the nouns with words for victory, armies, and battle, which add to their connotations in ways accessible to a modern reader. For instance, Judith's army bears "sigeþufas" [victory-banners] in line 201b of *Judith* before the battle even begins, thus signaling the eventual triumph of the Bethulians over the invading Assyrians.

Still, we can see a few connotative patterns. What we can tell about *segn*, *þuf*, *tacn*, and *beacen* comes mostly from context. *Segn* seems to be the most commonly used word for banner and is therefore probably the most generic term. *An Anglo-Saxon Dictionary* posits that a *þuf* bore a tuft of feathers on the top;[23] Michael D. J. Bintley theorizes that this tuft might have been not feathers, but tree branches.[24] Some archaeologists believe that the iron stand at the Sutton Hoo burial might have been a *þuf*.[25] Whatever its configuration, *þuf* clearly designated a particular type of banner, but one that could also be called a *segn*, since, as we have seen, the words are used as appositives. The translation of Bede quoted above indicates that a *þuf* could also be a *tacn*, but given the more common definitions of *tacn* as a sign or a symbol,[26] *tacn* may suggest identification. In the quotation from Bede cited above, Eadwine's banner always travels with him and precedes him in his travels; it is his symbol and part of his royal iconography, as are objects such as the whetstone scepter found at Sutton Hoo.[27] The connection of a banner to a particular person is consistent with Jones's assertion that banners were used as identification before the advent of heraldry.[28] *Beacen*, on the other

23 Ibid., 1075.
24 Michael D. J. Bintley, "Recasting the Role of Sacred Trees in Anglo-Saxon Spiritual History: The South Sandbach Cross 'Ancestors of Christ' Panel in Its Cultural Contexts," in *Trees and Timber in the Anglo-Saxon World*, ed. Michael D. J. Bintley and Michael G. Shapland (Oxford: Oxford University Press, 2013), 211–27, at 223–24.
25 Angela Care Evans, *The Sutton Hoo Ship Burial* (London: British Museum Press, 1986), 85; Martin Carver, *Sutton Hoo: Burial Ground of Kings?* (Philadelphia: University of Pennsylvania Press, 1998), 27, 169. It is important to note, however, that the function of the stand has not been conclusively determined; the British Museum website identifies this object only tentatively as "standard?"; "The Sutton Hoo Standard," www.britishmuseum.org/research/collection_online/collection_object_details.aspx?objectId=88889&partId=1, accessed June 30, 2019. Evans reports several other theories about its function, but concludes that "with no direct documentary evidence, and no parallels, the interpretation of the stand can never be more than theoretical" (85).
26 Bosworth and Toller, *Anglo-Saxon Dictionary*, 966–67.
27 Evans, *Sutton Hoo Ship Burial*, 83–85; Carver, *Sutton Hoo: Burial Ground*, 170.
28 Jones, "Identifying," 157–58, 166; Jones, *Bloodied Banners*, 38.

hand, probably suggests brightness, a connotation often underscored by surrounding adjectives. In *Beowulf*, for instance, the *segn* found in the dragon's hoard is the "bēacna beorhtost" [Brightest of banners] (2777a), and in *Elene*, in which the cross becomes a banner or a standard, it is associated with "leoht" [light] (163a). This brightness may be connected with the golden materials used for banners, which I discuss below.

Two of the banner words, *guðfana* and *cumbol*, seem to carry specifically military connotations. *Guðfana* is often used for banners taken as military trophies. In *The Anglo-Saxon Chronicle*, year 879, for instance,

> 7 þæs ilcan wintres wæs Inweres broðor 7 Healfdenes on Westsexna rice mid .xxiii. scypa, 7 hine man þær ofsloh 7 .dccc. manna mid him 7 .lx. manna his heres, 7 þær wæs se guþfana genumen ðe hie Hrefn heton[29]

> [And that same winter was Ivar's brother and Halfdan's in the kingdom of the West Saxons with twenty-three ships, and someone slew him there, and eight hundred men with him and sixty men of his army, and there the banner which they called the Raven was taken].

Similarly, in the Old English translation of Paulus Orosius's *History*, seven hundred "guðfonena" are seized after one battle, a fact reported with a high casualty count and clearly meant to emphasize the Romans' complete defeat.[30] Since the use of *guðfana* in the *History* and the *Anglo-Saxon Chronicle* do not depend on alliteration, we can conclude that the kenning *guðfana* is used for military banners specifically—and prestigious ones at that, since their capture is recorded. *Cumbol*, too, seems to have some military associations, though it is only used in poetry.[31] Most instances of *cumbol* appear in military contexts, such as in *Beowulf* in lines 1022a and 2505b, where Beowulf receives a battle-standard and later kills a standard-bearer; in *Andreas*, where the apostles' spiritual battles and warriors' armies are both accompanied by the *cumbol*,[32] and in *Judith* and *Elene*, where the armies carry *cumbol* (*Judith*, 332a; *Elene*, 25a, 75, 107a, 259a, all in kennings). The examples of *cumbol* are so few, however, that it is difficult to determine anything more specific.

While the connotations of these words are obscure, we can deduce a few important points about the appearance and construction of the banners that *segn*, *cumbol*, *tacn*, *beacen*, *þuf*, and *fana* designated. Granted, there is little discussion of Anglo-Saxon banners in archeological or textile research, and we have no extant examples of these objects. Yet we have several descriptions of banners in the surviving corpus of Old

29 "Manuscript B: Cotton Tiberius A.VI," *The Anglo-Saxon Chronicle: An Electronic Edition*, ed. Tony Jebson, http://asc.jebbo.co.uk/b/b-L.html, accessed July 18, 2018.

30 Janet Bately, ed., *The Old English Orosius*, Early English Text Society, supp. ser. 6 (Oxford: Oxford University Press, 1980), 84.

31 *Dictionary of Old English: A to I*, ed. Angus Cameron et al., online ed. (Toronto: Dictionary of Old English Project, 2018), http://tapor.library.utoronto.ca/doe, s.v. "cumbol."

32 Kenneth R. Brooks, ed., *Andreas and The Fates of the Apostles* (Oxford: Clarendon, 1961), lines 4b and 1204a.

English. These are generally brief, where they occur at all, except for the elaborate description of Cnut's banner in the Latin *Encomium Emmae Reginae*[33] and the highly symbolic detail of the banner in *The Prose Dialogue of Salomon and Saturn*.[34] Yet taken together, these two detailed descriptions and the brief descriptions elsewhere tell us something about what banners looked like and how they were constructed in Anglo-Saxon England.

Most importantly for our study here, these banners are clearly textile creations. Recall that *segn, fana, guðfana, tacn, beacen*, and *þuf* all gloss the Latin *vexilla*, specifically a textile standard, and that *cumbol*, the only remaining Anglo-Saxon banner word not specifically glossed as *vexilla*, is synonymous with the others. Moreover, the literary records also indicate that these objects were made of cloth, either partially or completely. The detailed description of Cnut's banner in the Latin *Encomium Emmae Reginae* specifies that the banner is cloth:

> Erat namque eis uexillum miri portenti ... Enimuero dum esset simplissimo candidissimoque intextum serico, nulliusque figurae in eo inserta esset [i]mago, tempore belli semper in eo uidebatur coruus ac si intextus ...

> [Now they had a banner of wonderfully strange nature ... For while it was woven of the plainest and whitest silk, and the representation of no figure was inserted into it, in times of war a raven was always seen as if embroidered on it ...][35]

However strange Cnut's banner is, it is made of cloth, and prestigious cloth at that—white silk. The banner also appears to sport embroidery, a specifically textile decoration. Other banners in Anglo-Saxon literature are also described as textile constructions. The very detailed description of a banner in *The Prose Dialogue of Salomon and Saturn* also mentions cloth: "hafað gyldene fonan, and sēo fane is mid xii godwebbum ūtan ymbhangen" [it has a golden banner, and the banner is decked with twelve fine cloths outside];[36] the banner is adorned with fine cloth in addition to its own principal textile. In Bede's *Ecclesiastical History*, the banner above King Oswine's tomb is likewise adorned with "godwebbe": "mid gold 7 mid godwebbe gefrætwad" [adorned with gold and fine cloth].[37] This *godweb* is, like the white silk of Cnut's banner, a prestige textile; *godweb* was a luxury fabric, a "thick and iridescent" cloth, possibly shot silk tafetta.[38] The Old English *godweb* glosses the Latin *purpura* [purple cloth][39]—and

33 Alistair Campbell, trans., *Encomium Emmae Reginae*, Camden Third Series 72 (London: Royal Historical Society, 1949), 24–25.
34 "The Prose Dialogue of MS A," in *The Poetical Dialogues of Solomon and Saturn*, ed. Robert J. Menner (New York: Modern Language Association of America, 1941), 168–71, at 170.
35 Campbell, *Encomium*, 24–25.
36 Menner, "Prose Dialogue," 170.
37 Miller, *Bede's Ecclesiastical History*, 184.
38 Gale R. Owen-Crocker, *Dress in Anglo-Saxon England: Revised and Enlarged Edition* (Woodbridge, UK: Boydell, 2004), 211, 302.
39 Ibid.

indeed, the Old English translator of Bede uses *godweb* to render *purpura*[40]—but Gale Owen-Crocker tells us that English records of church cloths include red, white, green, and black *purpura* as well.[41] Whatever the color, the banners clearly are constructed of these expensive and luxurious fabrics that indicate the banners' wealth and value, both real and symbolic.

The most common detail about banners in Old English also indicates their wealth and value: These banners are golden. This detail is nearly universal among banners described in the Anglo-Saxon period; according to the *Encomium Emmae Reginae*, only Cnut has a white banner. Scyld's funeral banner, the banner which Beowulf receives from Hrothgar, and the banner that Wiglaf later finds in the dragon's hoard are all golden (47b, 1021a, 2767a). King Oswine's banner in the Old English translation of the *Ecclesiastical History* is also golden.[42] The lion banner of Judah in *Exodus* is "gyldenne" as well (321b). The banner in *The Prose Dialogue of Salomon and Saturn* is excessively golden, wearing gold rings like a queen:

> hafað gyldene fonan, and sēo fane is mid xii godwebbum ūtan ymbhangen, and ānra gehwylc godweb hangað on hundtwelftigum hringa gyldenra.[43]

> [It has a golden banner, and the banner is decked with twelve fine cloths outside, and each one of the cloths hangs on one hundred twenty golden rings.]

The gold in these banners marks them as prestigious treasures; indeed, the spoils taken by the Hebrew army in *Exodus* are described in much the same way as banners:

> Heo on riht sceodon
> gold and godweb, Iosepes gestreon,
> wera wuldorgesteald (587b–89a)

> [They properly divided
> Gold and fine cloth, Joseph's treasure,
> Glory-possessions of men]

Though the *Exodus* poet is speaking of treasures generally and collectively, these treasures, like Oswine's banner in the *Ecclesiastical History* and the mysterious banner in *The Prose Dialogue of Salomon and Saturn*, consist of "gold and godweb." Clearly, the gold in these banners associates them with other golden treasures and emphasizes their status as treasures.

These descriptions may inspire a picture of a gilded metal object, but Anglo-Saxon textiles could indeed be gold. Golden fabric is well documented in Anglo-Saxon England; Owen-Crocker gives several examples of luxury fabrics such as silks woven, embroidered, or printed with gold, and notes that Edward the Confessor was

---

40 Bede, *Historiam Ecclesiasticam Gentis Anglorum*, 3.11.
41 Owen-Crocker, *Dress*, 302.
42 Miller, *Bede's Ecclesiastical History*, 184.
43 Menner, "Prose Dialogue," 170.

buried with a gold silk garment.[44] Moreover, in *Beowulf*, the *web* in Heorot are also gold-adorned and shine just like the banners: "Goldfāg scinon / web æfter wāgum" [The gold-adorned *web* shone on the walls] (994b–95a), and these *web* are definitely textiles. Generally, the word *web* is translated as "tapestries," but it designates woven work, and is related to the verb *webbian*, to weave, and the nouns for weavers, *webba*, *webbe*, and *webbestre*.[45] The dragon's golden banner in *Beowulf* also seems to be woven, since it is "hondwondra mǣst" [the greatest of hand-wonders] (2768b) and "gelocen" [locked or wound or intertwined] (2769a). Unfortunately, Old English literature does not give us further descriptive examples, but from these, we can see that these banners are not gold metal, but gold cloth.

The banners, possibly because of their golden thread, shine. Certainly, the word *beacen*, because of its other meanings, implies brightness, but many descriptions of banners, either symbolic or actual, indicate that banners actually shine. When Constantine talks of the cross in *Elene*, he asks,

> 'þe þis his beacen þæs,
> þe me spa leoht oðypde   7 mine leode ᵹenerede,
> tacna torhtost   7 me tir forᵹeaf,
> piᵹsped pið praðum   þurh þæt plitiᵹe treo'.
> Hio him andspare   æniᵹe ne meahton
> aᵹifan toᵹenes   ne ful ᵹeare cuðon
> speotole ᵹesecᵹᵹan   be þam siᵹebeacne (162b–68)

> ["Whose banner (or beacon) this was
> That appeared so light to me and saved my people for me,
> Most splendid of banners (or signs), and gave me glory
> War-success against wrath through that shining tree."
> None might answer to him,
> Give in return, nor full eagerly make known,
> Say clearly, about the victory-banner.]

Whether Constantine is speaking of the visionary cross he saw in a dream before battle or the ensign of the cross that he later constructs for the battle, two things are certain. First, the poet constructs the cross not only as symbol, but specifically as a banner through diction. The "siᵹebeacne" of the final line of the quotation is certainly a kenning for a banner. Secondly, that cross-banner is quite bright: It is "plitiᵹe" [bright or shining] and "torhtost" [most spendid] and appears as light itself, "spa leoht oðypde." Similarly, the miraculous pillar in *Exodus* (which actually does shed light) is likened to a shining banner when that poet calls it a *fana*: "Fana up gerad, / Beama beorhtost" [The banner rode up / Brightest of beams] (249b–50a). Some banners not only shine, but *glow*. The banner in *The Prose Dialogue of Salomon and Saturn* is so bright by virtue of one of its *godweb* adornments that it dispels the dark: "Ond ðæt

---

44 Owen-Crocker, *Dress*, 299.
45 Bosworth and Toller, *Anglo-Saxon Dictionary*, 1180–81.

ǣreste godweb is hāten *aurum celæstum*, ðām ðīostro ne magon cxxtigum mīla nēah gehleonian" [And that first cloth is called *aurum celæstum*, near which darkness may not rest (within) 120 miles].[46] Similarly, the banner which Wiglaf finds in the dragon's hoard in *Beowulf*, like the pillar of fire and Constantine's cross, actually gives off light: "of ðām lēoma stōd" [from it, a gleam stood] (2769b). Granted, these are miraculous banners, but in practical terms, the golden decoration or cloth of the banners would certainly shine in sunlight or candlelight.

The banners are also richly made and decorated, in addition to the gold; the diction of adornment surrounds them in the texts. The banner in *The Prose Dialogue of Salomon and Saturn* is golden and hung with *godweb* and rings; Oswine's banner is likewise golden, hung with cloth, and "gefrætwad" [adorned].[47] Heorogar's banner in *Beowulf* is "hroden" (1022a), another word meaning "adorned." These decorations are not often described; besides gold, the only adornment specifically mentioned are animal motifs. We are told that Heorogar's banner has a boar's head: "eaforhēafodsegn" [boar's-head banner] (2152b). Constantine also has a "Eofurcumble" [boar-banner], and his mother Elene carries one later with her army (*Elene* 76a; 259a). The banner of Judah in *Exodus* shows a lion:

> Hæfdon him to segne,   þa hie on sund stigon,
> ofer bordhreoðan   beacen arᴁred
> in þam garheape,   gyldenne leon,
> drihtfolca mᴁst,   deora cenost. (319–22)

> [They had as their banner, when they rose to sea,
> Over the shield-phalanx, a banner raised up,
> In the spear-troop, a golden lion,
> Best of troop-folk, bravest of the beasts.]

This description of an animal-adorned banner indicates the purpose of the zoomorphic decorations: The animals' ferocity and bravery are associated, through the banner, with the people. The people of Judah are the *best* troops and are therefore associated with the *bravest* animal. Documented banners belonging to historical figures also have animal motifs, particularly the raven. In the *Encomium Emmae Reginae*, Cnut's banner bears a raven, as noted earlier.[48] In *The Anglo-Saxon Chronicle*, quoted above, we are told that the English defeat the invaders and seize the banner called the Raven; interestingly, the chronicler thought the banner and its decoration worth noting, but not the invading leaders' names. The raven carries a double significance: Ravens are not only associated with the Norse god Odin, but also are one of the "beasts of battle," the carrion beasts often mentioned in Old English poetry before and after battles. Through that association, those who carry the banner of the raven are associated with victory,

---

46 Menner, "Prose Dialogue," 170.
47 Miller, *Bede's Ecclesiastical History*, 184.
48 Campbell, *Encomium*, 24–25.

with the feeding of ravens (and ironically, in the chronicle, these victory-minded invaders are defeated). Similar animal-motif flags are also attested later in the Bayeux Tapestry, including one with a raven.[49]

Despite these descriptions of the designs, we cannot know for certain what these banners looked like. No Anglo-Saxon banners remain; any banners buried with Anglo-Saxon rulers (or sent to a watery grave, as Scyld's banner is in *Beowulf*) have been destroyed by time and the elements along with the rest of the textiles. Nor can we know whether the objects denoted by these words changed over the Anglo-Saxon period, nor whether these objects changed materially between the composition of *Beowulf*[50] and the creation of its manuscript around the year 1000.[51] Still, we can look to the depictions of banners in Anglo-Saxon and insular artwork of the late tenth and early eleventh century to get an idea of how a late Anglo-Saxon audience, at least, might have pictured banners. British Library MS Additional 24199, produced at Bury St. Edmunds in the early eleventh century, about the same time as the *Beowulf* manuscript, includes men carrying banners in its illustrations of *Psychomachia* (fig. 1.1).[52] These banners do not look like Roman standards, but rather like flags with attached pennants, and are carried upright on a pole. These banners closely resemble several banners in the Bayeux Tapestry, including one banner associated with William of Normandy (fig.

49 Renn, "Burhgeat and Gonfanon," 78–79, 83; Martin K. Foys, *Bayeux Tapestry* (Saskatoon, Saskatchewan: Scholarly Digital Editions, 2011), panels 117 and 125; Jones, *Bloodied Banners*, 34.

50 The date of *Beowulf*'s composition is a fraught and complicated question and has been much disputed since 1980 even though Robert E. Bjork and Anita Obermeier declared, in their concise review of the scholarship, that determining the date of the composition of *Beowulf* is "impossible"; "Date, Provenance, Author, Audiences," in *A Beowulf Handbook*, ed. Robert E. Bjork and John D. Niles (Lincoln, NE: University of Nebraska Press, 1997), 13–34, at 18. Scholars have proposed composition dates as early as the year 340 and as late as 1025, based on historical, cultural, and literary approaches, while linguistic studies tend to date the poem to the seventh or eighth century; Bjork and Obermeier, "Date," 18, 13, 26–27; Andy Orchard, *A Critical Companion to* Beowulf (Cambridge: D.S. Brewer, 2003), 6. In 2007, Roberta Frank challenged many of the assumptions on which the linguistic arguments are built; "A Scandal in Toronto: *The Dating of 'Beowulf'* a Quarter Century On," *Speculum* 82, no. 4 (2007). More recently, Leonard Neidorf proposed a very specific date of ca. 685–725 in *The Transmission of* Beowulf: *Language, Culture, and Scribal Behavior* (Ithaca, NY: Cornell University Press, 2017), 4, and his 2014 edited anthology, *The Dating of* Beowulf: *A Reassessment* (Cambridge, UK: D.S. Brewer, 2014) predictably includes essays that also support an eighth-century date. Without a definitive date of composition, it is impossible to make any assumptions about the expectations of the poem's original audience regarding banners.

51 "*Beowulf*," British Library, www.bl.uk/collection-items/beowulf, accessed July 10, 2019; Orchard, *Critical Companion*, 20; Bjork and Obermeier, "Date," 17. Although the date of the poem's composition is highly debated, scholars all seem to agree on an early-eleventh-century date for the manuscript.

52 Prudentius, *Psychomachia*, London, British Library, MS Additional 24199. A contemporary version of *Psychomachia* (British Library, MS Cotton Cleopatra C.VIII, 30v) also shows what may be banners, though it is difficult, even with various digital photographic enhancements, to determine whether these are banners or simple pennants.

Fig. 1.1: Luxury dancing; men holding banners at right (London, British Library, MS Additional 24199, 18r). Photo: The British Library, by permission.

1.2).[53] The Bayeux Tapestry is, of course, later than the *Beowulf* manuscript, and a Norman work, but the similarity between the banner in MS Additional 24199 and those in the Bayeux Tapestry may indicate a continuous tradition of banner construction in the tenth and eleventh centuries which included not only these flag-like banners but also animal banners similar to Harold of Wessex's dragon or wyvern banner (fig. 1.3).[54] We cannot know for certain what the original audience of *Beowulf* would have pictured when the poet used words like *segn* and *cumbol*, but the audience of the early-eleventh-century manuscript of the poem would have most likely pictured these.

Anglo-Saxon banners must have been incredibly important culturally. The sheer number of words for banners—six, plus all the associated kennings—indicates that, like kings, warriors, and swords, banners were important enough to Anglo-Saxon audiences to require a considerable stock of poetic words for them. The frequent mention of banners and their descriptions also indicate their significance. We can deduce a few of the Anglo-Saxon cultural associations with banners. First, banners are almost always connected with royalty. Most banners appear with kings and are "symbols of rank."[55] Bede's two examples of banners belong to kings and symbolize their kingly power: Eadwine's banner precedes him and signals his nobility, and Oswine's banner sits over his tomb specifically as a reminder of his royalty.[56] In *Beowulf*, Scyld Scefing, the progenitor of the Danish kings, likewise has a banner on his funeral ship (47–48a). In *Elene*, Constantine and Elene both have boar's-head banners (76a and 259a), as do Heorogar and later Beowulf and Hygelac (2152b), and the Pharoah in *Exodus* is designated as the "segncyning" [banner-king] (172a).[57] Raw also notes that Satan's desire to acquire a banner in *The Poetical Dialogue of Solomon and Saturn* symbolizes his aspirations to rule:[58]

> ōðer him ongan wyrcan ðurh dier[n]e cræftas
> segn and sīde byrnan,   cwæð ðæt hē mid his gesīðum wolde
> hīðan eall heofona rice   and him ðonne on healfum sittan (443b–45)[59]

[… the other (Satan) began to strive through secret crafts
For the banner and wide byrnie; he said that he with his company would
Plunder all heaven-kingdom, and then sit with him at his side].

Granted, some banners are associated with peoples or armies, as is the lion of Judah in *Exodus* (321b), but most banners belong to kings, potential kings (such as Beowulf and Satan), and, in Elene's case, a queen.

53 Jones, *Bloodied Banners*, 34.
54 Ibid.; Renn, "Burhgeat and Gonfanon," 78. Renn identifies this banner as a wyvern, which may represent the dragon of Wessex; Jones identifies this banner as a dragon. See also Jones, *Bloodied Banners*, 34.
55 Raw, "Royal Power," 172.
56 Miller, *Bede's Ecclesiastical History*, 144–46 and 184.
57 Raw, "Royal Power," 172.
58 Ibid.
59 Menner, *Poetical Dialogues*, lines 443b–45.

Fig. 1.2: William of Normandy, seated with a banner. Photo: *The Bayeux Tapestry*, ed. Martin K. Foys (Scholarly Digital Editions, 2011), www.sd-editions.com/bayeux, panel 117, used by permission.

Fig. 1.3: The death of King Harold; a warrior holds a wyvern or dragon banner. Photo: *The Bayeux Tapestry*, panel 168, used by permission.

Another cultural association of banners is a military one, a link with armies and battles. King Hygelac in *Beowulf* is reported to fight two battles, and in both cases, his military activity is associated with banners, as I will discuss in more detail below (1204 and 2958b–59). King Eadwine in the *Ecclesiastical History* bears his banner into battle and everywhere else. In *Elene*, the Huns "hofon herecombol" [raised army-banners] before their invading host (25a). Banners are mentioned as troops go into battle so predictably that, like the beasts of battles, they form part of the poetic conventions of warfare. Indeed, sometimes banners are linked to the description of the beasts of battle. Soon after the description of the beasts of battle in *Elene* (111–13), Constantine and his defending Romans raise their cross-banner before fighting the Huns: "þa þæs þuf hafen, / segn for speotum" [then the banner was raised, / The banner before the troops] (123b–24a). The Bethulians in *Judith* march into battle with banners:

> Stopon cynerofe,
> secgas and gesiðas,   bæron sigeþufas,
> foron to gefeohte   forð on gerihte,
> hæleð under helmum,   of ðære haligan byrig
> on ðæt dægred sylf. (200b–204a)

> [The royally-brave ones advanced,
> Warriors and companions bore victory-banners,
> (They) went to the fight straight forth,
> Heroes under helmets from the holy city,
> In that same daybreak.]

Immediately after these war preparations, the beasts of battle—wolf, raven, and eagle— are described waiting for their upcoming feast of fallen Assyrians (*Judith* 205b–12a). The beasts of battle in lines 162–69 of *Exodus* also closely follow the mention of the Pharoah's banner in line 160. The banners, like the beasts of battle, signal not only the approaching army but the approaching fight.

Finally, banners in Old English poetry and prose often have magical powers. Donald Meek hypothesizes that banners in early literature generally "seem to have some innate power" which "may derive from early cultic or religious functions and related pageantry."[60] Meek cites early Christian banners associated with the cross, as they are in Fortunatus's hymn "Vexilla regis prodeunt."[61] Obviously, Constantine's hastily constructed cross-banner in *Elene* carries this religious power, but his banner promises victory in the face of an almost-certain defeat: "Mid þys beacne ðu / on þam frecnan fære feond oferswiðeð, / ʒeletest lað perod" [With this banner thou / In the dangerous peril shalt overpower the enemy, / Oppress the hateful troop] (92b–94a). And it delivers the victory later in line 126b of *Elene*, three lines after the cross-banner

---

60 Donald Meek, "The Banners of the Fian in Gaelic Ballad Tradition," *Cambridge Medieval Celtic Studies* 11 (Summer 1986): 29–69, at 33.
61 Ibid.

arrives on the field in line 123b. In contrast, Orosius notes an instance in which the inability to raise a banner guarantees the defeat of its army;[62] this banner, like Constantine's, has power to win, or lose, battles. In the *Encomium Emmae Reginae*, Cnut's banner, in contrast, can magically predict the results:

> Enimuero dum esset simplissimo candidissimoque intextum serico, nulliusque figurae in eo inserta esset [i]mago, tempore belli semper in eo uidebatur coruus ac si intextus, in uictoria suorum quasi hians ore excutiensque alas instabilisque pedibus, et suis deuictis quietissimus totoque corpore demissus.

> [For while it was woven of the plainest and whitest silk, and the representation of no figure was inserted into it, in times of war a raven was always seen as if embroidered on it, in the hour of its owners' victory opening its beak, flapping its wings, and restive on its feet, but very subdued and drooping with its whole body when they were defeated.][63]

Cnut's banner has several important features. Besides the popular raven design,[64] the flag magically changes its decoration not only *for* battle, but *because of* the battles. While the raven's predictions cannot give victory as the cross-banner does, it at least helps Cnut avoid defeat by forewarning him. Compared with these banners, the banner in the dragon's hall in *Beowulf* has a relatively tame magical power:

> Swylce hē siomian geseah   segn eall gylden
> hēah ofer horde,   hondwundra mǣst,
> gelocen leoðocrǣftum;   of ðam lēoma stōd,
> Þæt hē þone grundwong   ongitan meahte,
> wrǣtte giondwlītan … (2767–71a)

> [Likewise, he saw hanging a banner, all golden,
> High over the hoard, best of hand-wonders,
> Intertwined with song-craft; from it, a gleam stood
> So that he the ground-plain might see,
> Look over the artwork …]

Old English banners generally shine, as we have seen, but this one glows in the dark, and this glow connects it to the presumably holy banner in *The Prose Dialogue of Salomon and Saturn*, whose *godweb* drives darkness away. Indeed, *godweb* itself may have divine connotations,[65] and, if so, the magical properties of the banners may be woven into their very fabric: They may all be "gelocen leoðocrǣftum" [intertwined with song-craft]. While only literary banners possess magical powers, most banners

---

62 Bately, *Old English Orosius*, 136.
63 Campbell, *Encomium*, 24–25.
64 Meek ("Banners of the Fian," 34) notes that several sagas and chronicles assign raven banners to Scandinavian kings.
65 Owen-Crocker, *Dress*, 302.

convey a symbolic and cultural power of signaling defeat, victory, and control of peoples and territories, and of regal authority and prestige. While the banners of Oswine, Eadwine, the Pharoah, and the tribe of Judah may not be actually magical as Cnut's banner, Constantine's banner, and the banner in the dragon's hoard are, they have power nonetheless.

THE BANNERS IN *BEOWULF*

The poem *Beowulf* includes three prominent banners: Scyld's funeral banner; Heorogar's banner, which Hrothgar gives to Beowulf and Beowulf gives to Hygelac; and the banner that Wiglaf finds in the dragon's hoard. Elsewhere, the poem briefly mentions that King Hygelac's banners overrun the Swedes (2958–59); he later dies fighting the Frisians under a banner (1204–5a). During same feud, Beowulf kills the Hugas' standard-bearer, Dæghrefn (2501–8a). The banners in *Beowulf* share the general characteristics of Old English banners: They are golden textiles, sometimes have animal motifs, and are, as even the brief catalog above shows, associated with royalty and warfare. In *Beowulf*, however, the banners do not signal upcoming battles but signify military conquest; furthermore, the banners are more specifically regarded as treasures in *Beowulf*, and the giving and receiving of these banners as treasure indicates not only prowess, but royal succession.

    Beowulf's first banner appears very early in the poem, at the funeral of Scyld Scefing, the progenitor of the Danish kings:

> Þā gȳt hīe him āsetton   segen gyldenne
> hēah ofer hēafod,   lēton holm beran,
> gēafon on gārsecg;   him wæs geōmor sefa,
> murnende mōd. (47–50a)

> [Then, further, they set a golden banner,
> High over (his) head, (they) let the sea bear him,
> Gave (him) into the sea; (there) was sadness in mind for them,
> Mourning in spirit.]

The banner seems typical of banners in Old English poetry: It is "gyldenne," and it belongs to a king. Like Oswine's banner in the *Ecclesiastical History*, the banner marks a dead king's grave and reminds us of his royalty. But this banner also signals military might and conquest. The poet tells us emphatically that Scyld became a king by conquering his neighbors:

> Oft Scyld Scēfing   sceaþena þrēatum,
> monegum mǣgþum   meodosetla oftēah,
> egsode eorl[as],   syððan ǣrest wearð
> fēasceaft funden.   Hē þæs frōfre gebād:

wēox under wolcnum,   weorðmyndum þāh,
oð þæt him æghwylc   þāra ymbsittendra
ofer hronrāde   hȳran scolde,
gomban gyldan.   Þæt wæs gōd cyning. (4–11)

[Often, Scyld Scefing, troops of enemies,
Many tribes, deprived of mead-seats,
Terrified earls, since first he was
Found destitute. For that, he lived to see comfort;
Grew under the clouds, prospered with honor-memories,
Until every one of the border-sitters
Over the whale-road had to obey (him),
Give (him) tribute. That was a good king.]

Scyld is not royal by birth, but "fēasceaft funden"—found, and helpless or destitute at that. He becomes king by conquest, as the obedience and tribute of all his neighbors (the "ymbsittendra") indicate. Scyld is defined by his conquests; we hear nothing else about his reign. Moreover, Scyld's conquests not only make him king, but make him a *good* king, one of the few kings so described in the poem.[66] As a good king, he defended his people with military might.[67] While his banner serves as a reminder of his royalty, it also reminds us of the military conquests that made him royal.

The poet also associates Scyld's banner directly with treasure. Scyld's banner is placed on his funeral ship among "mādma mænigo" [many treasures] (41a). The objects on this ship are repeatedly designated as treasures, not only in line 41a, but later: "mādma fela" [many treasures] (36b) and "þēodgestrēonum" [people-treasures] (44a). Scyld is being sent off with prestige military equipment, "hildewǣpnum ond heaðowǣdum" [war-weapons and battle-armor] (39), but the only specific treasure which the poet mentions is the banner (47b). The poet's specificity here indicates first that the banner is not only a royal treasure but also a military one, part of Scyld's war equipment, like the weapons and armor. Secondly, the specific mention of this one treasure shows us that the poet wants us to recognize the banner's importance, an importance emphasized with a few details. Granted, these details are sparse: The banner is golden, set at Scyld's head, and high. Yet that is more detail than the poet offers about the generic treasures or the war-weapons and battle-armor. Clearly, the poet wants us to notice the banner and singles it out as important. A banner is a treasure worthy of, and appropriate to, a conquering king, and like Oswine's banner, it is set on Scyld's ship to indicate his continued royal power.

We see the same pattern of a banner indicating conquest and treasure in the episodes surrounding the banner which Hrothgar presents to Beowulf:

---

66 The others are Hrothgar, despite his inability to cope with Grendel, and Beowulf (863b and 2390b).

67 Leo Carruthers, "Kingship and Heroism in *Beowulf*," in *Heroes and Heroines in Medieval English Literature*, ed. Leo Carruthers (Cambridge, UK: D. S. Brewer, 1994), 19–29, at 19.

> Forgeaf þā Bēowulfe   brand Healfdenes,
> segen gyldenne   sigores tō lēane,
> hroden hildecumbor,   helm ond byrnan.
> Mǣre māðþumsweord   manige gesāwon
> beforan beorn beran. (1020–24a)

> [(Hrothgar) then gave Beowulf the sword of Healfdene,
> A golden banner of victory as a gift,
> Adorned war-banner, a helm and byrnie.
> A famous treasure-sword, many saw
> Borne before the hero.]

Beowulf later gives this banner to his uncle and king, Hygelac:

> Hēt ðā in beran   eaforhēafodsegn,
> heaðostēapne helm,   hāre byrnan,
> gūðsweord geatolic,   gyd æfter wræc (2152–54)

> [(Beowulf) commanded to be borne inside then the boar's-head banner,
> The battle-steep helm, the gray byrnie,
> Adorned battle-sword, he afterwards told the story.]

This banner shares many characteristics with Scyld's. It is, as usual, golden and decorated and royal: Beowulf tells us that the banner belonged to Heorogar, King Hrothgar's brother and predecessor on the Danish throne (2155–62). It may even carry an imperial connotation, since it is a "eaforhēafodsegn," a boar's-head banner, like Constantine's in *Elene*. And like Scyld's banner, it is given some prominence, partially through its description and partially through diction and poetics. Like Healfdene's sword, this banner is named twice in the first passage and once in the second. Unlike the sword, the banner is given two kennings ("segn … sigores" and "hildecumbor") in the first passage, and both kennings fall on stresses in the poetic line and then alliterate; the very workings of the poetics underscore the importance of the banner (and the sword). The elaborate kenning "eaforhēafodsegn" in line 2152b, which comprises an entire half-line, also emphasizes the banner. As with Scyld's banner, the poet clearly wants his audience to notice this banner and stresses its presence.

And like Scyld's banner, Heorogar's banner occurs in the context of both conquest and treasure. Its very designations as "segen gyldenne sigores" [a golden banner of victory] and "hildecumbor" [war-banner] associate it at least with military conquest. More importantly, Hrothgar gives the banner to Beowulf because of his conquest of Grendel, who had usurped the royal hall, Heorot. The banner, like Scyld's, is also clearly treasure. The poet designates the banner as one of four fabulous "mādmas" [treasures] (1027b) which give Beowulf standing among warriors: "for scēotendum scamigan ðorfte" [he need not be ashamed before the archers] (1026). The banner is also clearly a military treasure, as its inclusion among other military equipment demonstrates. It comes to Beowulf with other battle gear: a sword, a mail shirt, and a helmet, and later, warhorses and a war saddle (1035–41a). With the banner, and the other treasures, Hrothgar has not only given treasure, as a king should do,[68] but has acknowledged and rewarded Beowulf's conquest with a banner and war equipment that will enable him to conquer others.

Heorogar's banner is not merely royal, but may indicate inclusion in royal succession. It seems to have been passed down among the Danish kings: The possessive "Healfdenes" in line 1020b may apply to the banner as well as the sword and indicate that, like the sword, it belonged to Hrothgar's father. Later, Beowulf tells us that the banner belonged to Heorogar, King Hrothgar's elder brother and predecessor on the Danish throne (2155–62).[69] Hrothgar apparently inherited the banner (and sword and armor) along with his kingship, and he gives it to Beowulf, the grandson of a king and a future king, who gives it to Hygelac, another king. These facts alone do not necessarily constitute succession, but if Raw is correct, banners form part of the king's regalia,[70] and Hill and Raw both believe that this particular banner is not a personal standard but a national or royal one.[71] Both Hill and M. J. Swanton posit that Hrothgar's giving of the banner, sword, and royal arms to Beowulf places Beowulf in the royal line of Denmark.[72] Like King Hygelac's dynastic gift of King Hrethel's sword to Beowulf later,[73] the gift of the royal battle gear publicly includes, and visually marks, Beowulf as part of the line of succession. Beowulf neatly deflects this claim on his loyalty and rejects his place in the Danish royal house by giving these treasures to Hygelac,[74] but this does not change the fact that the banner, like the sword and the other war-treasures, establish his inclusion in the royal succession.

The poem does not indicate the fate of Heorogar's banner. During the references to an ongoing feud between the Swedes and the Geats, however, the poet refers to banners three times, and these banners, though not specifically treasures, signal military conquest and have implications for succession. These references do not occur together or chronologically, but placed in order, they form the story of Hygelac's feud with the Swedes. Initially, Hygelac triumphs over his Swedish enemies beneath banners:

---

68 Peter Fox, *An Introduction to Anglo-Saxon Kingship* (Hockwold cum Wilton, UK: Anglo-Saxon Books, 2004), 22–23; Carruthers, "Kingship and Heroism," 19; Richard P. Abels, *Lordship and Military Obligation in Anglo-Saxon England* (Berkeley: University of California Press, 1988), 11.

69 In lines 2155–62, Beowulf claims that Hrothgar told him to tell Hygelac that King Heorogar had once owned the banner, sword, helmet, and armor, and did not wish to give them to Heorogar's son. This command, however, does not appear in the scene in which Hrothgar gives the items to Beowulf, and the only owner mentioned in the gift-giving scene, as we see in the quotation, is Healfdene. It is likely that Heorogar inherited these items from his father, Healfdene, however, and both claims about the origins of the items may be true.

70 Raw, "Royal Power," 172–73.

71 Ibid.; John M. Hill, *The Cultural World in* Beowulf (Toronto: University of Toronto Press, 1995), 100.

72 Hill, *Cultural World*, 99–100; Swanton, *Crisis and Development*, 115.

73 Swanton, *Crisis and Development*, 134; Creed, "*Beowulf*'s Fourth Act," 94.

74 Hill, *Cultural World*, 100.

> Þā wæs ǣht boden
> Swēona lēodum,   segn Higelāces
> freoðowong þone   forð oferēodon,
> syððan Hrēðelingas   tō hagan þrungon. (2957b–60)

[Then pursuit was offered
To the people of the Swedes, the banner of Hygelac
Overran the peace-plain,
After the Hrethelings pressed to the fortress.]

In a later battle, Beowulf kills a Frisian standard-bearer, which I will discuss shortly, and Hygelac dies beneath his banner while wearing the Brosing necklace which Beowulf received from Queen Wealtheow:

> Þone hring hæfde   Higelāc Gēata,
> nefa Swertinges   nȳhstan sīðe,
> siþðan hē under segne   sinc ealgode,
> wælrēaf werede;   hyne wyrd fornam
> syþðan hē for wlenco   wēan āhsode,
> fǣhðe tō Frȳsum. (1202–7a)

[Hygelac of the Geats had the ring (the Brosing necklace),
The nephew of Swerting, on the last journey
After he defended treasures under the banner,
Guarded slain-spoils. Fate took him
After he for pride sought out trouble,
The feud against the Frisians.]

Certainly, these banners are royal, the king's banners. Taken together, these quotations link banners to military conquest. Hygelac conquers the Swedes' "freoðowong" [peace-place] specifically under his banners; indeed, his *segn*, not Hygelac himself, storms the fortress. Clearly, *segn* is used metonymically for the troops, as it is in *Exodus* when Pharoah's treasure is distributed among the Hebrews: "Ongunnon sælafe segnum dælan" [They began to divide the sea-leavings among the banners] (585). Hygelac's banner is his army, and here, it is a *conquering* army, a conquering banner. Yet Hygelac is conquered in turn, significantly "under segne" [under the banner]. These two banners are not depicted as or associated with treasures directly. Yet there is an indirect association: Hygelac loses the prestigious Brosing necklace when he dies beneath his banner, a treasure not only royal but divine: The original Brosing necklace belonged to the goddess Freyja. These banners are also indirectly associated with succession: These battles affect the deposition and ascension of the Swedish kings, and when Hygelac dies under his banner, his son, and later his nephew Beowulf, succeed him.

During Hygelac's fatal battle against the Frisians, Beowulf kills a warrior named Dæghrefn (Day-Raven), the "cumbles hyrde" [banner's guardian] (2505b). The poet connects Beowulf's triumph over this standard-bearer with military might and with treasures. Just before fighting the dragon, Beowulf tells Wiglaf and his other thanes of this victory:

> … ond swā tō aldre sceall
> sæcce fremman,   þenden þis sweord þolað
> þæt mec ǣr ond sīð   oft gelǣste,
> syððan ic for dugeðum   Dæghrefne wearð
> tō handbonan,   Hūga cempan—
> nalles hē ðā frætwe   Frēscyninge,
> brēostweorðunge   bringan mōste,
> ac in campe gecrong   cumbles hyrde,
> æþeling on elne;   ne wæs ecg bona,
> ac him hildegrāp   heortan wylmas,
> bānhūs gebræc. (2498b–2508a)

> [… and so I shall ever
> Do battle, as long as this sword survives,
> Which often served me, before and since,
> After I, before the troops, became to Day-Raven
> The champion of the Hugas, as a hand-bane.
> To the Frisian king, he not at all
> Might bring breast-worthy treasures,
> But in the fight, the guardian of the banner,
> The prince in strength, died; nor was it edge-bane,
> But battle-grip broke his heart-swelling,
> His bone-house, for him.]

Beowulf's triumph against Dæghrefn is clearly noteworthy. It forms part of Beowulf's boast to kill the dragon, and, while Beowulf mentions youthful battles several times, he specifically mentions only the defeat of Grendel and the defeat of Dæghrefn. Dæghrefn must be a prestigious and worthy enemy, as important and difficult to defeat as Grendel, and like Grendel, slain without weapons. The poem gives us other clues about Dæghregn's importance: He, like Beowulf, is an "æþeling," a term indicating royal blood and generally rendered "prince." Dæghrefn is also a *cempa*, a champion, of his people, and, more importantly, the "cumbles hyrde" [the banner's guardian]; once again, we have the association of banners and royalty. His position as standard-bearer, however, may be more important here. Dæghrefn's very name, literally Day-Raven, underscores his link with the banner he carries; it bears remembering that Cnut had a raven banner, and the Saxons took a raven banner from Danish invaders.[75] Dægh-refn's position as standard-bearer also makes him emblematic of the Hugas themselves. Beowulf's defeat of Dæghrefn marks not just the downfall of the warrior himself, but

---

75 Campbell, *Encomium*, 24; Jebson, "Manuscript B," 879.

conquest of the Hugas; once again, military conquest in *Beowulf* is signaled by banners. And that conquest is total and brutal: Beowulf breaks the standard-bearer, the champion and prince of his people entrusted with the emblem of his tribe, with his bare hands.

The poet also connects banners with treasure in the Dæghrefn episode. If we accept the poem's stance that banners are treasures, certainly Beowulf acquires the Hugas' banner when he kills their standard-bearer, though the poem does not explicitly state this, nor that Dæghrefn's banner is a treasure. But in the larger speech quoted above, Beowulf reminds us that Dæghrefn will not be able to return "frætwe … brēost-weorðunge" [breast-worthy treasures] to the Frisian king (2503–4). Moreover, Beowulf boasts that he will continue to fight with the sword

> þæt mec ǣr ond sīð   oft gelǣste
> *syððan* ic for dugeðum   Dæghrefne wearð
> tō handbonan,   Hūga cempan (2500–2502; my emphasis)

> [Which often served me, before and since,
> *After* I, before the troops, became to Day-Raven
> The champion of the Hugas, as a hand-bane.]

The text here connects Beowulf's sword Nægling, with which he fights the dragon, directly with the defeat of Dæghrefn, implying that Beowulf gained Nægling, a prestigious, named sword, through his conquest of Dæghrefn the banner-carrier; the sword may even have belonged to the standard-bearer himself. Conquest of a banner here, as with Hygelac, means the loss of treasure for the defeated, and treasure gained by the victor.

The final banner in the poem is the one that Wiglaf finds among the dragon's hoard, and it, like Scyld's banner and Heorogar's, is explicitly linked with treasure and conquest, and also has clear implications for succession. This banner is described in some detail:

> Swylce hē siomian geseah   segn eall gylden
> hēah ofer horde,   hondwundra mǣst,
> gelocen leoðocræftum;   of ðām lēoma stōd,
> þæt hē þone grundwong   ongitan meahte,
> wrǣtte giondwlītan. …
> Ðā ic on hlǣwe gefrægn   hord rēafian,
> eald enta geweorc   ānne mannan,
> him on bearm hladon   bunan ond discas
> sylfes dōme;   segn ēac genōm,
> bēacna beorhtost. (2767–71a, 2773–77a)

> [Likewise, he saw hanging a banner, all golden,
> High over the hoard, best of hand-wonders,
> Intertwined with song-craft; from it, a gleam stood

So that he the ground-plain might see,
Look over the artwork …
Then I learned the hoard in the hill (was) plundered,
Old work of giants, by one man.
He loaded into his lap cups and dishes
At his own judgment; he also took the banner,
The brightest of banners (or beacons).]

This banner is certainly a treasure, found among other treasures, including jewels, arm-rings, gold, assorted tableware, and helmets (2756–64a and 2775). This hoard is specifically designated as treasures, "Sinc" (2764a), and the banner is also included among the "māðmum" [treasures] which Wiglaf brings to Beowulf (2788–90a). The banner is the most important treasure in the hoard, since it, like Scyld's banner, is the only treasure specifically described. The level of detail in this description is also important. As usual, the banner is "gylden" [golden], but this banner is also tall: "hēah" [high]. It is well made, the "hondwundra mæst" [best of hand-wonders], and even magical, for it is "gelocen leoðocræftum" [intertwined or locked with song-craft] and glows so brightly that Wiglaf can see by its light. Like the banner in *The Prose Dialogue of Salomon and Saturn*, this banner dispels darkness, and its radiance also recalls the brightness associated with the cross-banner in *Elene*, another banner designated as a "beacen" (100b and 162b). Only one other object in *Beowulf* merits this level of detailed description: the giant-made sword found in the hall of Grendel's mother (1557–64, 1615, 1662–63a, and 1688–98a). Not only is the banner a treasure, it is a noticeable and important one.

Like the giant-made sword, the banner in the dragon's hoard also signals conquest. The giant-made sword appears almost miraculously as a means for Beowulf to conquer Grendel's mother[76] and then serves as a symbol of Beowulf's conquest of both Grendel and his mother. Similarly, this banner appears after the conquest of the dragon when it is taken back to Beowulf as a token of his and Wiglaf's victory. And like Dæghrefn's banner, this one is a territorial or national symbol, one of the "tribal possessions" of a people long lost whose treasure the dragon has usurped.[77] The banner, like the rest of the treasure in the hoard, shows Beowulf and Wiglaf's re-conquest and control of their own territory. As the giant sword in Grendel's mother's hoard appears as a gift from God,[78] and the vision of the cross appears (and becomes a banner) in *Elene*, both signaling upcoming victories, the banner appears unexpectedly, a glowing symbol of conquest, in the dragon's hoard, as a confirmation of the victory over the dragon.

The banner in the dragon's hoard is not directly connected with royalty, aside from the fact that Wiglaf recovers it for his king,[79] but the banner certainly carries impli-

76 Swanton, *Crisis and Development*, 99.
77 Raw, "Royal Power," 172–73.
78 Swanton, *Crisis and Development*, 99.
79 Atkinson argues that the poem constructs the dragon as a king; Stephen C. B. Atkinson, "*Oð Ðæt an ongan … draca ricsian*: Beowulf, the Dragon, and Kingship," *Publications of the Missouri*

cations for succession, as Heorogar's does. Just as Beowulf receives a golden banner from Hrothgar as a reward for conquering Grendel, Wiglaf receives a golden banner when he defeats the dragon,[80] and this banner, like the one Beowulf receives, places Wiglaf in the line of succession. In the scene just before Wiglaf enters the hoard, the dying Beowulf brings up the problem of his successor:

> Nū ic suna mīnum   syllan wolde
> gūðgewǣdu,   þǣr mē gifeðe swā
> ǣnig yrfeweard   æfter wurde
> līce gelenge. (2729–32)

> [Now I would give to my son
> War-weeds, if it were so granted to me,
> If any inheritance-guardian had afterwards remained
> Belonging to my body.]

The "gūðgewǣdu" [war-weeds] that Beowulf wishes to leave to a son include a golden neck-ring, a helmet, and his armor (2809–12), items that recall Hrothgar and Wealtheow's gifts to Beowulf—Heorogar's helmet and armor, and the Brosing necklace, "dynastic treasures" that, according to Hill, placed Beowulf in the Danish succession.[81] These items constitute not only a personal inheritance, but, like Hrothgar's gifts, indicate succession. Only the sword and banner are missing. Beowulf's sword Nægling is broken, shattered by his own brute strength on the dragon's head (2677b–82a), and cannot be passed on, but immediately after Beowulf laments the lack of a son, Wiglaf finds the glowing banner in the dragon's hoard. Since a golden banner is part of a king's regalia,[82] the banner signals that God is choosing Wiglaf as king just as the visionary cross, which becomes Constantine's banner, signifies God's endorsement of Constantine as emperor in *Elene*. When Wiglaf returns with the banner, Beowulf gives Wiglaf the "items which belong to the king in virtue of his office … ornaments and military equipment," the same items which Hrothgar gives to Beowulf,[83] and notes that Wiglaf is the last of their family (2813–16a). While Beowulf does not specifically give Wiglaf the banner, it remains with Wiglaf, and when the cowardly thanes find him later (2846–52a), they see him wearing Beowulf's regalia and holding the dead king beneath the golden banner from the hoard. If the banner, armor, and helm indicate succession as Hill posits, then the visual cues here show that Wiglaf has received Beowulf's endorsement as his successor.

Philological Association 11 (1986): 1–10, at 1–4. But the banner in the dragon's hoard does not technically belong to the dragon but to a long-dead people; Raw, "Royal Power," 172–73; *Beowulf*, 2231b–46.
80 McNabb, "Eldum Unnyt," 152.
81 Hill, *Cultural World*, 99.
82 Raw, "Royal Power," 172.
83 Ibid.

CONCLUSION

Banners clearly carry more importance in Anglo-Saxon culture and literature than critics have previously remarked, and they deserve more careful study than they have previously received. Their appearance in poetry and prose in connection with royalty and battle indicates that banners were important cultural symbols, objects so heavily invested with meaning that not only poets but also Bede and the chroniclers who composed *The Anglo-Saxon Chronicle* and the *Encomium Emmae Reginae* include accounts of important banners. The banners' occasional magical properties also demonstrate their presumed power to win, lose, or predict the outcome of battles. While this power may have been only symbolic, the depictions of the cross-banner in *Elene*, Cnut's raven banner in the *Encomium*, and Eadwine's royal banner which seems to keep the peace show that this power was very real to the Anglo-Saxon audience.

My study of banners, and the banners in *Beowulf*, is preliminary. Many avenues for the study of Anglo-Saxon banners remain open to us. Further investigation of banners in particular works might illuminate the objects' importance and cultural functions as well as their significance to those texts. A systematic study of kennings might reveal more associations and attitudes surrounding banners. More research into Anglo-Saxon and insular depictions of banners in manuscripts and artwork could reveal banners' physical forms and variations. While archeological finds are improbable, a survey of banners in Anglo-Saxon charters, wills, and inventories might provide us with more information about materials and construction. Cross-disciplinary studies are certainly needed. When we, as literary, linguistic, art, and textile scholars, take up these banners, we are sure to discover much, not only about Anglo-Saxon banners and textiles generally, but about the material culture, thoughts, and values of the Anglo-Saxons themselves.

The Use of Curved Templates in the Drawing of the Bayeux Tapestry

Maggie Kneen and Gale R. Owen-Crocker

The Bayeux Tapestry is an eleventh-century embroidered frieze. It is 68.58 metres (225 feet) long in its present incomplete state[1] and averages 50 centimetres (19.7 inches) in width, including borders. It is constructed of nine pieces of linen, the first two of which are much longer than the subsequent ones,[2] joined by almost invisible seams so as to appear continuous. The Tapestry is world famous; it is listed on the international UNESCO Memory of the World Register, and it receives about 400,000 visitors per year in Bayeux, northern France, where it has been since at least the fifteenth century, probably much longer.[3] However, it was probably designed in Canterbury, in southeast England, since its graphic style resembles the manuscript art of that area and it borrows images from manuscripts known to have been made and kept in Canterbury, in the libraries of St. Augustine's Abbey and Christ Church Cathedral (see below, pages 53–54);[4] it references specific persons associated with and known patrons of St. Augustine's; and it depicts Mont Saint-Michel, the previous home of the first Norman

Maggie Kneen presented parts of this paper at the Leeds International Medieval Congress in July 2014 (see note 25, below). The idea stems from her Master's dissertation, a degree gained at the University of Manchester in 2011 under the supervision and tutelage of Professor Gale Owen-Crocker. The ongoing research presented here has been greatly expanded since then. This paper has been shaped by the collaboration of Kneen and Owen-Crocker, with the invaluable input of Robin Netherton, without whose editing skills the paper would have been incomplete. Thanks go to her.

1 According to the measurements for the individual sections given by Isabelle Bédat and Béatrice Girault-Kurtzeman, "The Technical Study of the Bayeux Tapestry," in *The Bayeux Tapestry: Embroidering the Facts of History*, ed. Pierre Bouet, Brian Levy, and François Neveux (Caen, France: Presses Universitaires de Caen, 2004), 83–109, at 86. As Christopher Norton points out, their total of 68.38 metres is incorrect; Christopher Norton, "Viewing the Bayeux Tapestry, Now and Then," *Journal of the British Archaeological Association* 172, no. 1 (2019): 1–47, at 5.

2 Respectively 13.7 metres (44 feet, 11 inches), 13.9 metres (45 feet, 7 inches), 8.19 metres (26 feet, 10 inches), 7.725 metres (24 feet, 4 inches), 5.52 metres (18 feet, 1 inch), 7.125 metres (23 feet, 4 inches), 7.19 metres (23 feet, 2 inches), 2.8 metres (9 feet, 2 inches), 2.43 metres (7 feet, 11 inches).

3 It is mentioned in an inventory of the treasure of Bayeux Cathedral, written in 1476, but may have arrived there as the property of Bishop Odo of Bayeux, in the 1070s or 1080s.

4 The two are a short walk apart, the abbey outside the city walls and the cathedral within.

abbot of St. Augustine's (see below, page 56).[5] It may also have been embroidered in southern England.[6]

Every person viewing the Bayeux Tapestry is struck by its vitality. The assumption follows that the drawing which underlay the embroidery was spontaneous, freehand, each figure drawn as a complete entity before the artist moved on to the next. Yet, this is probably an illusion. As Richard Gameson has pointed out, the artists of eleventh-century Anglo-Saxon manuscripts who were creating images of more than one colour were already accustomed to working piecemeal, necessarily drawing a single image in different stints and changing ink in the course of its composition,[7] though of course the act of creating a monochrome under-drawing might be more spontaneous and continuous.[8] There is no trace of under-drawing for the original embroidery visible now; it may have been washed out.[9] Commentators on the Tapestry tend to

5 Elizabeth Carson Pastan and Stephen D. White, with Kate Gilbert, *The Bayeux Tapestry and Its Contexts: A Reassessment* (Woodbridge, UK: Boydell, 2014), esp. White, "The Prosopography of the Bayeux Embroidery and the Community of St Augustine's, Canterbury," 82–104, and Pastan, "*Quid Faciat ... Scollandus*? The Abbey Church of St Augustine's c. 1073–1100," 260–87, at 284–85, where the scenes depicting Westminster Abbey and King Edward's death are linked to works "probably written in Canterbury" (285).

6 There are no documented eleventh-century embroidery workshops near Canterbury, which is in southeast England, but that does not mean they did not exist. Specific suggestions about an English place for the embroidery have focused on the nunneries of Wilton and other convents in the southwest of England known to have housed widows and orphans of the Battle of Hastings; Carola Hicks, "The Patronage of Queen Edith," in *The Bayeux Tapestry: New Approaches*, ed. Michael Lewis, Gale R. Owen-Crocker, and Dan Terkla (Oxford: Oxbow, 2011), 5–9, at 8–9; Patricia Stephenson, "Where a Cleric and Ælfgyva ...," in the same volume, 71–74, at 72–73. The Nunnaminster at Winchester and nearby convents are suggested by Jan Messent, *The Bayeux Tapestry Embroiderers' Story* (Thirsk, UK: Madeira Threads, 1999). For theories about continental manufacture see note 36.

7 Richard Gameson, *The Role of Art in the Late Anglo-Saxon Church* (Oxford: Clarendon Press, 1995), 13.

8 Various early-eleventh-century artists who created the coloured line drawings in the Harley Psalter (London, British Library [henceforth BL], MS Harley 603), which is partially copied from the ninth-century monochrome Utrecht Psalter, employed, in different places, hardpoint (stylus), leadpoint, and tracing to prepare under-drawings which were subsequently inked in; William Noel, *The Harley Psalter* (Cambridge: Cambridge University Press, 1995), 33–36, 60, 61, and note 74. Leadpoint was also used in the early-eleventh-century Old English Hexateuch (BL MS Cotton Claudius B.iv); Michelle P. Brown, *The Lindisfarne Gospels: Society, Spirituality and the Scribe* (London: British Library, 2003), 217 and fig. 84 (and also fig. 81 for an example of leadpoint from the Harley Psalter). Both these manuscripts influenced the graphics of the Bayeux Tapestry.

9 Simone Bertrand, *La Tapisserie de Bayeux et la Manière de Vivre au Onzième Siècle*, Glossaire de Bayeux: Introductions à la Nuit de Temps 2 (La Pierre-qui-Vire: Zodiac, 1966), 38, claims the Tapestry has been washed at least twice, which could have eradicated all trace of drawing. It is hoped that the new Anglo-French research study, begun in 2017, might find some evidence of ink, metal, or charcoal underlying the embroidery. There is red under-drawing, visible under some dark blue and green inscriptions, but those inscriptions are modern restorations and the under-drawings the guidelines for them; ibid., 37–38, and Bertrand, "A Study of the Bayeux Tapestry," in *The Study of the Bayeux Tapestry*, ed. Richard Gameson (Woodbridge, UK: Boydell, 1997), 31–38, at 37 (originally published as "Étude sur la Tapisserie de Bayeux," *Annales de*

refer to "the artist" or "the designer" as if a single hand were responsible for the whole design and drawing. That neither the assumption of spontaneity nor that of the single artist is accurate is gradually being recognised. In recent studies Gale Owen-Crocker identifies different hands and geometric design principles involving both squares and "golden sections."[10] Patrick Arman Savidan recognises different stylistic approaches, though attributing them to the embroidery teams; he also asserts that horses with riders were each drawn with three stencils/templates.[11] François Murez relates the Tapestry to a long tradition of composition by means of squares and rectangles.[12]

The collaboration which produced the present article is a result of the independent desire of both authors to test the possibility that the Bayeux Tapestry cartoon was drawn with the use of artists' tools, which may have taken the form of templates, stencils, and grids of square and rectangular shapes. Gale Owen-Crocker, a long-time Bayeux Tapestry scholar, was alerted to this possibility by an inspirational graduate student, the late Patricia Cooper (who had examined geometric composition in Anglo-Saxon manuscript art for both her M.A. dissertation and her Ph.D., creating effective templates and stencils from wax for her experiments),[13] but, lacking skills or training in graphic design herself, felt unable to take the matter to the necessary level. Meanwhile, Maggie Kneen, a professional illustrator who had worked on the Bayeux Tapestry for her own M.A. in Medieval Studies, was also speculating about the use of templates. She was eager and competent to undertake the necessary practical work, which involved tracings and comparisons of individual shapes throughout the Tapestry. Following experiments with stencils, it was decided to focus on templates.[14] How-

---

Normandie 10 [1960]: 197–206). For further discussion of possible under-drawing and how it might have been made, see pages 59–64 below.

10 Gale R. Owen-Crocker, "The Bayeux Tapestry: Faces and Places," in Lewis, Owen-Crocker, and Terkla, *Bayeux Tapestry: New Approaches*, 96–104; Owen-Crocker, "La Tapisserie de Bayeux: L'Art du Récit Linéaire," in *L'Invention de la Tapisserie de Bayeux: Naissance, Composition et Style d'un Chef-d'Œuvre Médiéval*, ed. Sylvette Lemagnen, Shirley Ann Brown, and Gale R. Owen-Crocker (Bayeux, France: Point de Vues / Ville de Bayeux, 2018), 94–107. All chapters in this volume are followed by synopses in English.

11 Patrick Arman Savidan, "L'Invention Plastique d'une Conquête," in Lemagnen, Brown, and Owen-Crocker, *L'Invention*, 289–309.

12 François Murez, "La Géométrie Construit l'Espace et Rythme le Temps dans la Tapisserie de Bayeux," in Lemagnen, Brown, and Owen-Crocker, *L'Invention*, 124–47.

13 The M.A. dissertation, "The Illustrated Old English Hexateuch: A Reappraisal," identified repeated shapes which might have been made with templates, stencils, and even stamps in part of the Old English Hexateuch (BL MS Cotton Claudius B.iv), but is no longer available. The doctoral thesis is Patricia Cooper, "Christian Irish/Anglo-Saxon Illuminated Manuscripts: Divine Intervention or Inspired Technique" (Ph.D. thesis, University of Manchester, March 2013). At the suggestion of the examiners, the Ph.D. degree was awarded posthumously on the basis of an uncorrected typescript.

14 A stencil consists of a thin sheet from which shapes have been cut out, held together by narrow, solid strips called ties. The pattern is transferred by drawing along the edges of the perforations. A template is a thin sheet cut into a specific shape. The pattern is transferred by drawing round the outside of it. In November 2014 Gale Owen-Crocker delivered two three-hour workshops on the Bayeux Tapestry at the Textile Research Centre, Leiden, the Netherlands,

ever, it became apparent that some shapes used on the Tapestry (called here "strip" and "bulbous") were seemingly hybrids of stencils and templates (see pages 42–46).

THE RESEARCH QUESTIONS

The researchers asked themselves:

- Is there evidence in the Tapestry for the systematic use of templates?
- What repeated shapes can be identified?
- Are the same templates used in all nine sections of linen?
- Are the same templates used in the borders?
- Are the same templates used in sections which appear to be created by different hands?
- How do our findings develop our understanding of how the Tapestry was designed?

The original plan had been to focus on the constituent parts of items that recur in the Tapestry; birds and horses were chosen. However, it soon became obvious that identical shapes were used across a range of image types: For example, birds' wings were found to have identical dimensions to kite-shaped shields, while stallions' phalluses were clearly created from the same model as buds on trees. Owen-Crocker and Kneen therefore rapidly decided to concentrate on the shapes themselves, rather than their use as sections of images, and agreed to work initially on curves, incorporating work Kneen had already done on architecture in the Bayeux Tapestry for her M.A. thesis.[15] This had demonstrated that the same arched templates had been used for architecture throughout the whole length of the Tapestry, in a range of sizes extending from the tiniest of curved roof-tiles to the various-sized windows, doorways, and arches. The

---

each to fifteen members of the general public, in the course of which each participant began to embroider one border creature from the Bayeux Tapestry, of approximately one-third size, using embroidery kits prepared by Gillian Vogelsang Eastwood to specifications by Alexandra Lester-Makin employing stencils prepared by Maggie Kneen. Eastwood used the stencils and a sharp pencil to draw the cartoons onto the cloth. The participants were given a choice of a bird, a lion, or a dragon, subjects of various levels of difficulty. Participants could finish the work in their own time, and could make a second pattern from one of the other stencils if they wished to do another. Even participants completely inexperienced in embroidery produced creditable results, but the discrepancy between the proportions of the ties and the single-stem stitch lines, and the adjustments that had to be made because of this, convinced Owen-Crocker that this method was not that used in the original work.

15 Maggie Kneen, "'Hestenga Ceastra': The Buildings of Hastings on the Bayeux Tapestry and their Rôle in the Norman Conquest" (M.A. thesis, University of Manchester, 2011). Elizabeth Pastan has described the buildings as "a unifying presence" which "work within and support the narrative" in her chapter "Representing Architecture" in Pastan and White, *Bayeux Tapestry and its Contexts*, 183–209, at 187 and 188 respectively (a revised version of her "Building Stories: The Representation of Architecture in the Bayeux Embroidery," *Anglo-Norman Studies* 33 [2011]: 150–85). The compositional unity demonstrated below supports and gives another dimension to this view.

largest of this set of arches were used for the great mottes upon which all six castles of the Tapestry stood.

Following the study of curves, it became possible to return to image types, and accordingly, short studies of dragons and horses are presented here. This is followed by discussion of the probable workshop and some issues relating to the composition of the design.

ARCHES

It became evident that there was a sequence of arches of the same proportions but of different sizes (fig. 2.1), and that they were used throughout the Tapestry. Comparison with the arches in the Harley Psalter, which was still in the process of being made in Canterbury when the Bayeux Tapestry was most probably being designed there,[16] suggests that the arches on the Tapestry were made using templates which, judging from their occasionally wavering or off-centre outlines, had probably been both drawn and cut by hand and eye, by simply drawing around the arch or curve of an existing template in a concentric fashion, but leaving a consistent gap between the two in order to create the next size up; whereas those of the manuscript are more accurately

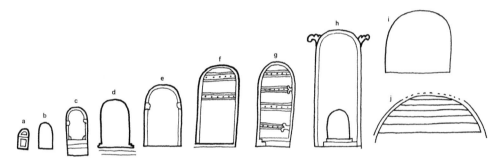

Fig. 2.1: Arches made with templates on the Bayeux Tapestry. (a) Dol and Rennes castle gateways, Scene 18. (b) Bayeux Castle gate, Scene 22; upper door of burning house, Scene 47. (c) Door of Westminster Hall, Scene 1; reused many times elsewhere. (d) Bosham church outer arch, Scene 3; cauldron, Scene 42. (e) Arches of Harold's hall in Bosham, Scene 3; dome of Bayeux Castle, Scene 22. (f) Apse of Church of St. Mary, Hastings, Scene 47. (g) Great door, representing William's exit from Hastings, Scene 47. (h) Dover Tower, Scene 24. (i) Bayeux motte interior, Scene 22. (j) Motte of Hastings Castle, Scene 45. Drawing: Maggie Kneen.

16 BL MS Harley 603. Harley 603 is thought to have been made at Christ Church, Canterbury. It was begun in the early years of the eleventh century and work on it continued intermittently for about a hundred years. The central part of the text (fols. 28r–49v) was not written until the third or fourth quarter of the eleventh century, and illustrations were added to part of that later, into the early twelfth century; Noel, *Harley Psalter*, 137–40, 210–11. It was never completed. The Bayeux Tapestry was begun at some time after 1066 and probably completed within twenty years.

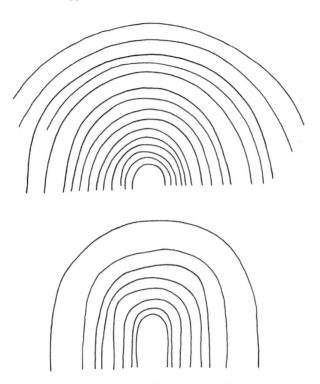

Fig. 2.2: Top: The regular, concentric arches of Hand F of the Harley Psalter (ca.1025–50). Bottom: a selection of those from the Tapestry. Drawing: Maggie Kneen.

concentric, as if either drawn onto the parchment using tools such as dividers, or drawn around templates that were made using these (fig. 2.2). Where any images of the Tapestry are concerned, however, unintentionally crooked or eccentric lines may have been caused by uneven stress upon the linen, which could have happened during the embroidery process, by the subsequent weight of the embroidery, by suspension of the hanging, or by pulling on the fabric during patching and other repair work.

The smallest arches are used right from the start of the Tapestry to represent the most diminutive roof-tiles[17] and windows, and in one instance, the hinges of a door (fig. 2.3). Although employed in many different ways (as evident from the figures and furnishings in fig. 2.3), architecturally the arched templates were also used for various-sized apertures: an apse, the great gate representing the exit from the *burh* of Hastings (W51, Scene 47),[18] and at the English port, a whole tower (see fig. 2.9). The

17 Possibly these represent wooden shingles rather than tiles made of clay or slate. The composition of Bayeux Tapestry roofs and opinions on them are discussed in Michael John Lewis, *The Archaeological Authority of the Bayeux Tapestry*, British Archaeological Reports, British Series 404 (Oxford: John and Erica Hedges, 2005), 36–37 and note 231.
18 In this article, the letter W followed by a number refers to plates in David M. Wilson, *The Bayeux Tapestry* (London: Thames and Hudson, 1985), in each case a double-page spread.

Fig. 2.3: The opening scene of the Bayeux Tapestry (W1, Scene 1) showing template construction in red. The roof above King Edward's head, broken in the middle by a roof boss into what looks like a low-pitched roof, does not have the appearance of a curve, but is in fact made from one of the biggest curves on the Tapestry, which was also used for King Edward's palace roof on W28, Scene 25. The underside of the left-hand span of the roof in the opening scene matches the wide curve of the ceiling beam of the new King Harold's building on W32, Scene 32, which is almost directly beneath the comet. There are so many different curved templates used in this scene that the authors have chosen to illustrate just a typical selection. Photo: By special authorization of the City of Bayeux. Overdrawing: Maggie Kneen.

Fig. 2.4: Bosham Church (W3, Scene 3) showing template construction in red. Several different curved templates have been used to create the features of this building. Photo: By special authorization of the City of Bayeux. Overdrawing: Maggie Kneen.

roofs of the side-aisles of King Edward's palace are covered with two different sizes of small tile. Those on the right-hand side are larger. These are the same size as the topmost row of tiles on the Bosham Church roof (fig. 2.4), which are slightly smaller than the three rows below them, thus seeming to give a sense of distance and perspective and suggesting a degree of architectural observation. This apparent visual acuity may simply have been derived from manuscript illustration, although we also witness this sense of distance in the diminution of some ships, human figures, horses, and even buildings elsewhere in the Tapestry, an early form of perspective created by the simple reduction in size of an image, often seen in late Antique and medieval art. On

The scene numbers are a convenience but have no historic value. They are written, in ink, in a modern hand, on the backcloth of the Bayeux Tapestry, which is sixteenth-century cloth; Gabriel Vial, "The Bayeux Embroidery and Its Backing Strip," in Bouet, Levy, and Neveux, *Bayeux Tapestry*, 111–16. The numbers were added some time after the addition of the present, nineteenth-century, lining, since the ink has leaked onto this lining; Shirley Ann Brown, *The Bayeux Tapestry: Bayeux, Médiatheque Municipale: MS 1: A Sourcebook*, Publications of the Journal of Medieval Latin 9 (Turnhout, Belgium: Brepols, 2013), xviii–xix. The numerals appear in some editions of the Tapestry, including the one-seventh-size folding pull-out versions on sale in Bayeux. Wilson's numbers are plate numbers, their dimensions dependent on the frames of the available photographs, which inevitably cut through "scenes."

the roof of Bosham church, the height of the two top rows of tiles together equal the height of the clerestory windows below them; and the two minuscule windows in the lower right-hand turret are made from the same template as the very small roof-tiles on Edward's palace in Scene 1. The Bosham feasting hall roof (W3–4, Scene 3) makes use of both sizes of tile found on the church roof, but although beginning in neat and orderly fashion on its left-hand side, like Edward's palace, again becomes somewhat random in arrangement towards the right.

It is evident that buildings, wherever they occurred in the Tapestry, were constructed using the same arched templates. Thus, the last remaining built structure on the Tapestry, the church at Hastings (W51, Scene 47, which is in the fifth section of linen), uses exactly the same templates for the same purposes as the first buildings on the Tapestry, with the addition of an apse roof-line. The three English cottages in W45–46, Scenes 40–41 (two of which are visible in fig. 2.5), are the least obvious examples, but they all have arched doorways, and the first has a section of tiled roof. The third of these has bow-shaped walls as a result of having been made with a curved, arched template that seems to be closest in shape to that used for the top part of the tower building at the English port (see fig. 2.9); the same template was also used for many of the curved prows and sterns of the ships, from the first on W4, Scene 4, up to the last on W44, Scene 39, where William's fleet beaches at Pevensey. Expanses of roof-tile appear often on the first five sections of the Tapestry, even where a building is indicated only by supporting posts and a roof, up to the departure of William and his army from Hastings for battle (W51, Scene 47); after that, there is no architecture to warrant any roofing.

Arches were used not only for architectural elements in the rounded Anglo-Norman, Romanesque style but also for other objects within the design. A rule of composition emerges: When used to draw static items like architecture and landscape, the arched templates were always used in perpendicular fashion; to illustrate things that could move, or be moved, such as tools, seat cushions, vessels, prows of ships and their sails, figureheads, and oars, also anatomical details of birds and beasts in the borders, the curved, arched templates might be used at any angle. Containers, including the cauldron and the pony's pannier as the Normans prepare for their feast at Hastings (fig. 2.5) and vessels for food and drink (W3, Scene 3; W47–48, Scene 43) are simply arches used upside down, with a further, unique use as Bishop Odo's headgear as he rides on the Brittany Campaign (W18–19, Scene 16).[19] A section illustrating events around Hastings (fig. 2.6) demonstrates the use of arched templates not only for the

---

19 Usually considered to represent Duke William, but identified as Odo in Gale R. Owen-Crocker, "Brothers, Rivals and the Geometry of the Bayeux Tapestry," in *King Harold II and the Bayeux Tapestry*, ed. Owen-Crocker, Publications of the Manchester Centre for Anglo-Saxon Studies 3 (Woodbridge, UK: Boydell, 2005), 109–23, at 113, reprinted in Owen-Crocker, *The Bayeux Tapestry: Collected Papers* (Farnham, UK: Ashgate, 2012), as chapter 8 with additional pages of images, 124–32. Arthur C. Wright, *Decoding the Bayeux Tapestry: The Secrets of History's Most Famous Embroidery Hidden in Plain Sight* (Barnsley, UK: Pen & Sword Books, 2019), also identifies the figure as Odo (35) and suggests that the man wears "a 'harness-cap' or padded lining" on his head (117).

HIC·COQVI
TVR·CARO

HIC·EST:VVAD·ARD:

Fig. 2.5: English cottages and part of pillaging scene showing a pannier-laden pony and a cauldron (W45–46, Scenes 40–41), showing template construction in red. Photo: By special authorization of the City of Bayeux. Overdrawing: Maggie Kneen.

Fig. 2.6: Section of the Tapestry from the building of Hastings Castle to the firing of a building (W50, Scenes 45–47), showing template construction in red. Photo: By special authorization of the City of Bayeux. Overdrawing: Maggie Kneen.

motte of Hastings Castle (left) and the burning house (right), but also for details of garments, a cushion, and the bodies of border creatures.

A simple arch could have its vertical height altered to make it a taller or a shorter shape (fig. 2.7, left). Furthermore, there are two subgroups of arch templates, distinguished from each other in that one type of template consisted of a plain, solid "tongue" of material with a single outer curve, whilst the other was like the same tongue but with its centre cut away to create a flat arched "strip," almost like a straight-sided horseshoe or the arched architrave surrounding a round-topped door (fig. 2.7, right). This second type therefore had both an inner and an outer curve, making it a hybrid of a template and a stencil, since one could draw around both the outside and the (perforated) inside edges. Both of these types of arched template—"tongue" and "strip"—were used interchangeably on the Tapestry up to W52, Scene 48, where battle begins, after which point and up to the end of the Tapestry as we know it, the action takes place entirely in the open landscape where there are no buildings.

The "strip" templates were also utilised for narrow features such as the branches of trees, rims of shields, and plant-like decorations in the borders (fig. 2.8). The bear's tether in the bottom border of W12, Scene 11, is made from a curve used for the top left branch of the tree on W8 (the boundary between Scenes 7 and 8), and also fits the top left-hand side of the great gate template on W51, Scene 47. The reins of the blue-green horse at the rear on W11, Scene 10, are made from the same template as the steering oar used on Harold's returning ship (W26, Scene 23), but inverted; and the reins of the yellow horse in the foreground on W11, as well as the mane of the rear horse, correspond to the arching undercroft of the burning house (W50, Scene 47; fig. 2.6). The necks of the birds from the upper border above William's castle (W13, Scene 12) fit the arched doorway of the Westminster building (W1, Scene 1; fig. 2.3).

Tracing and overlaying arches on top of others for comparison reveals that, at the design stage of the Tapestry, a deliberate choice had been made as to which of the range of arched templates was to be used for each type of object. Experiments revealed that a sequence of arches which ran consecutively from the smallest arched shape up to that used for both the English port building (fig. 2.9), and William's castle roof (W13, Scene 12) was used for architecture, and also for shields hung along the sides of the ships (the latter at W5, Scenes 4–5; W26–27, Scene 23; W42–43, Scene 38, respectively in the first, second, and fourth sections of linen). A narrow band of arches above this size was allocated to provide the rounded shapes of horse's rumps and also the prow and stern curves of the major ships and their sails. The next sequence of large curves was used for hills, mottes, the enormous circular table at the Hastings feast (W48, Scene 43), and the roof of the exceptionally large *rotunda* building (W11–12, Scene 11). Even larger curves are those which indicate the expanses of roof representing palace interiors, where important conversations and a coronation take place (W28, Scene 25; W31–33, Scenes 30 and 33; and W34–35, Scene 35). From beginning to end of the Tapestry, the smallest of the arched templates also performed the task of representing the phalluses of priapic horses.

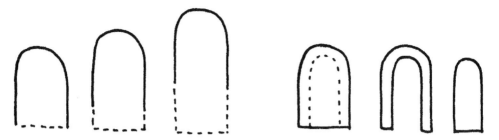

Fig. 2.7: Developed arches. Left: Arches elongated to make a taller shape. Right: "Tongue" and "strip" variations. Drawing: Maggie Kneen.

Fig. 2.8: Secondary uses of "strip" templates. Top left: Tree branches (W12, Scene 12). Top right: Horse reins (W11, Scene 10); one set of reins (red) is made from the template used for the ship's steering oar, W26, Scene 23. The other, and the outline of the horse's mane (blue), match the inner curve of Dinan motte, W23, Scene 19. Bottom left: Necks of birds (W13, Scene 12). Bottom right: A rope tying a bear to a tree (W12, Scene 11, lower border). Drawing: Maggie Kneen.

Fig. 2.9: The English port building (W27, Scene 24), showing single "tongue" arches in red and double "strip" arches in blue. Drawing: Maggie Kneen.

KITE SHAPES

The kite shape was made by closing the arch to a point at the bottom. One way to visualise this is to imagine taking the lower ends of an arch shape between thumb and forefinger and pinching them together to form a point. Kite-shaped templates were used numerous times for shields, but, less obviously, in their many different sizes they were also employed to form the wings of birds and dragons, the bodies of dogs, and other details in both the main register and the borders (fig. 2.10). The pointed ends of various sizes of these kite-shaped templates, usually the larger ones, were also used to create the outlines of castle ditches at Dol, Rennes, and Dinan (W21–23, Scenes 18–19), and at Hastings, and even the spades which dug these ditches (for an example, see the man pushing on his spade with his foot at the left side of fig. 2.6). Many of the folds on fabric and sails were also made by drawing around the pointed end of the larger kite-shaped templates.

Fig. 2.10: Kite shapes. Left: Shields from W23, Scene 19, and W71, Scene 57. Right: Birds' wings, top to bottom, from W1, Scene 1; W4, Scene 4; and W8, Scene 8. Drawing: Maggie Kneen.

BULBOUS SHAPES

In what may be a variation of the hollow, or "strip," type of arched template, there is a hollow, rounded, bulbous template (fig. 2.11)— another template/stencil hybrid— which was developed in a range of sizes, the largest being used for a unique, rounded, pollarded tree from the closing scene of the Hastings section of the Tapestry (W52, boundary between Scenes 47 and 48). Two other trees (on W57, Scene 50, and W73, Scene 58) are also recognizable as pollards, even if the draftsman responsible for designing them did not understand this; they are possibly simple copies of the one on W52. Other examples include the cupped horns of the ox lying (dead?) as the Normans pillage animals for food after their invasion (W45, Scenes 40–41), and the bushes of the only garden on the Tapestry, at the foot of the apsidal church at Hastings (W51, Scene 47).

This bulbous template was also used to create the line of the front hip joint and front leg of the majority of the horses and furthermore was also used to form the horse's head-shape from behind the jaw line to the nose, which explains the double line visible behind both the front hip joint and the jaw/cheek of the majority of the horses, also present in border animals.

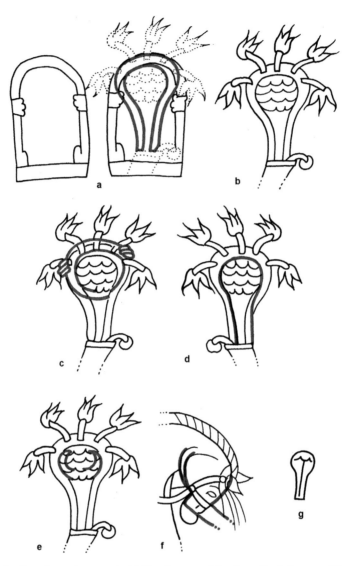

Fig. 2.11: "Bulbous" template use. (a–b) The shape used for the pollarded tree on W52, Scenes 47–48, appears to have developed from an arched template (the doorway is from W1, Scene 1; see fig. 2.3). (c) A rounded shape gazed through by a man on W45, Scene 41, as he assists in preparing the Hastings feast closely fits the same template, as marked here in red. (d) The front hip and leg of the first yellow horse on the Tapestry (W2, Scene 2), its shape marked here in red, is clearly also related to the same bulbous template. (e) So are the horns of an ox (W45, Scenes 40–41) which fit equally neatly within the hollow space within the tree template, as marked in red. (f) The front hip of the second yellow horse, also W2, Scene 2, and marked here in red, is demonstrably made from a template which perfectly fits the head of Harold's black horse which walks just in front of it. (g) A small bush from the foot of the church apse on W51, Scene 47 is a miniature version of the same series. Drawing: Maggie Kneen.

ASYMMETRICAL CURVED TEMPLATES

Whereas the arches and kite-shaped templates of the Tapestry are basically symmetrical, other curved shapes used in the Tapestry are asymmetrical, including architectural and decorative curlicues that arc in only one direction, and the curled and knotted tails of the dragons that appear on shields, as well as on battle pennants and in the bottom border. The leftmost shield dragon in W7, Scene 7, is contorted because the draftsman has misunderstood the template, so that although its head faces one way, its body, when compared to the others, has been reversed, its belly being where its back should be (fig. 2.12, left). W12, Scene 11, shows two shield dragons, both made from the same template, one adapted to fit a smaller space (fig. 2.12, center); the shield dragon on W15, Scene 13, is related to the two in the bottom border of W57, Scene 51 (fig. 2.12, right and bottom), one of which, although being created from the same template as the other, had the template reversed part way through the drafting of the final cartoon. The flexed bodies of many of the soldiers in action are also made from asymmetrical templates, but these have sharp angles as well as curves and so do not altogether fit into this category.[20]

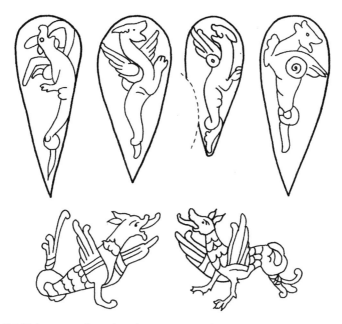

Fig. 2.12: Shield dragons and standing dragons. Top: A dragon shield from W7, Scene 7; a similar pair, both from W12, Scene 11; another shield from W15, Scene 13. Bottom: A confronted pair of scaly, freestanding dragons from W57, Scene 51. Drawing: Maggie Kneen.

20 Human bodies in the Tapestry are the subject of the next stage of this project.

One of the intrinsic qualities of a template (or a stencil) is that it can very easily be flipped over and used in reverse, upside-down, back-to-front, with several or all of these variations at once. Recognition of the flipping of some asymmetrical templates reveals some surprising effects as unrelated objects far apart are found to have been drawn with the same pattern piece. One case is the "drinking horn" template which reverses to become Archbishop Stigand's maniple, flips over to become the oliphant or "blowing horn" at the Hastings feast preparations (W47, Scene 43), and is further repurposed to form the decoration on some shields (W23, Scene 19; W69–70, Scene 56), for which the shape seems to have been flipped over and back again (fig. 2.13). From the undulating land- and seascapes, down to the decorative, coiling curlicues

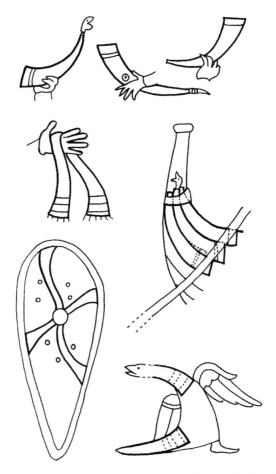

Fig. 2.13: Use of an asymmetrical template to make unrelated items: drinking horns (W3–4, Scene 3), "oliphant" or blowing horn (W47, Scene 43), the archbishop's maniple (W31, Scene 30), ship's curving timbers (W4, Scene 4), shield decoration (W23, Scene 19), a backward-facing bird (W31, Scene 29). Drawing: Maggie Kneen.

and the many tongues of the miniature beasts in the borders, asymmetrical curved templates had an important function in the making of the Tapestry.

DRAGONS

All nineteen dragons in the Bayeux Tapestry are made from related templates. This includes dragons probably taken from different models and sources: The large, single dragon in the lower border beneath Conan's escape from Dol (W21, Scenes 17–18) probably derives from a depiction of the constellation Coetus (a sea monster) in an astronomical drawing, like the adjacent border creatures beneath the quicksands episode and the horsemen storming Dol;[21] smaller, paired dragons with triple tongues may ultimately derive from a Vergilian simile referring to a triple-tongued snake.[22] In the Tapestry, wings, tails, and heads are all related in some way, some clearly made from identical templates even if the shape was rotated or flipped (fig. 2.14). All bodies with their knotted tails are related, if sometimes rather tenuously, but one can always find a connection to the same group of templates. The fact that the dragon parts are moved around a lot in relation to each other (i.e. body, head, tail, wings, and legs) shows that we are dealing with a set of shapes, rather like those for the horses (see below).

Fig. 2.14: A pair of dragons from the bottom borders of W43 and W44 (both in Scene 39) whose bodies, heads, wings, and base of tail are clumsily made from the same templates, reversed for a mirror image. Drawing: Maggie Kneen.

21 Cyril Hart, "The *Cicero-Aratea* and the Bayeux Tapestry," in Owen-Crocker, *King Harold II*, 161–78. Hart does not explicitly link the Bayeux dragon to the constellation drawings, but illustrates Coetus in BL MS Harley 2506, 42v (*sic*, should be 42r), at fig. 24c, and in Harley 647, 21v, at fig. 12. Both are viewable at the BL website, www.bl.uk/manuscripts (accessed Aug. 14, 2019).

22 *Aeneid* II, 475, where Pyrrhus is described as a triple-tongued snake, "linguis … ore trisulis"; Elizabeth M. Tyler, "'When Wings Incarnadine with Gold are Spread': The *Vita Ædwardi Regis* and the Display of Treasure at the Court of Edward the Confessor," in *Treasure in the Medieval West*, ed. Tyler (York: York Medieval Press, 2000), 83–107, at 94–99.

There are two slightly different types of composition in the dragons. Whereas the two-dimensional dragon designs on the kite shields in the central register have long, thin, conical or subconical, wormlike bodies (see fig. 2.12, top), those that are "free-standing" and represented as living, (fire)breathing creatures, although confined to the borders, have deeper ribcages and more significant wings and stronger legs (see fig. 2.12, bottom, and fig. 2.14). Of this latter three-dimensional type, only the two forming English battle pennants (W71, Scene 56) appear in the main register.[23]

One circular element which appears in the general dragon anatomy as a wing-pivot or a tail knot was also pressed into service for producing the testicles of horses or curlicue decoration. For example, both the spiralling shoulder-socket and tail-knot of the kite-shield dragon on W15, Scene 13, in the first linen section, have been made with the same template as several horse scrotums, such as that of the black horse on W16, Scene 14 (nearby but in the second section of linen); also, the eye of the wooden beast-head decorating the left-hand side of Harold's coronation throne (W32, Scene 33, third linen section) and the roundel sitting centrally at the top of Bayeux dome (W25, Scene 22, second linen section).

Finally, the curtain twisted around the bedstead of the dying King Edward (W30, Scene 27, third linen section) is a very large version of the dragon's knotted tail.

HORSES

All of the 190 equines depicted in the Tapestry[24] appear to have been built using sets of templates (up to eight separate pieces per horse) that could be articulated in relation to one another, giving the impression of vitality and movement by conferring a different position to every horse. Each component shape corresponds to a different anatomical part: head, neck, chest, rump, limbs, and tail (fig. 2.15).[25] The different elements of these sets could be disassembled and used interchangeably from horse to horse, as

---

23 Michael Lewis (private communication to Gale R. Owen-Crocker, Nov. 27, 2019) points out that these are often interpreted as wyverns (two-legged creatures similar to dragons). The authors are grateful to Professor Lewis for a number of helpful suggestions.

24 This figure includes border animals, donkeys, a pony, and winged and tethered equines, as well as the horses in the main register.

25 This material on horses was presented by Maggie Kneen in a paper titled "Designer Tools of the Eleventh Century: The Use of Templates on the Bayeux Tapestry" in a session called "Medieval Embroidery" at the 2014 International Medieval Congress, University of Leeds, UK. The authors have not, at this stage of their work, attempted to engage with Sarah Larratt Keefer's observations that the Tapestry depicts English Arab horses and Norman Iberian ones (Keefer, "Hwær Cwom Mearh? The Horse in Anglo-Saxon England," *Journal of Medieval History* 22, no. 2 [1996]: 115–34, at 129–32); that specific horses in the Tapestry derive from the Old English Hexateuch and the BL MS Cotton Cleopatra C.viii manuscript of Prudentius (Keefer, "Body Language: A Graphic Commentary by the Horses of the Bayeux Tapestry," in Owen-Crocker, *King Harold II*, 93–108, at 99, 103); or that the horses convey a subtle commentary in terms of details such as spurs, gender, and "priapism" (ibid., 95–97, 100–5), other than to note that whatever their appearance and size, all Tapestry horses are composed with templates.

Fig. 2.15: Curved templates used to make a horse, shown as a joined-up whole and with pieces separated. Drawing: Maggie Kneen.

can be seen from one horse on which the head is far too small for its body and another with a very short, cramped-up body yet long, gangly legs; others are impossibly stretched out (fig. 2.16). The variety of poses which the horses exhibit reveal that the anatomically shaped templates from which they were made were purposely designed to have significant overlap with the adjoining pieces, giving them ample capacity to stretch or contract, as necessary, thereby being able to display all stages of momentum from complete stasis to full gallop. The Tapestry designers seem to have made efforts to distinguish each animal from the next, and sometimes they achieved this by placing limbs or head at different angles. In addition, however, colour contrast is used to individualise horses in an overlapping row, disguising the fact that each animal has been drawn using similar sets of templates (for example W8, Scenes 7, right, and 8, left).[26]

Horses' rumps and tails are made using a variety of arched templates of both the solid and strip kind. As an example of a tail, the top layers of that of Vital's horse (W55,

26 "There are never two directly adjacent horses in the same colour, or a rider dressed in the same hue as his horse"; Gale R. Owen-Crocker, "Fur, Feathers, Skin, Fibre, Wood: Representational Techniques in the Bayeux Tapestry," in Owen-Crocker, *Collected Papers*, chap. 3, at 5.

Fig. 2.16: Ill-matched horse templates (W18, Scene 16; W8, Scene 8; W20, Scene 18).
Drawing: Maggie Kneen.

Scene 49) were made using an arched template that fits the left side of Hastings motte (W49–50, Scenes 45–46) and also has the same curve as the napes of the red horse on W54, Scene 49, and Guy's mule on W14, Scene 13, to name only two. The tail of the horse ridden by Harold as a *nuntius* (messenger) brings information that William's army has been seen (W56–57, Scene 50), is made from two strip curves, one which was also used to form the roof of the tower at the English port (fig. 2.9), although reversed, and the other from the top curve of the great gate at Hastings (W51, Scene 47). The tail of the red horse facing an English axe-man (W62, Scene 52), which also has a disproportionately small head but overly ample rump, is made from the kite-shaped template of its own rider's shield.

COMPOSITION OF THE DESIGN

The Bayeux Tapestry is now generally considered to be of English design. Not only does its Latin inscription include the Old English letters Æ and Ð and some Old English–derived word forms, as well as some Norman French ones;[27] also the style of its pictorial content and some specific use of models point to English design, and particularly to Canterbury. In the late tenth and early eleventh centuries, the monastic scriptoria of Canterbury, in Kent, southeast England, developed a style of illustrating narrative in their manuscripts with cycles of drawings which depicted lively human figures in buildings and landscapes, employing tools and furniture in apparently realistic ways: a style very different from the practice of illuminating manuscripts with decorative initials and elaborate but somewhat static depictions of significant biblical events and of saints, for which the Winchester School of painting is justifiably famous. Over the last seven decades, research has repeatedly linked the Bayeux Tapestry with Canterbury, showing that not only is the Tapestry's general graphic style similar to that of eleventh-century manuscripts made at St. Augustine's Abbey, Canterbury, such as the Old English illustrated Hexateuch[28] and an illustrated calendar,[29] but also that specific images from Canterbury manuscripts were used as models for figures, details, and *mises en scène*, especially the Hexateuch but also a copy of Prudentius's allegorical poem *Psychomachia*[30] and drawings of the constellations from a ninth-century Carolingian manuscript (Harley 647) and a tenth-century one from Fleury (Harley 2506), both of which were in Canterbury (see above, page 49). The Tapestry designer was also evidently familiar with the Utrecht Psalter, an influential ninth-century illustrated Carolingian manuscript,[31] which was brought to Christ Church, Canterbury, around the year 1000, and its partial copy, the Harley Psalter,[32] which was begun early in the eleventh century and was still being worked on in the 1070s and 80s when the Bayeux Tapestry was supposedly being made. The artist may also have known the late-tenth-century illustrations to Genesis rendered in Old English verse, in what

---

27 Gale R. Owen-Crocker, "The Embroidered Word: Text in the Bayeux Tapestry," *Medieval Clothing and Textiles* 2 (2006): 35–59, esp. 37 and 58, where she suggests "dictation by a Norman speaking Latin to an Englishman who wrote it down." Reprinted as chapter 6 in Owen-Crocker, *Collected Papers*.

28 BL MS Cotton Claudius B.iv, viewable at www.bl.uk/manuscripts (accessed Aug. 1, 2019).

29 In BL MS Cotton Tiberius B.v, viewable at www.bl.uk/manuscripts (accessed Aug. 1, 2019).

30 BL MS Cotton Cleopatra C.viii, viewable at www.bl.uk/manuscripts (accessed Aug. 1, 2019).

31 Utrecht, Netherlands, Universiteitsbibliotheek, MS 32 (Script eccl. 484), viewable at https://bc.library.uu.nl/utrecht-psalter.html (accessed Aug. 1, 2019).

32 BL MS Harley 603, viewable at www.bl.uk/manuscripts (accessed Aug. 1, 2019).

was probably also a Christ Church manuscript.[33] There are also parallels in Canterbury ivory carvings,[34] and a parallel for the script on a St. Augustine's, Canterbury, gravestone.[35] For these reasons and others, many scholars believe that the Tapestry was designed at St. Augustine's Canterbury.[36]

33 Oxford, Bodleian Library, MS Junius 11, viewable at https://digital.bodleian.ox.ac.uk (accessed Aug. 1, 2019). See Michael J. Lewis, "The Bayeux Tapestry and Oxford, Bodleian Library, Junius 11," in Lewis, Owen-Crocker, and Terkla, *Bayeux Tapestry: New Approaches*, 105–11.

34 The pioneering work in recognising Canterbury influence in the Bayeux Tapestry was that of Francis Wormald, "Style and Design," in *The Bayeux Tapestry: A Comprehensive Survey*, ed. Sir Frank Stenton (London: Phaidon, 1957). A firm case for St. Augustine's as the place of origin of the Tapestry, based on cumulative evidence, is made in the influential article by N. P. Brooks and H. E. Walker, "The Authority and Interpretation of the Bayeux Tapestry," in *The Study of the Bayeux Tapestry*, ed. Richard Gameson (Woodbridge, UK: Boydell, 1997), 63–110, at 70–78, first published in *Proceedings of the Battle Conference on Anglo-Norman Studies* 1 (1979): 1–34 and 549–60. Visual "quotations" from St. Augustine's manuscripts were enumerated by David Bernstein as a fundamental part of his argument that the Tapestry was designed in an environment resistant to Normanization; Bernstein, *The Mystery of the Bayeux Tapestry* (London: Guild Publishing, 1986), 39–46. (Bernstein employs the word "quotations" at 39, a term now often used to characterise the Bayeux design's use of models.) Cyril Roy Hart has been influential in adding to the corpus of Canterbury borrowings, and including astronomical drawings and ivories; Hart, "The Canterbury Contribution to the Bayeux Tapestry," in *Art and Symbolism in Medieval Europe: Papers of the 'Medieval Europe Brugge 1997' Conference* 5, ed. Guy de Boe and Frans Verhaege (Zellik, Belgium: Instituut voor het Archeologisch Patrimonium, 1997), 7–15; Hart, "The Bayeux Tapestry and Schools of Illumination at Canterbury," *Anglo-Norman Studies* 22 (1999): 117–67; and Hart, "*Cicero-Aratea*." For historiography and analysis of the thematic significance of individual cases of borrowing, see Gale R. Owen-Crocker, "Reading the Bayeux Tapestry through Canterbury Eyes," in *Anglo-Saxons: Studies Presented to Cyril Roy Hart*, ed. S. Keynes and A. P. Smyth (Dublin: Four Courts, 2006), 243–65, reprinted as chapter 4 in Owen-Crocker, *Collected Papers*; also, for the blending of sources ultimately Roman with details from Canterbury manuscripts, Owen-Crocker, "Stylistic Variation and Roman Influence in the Bayeux Tapestry," in *The Bayeux Tapestry Revisited*, ed. J. M. Crafton, *Peregrinations* 2, no. 4 (2009): 51–96, reprinted as chapter 5 in Owen-Crocker, *Collected Papers*; and for further parallels with the Hexateuch, Owen-Crocker, "Reading the Mind of the Bayeux Tapestry Master," in *Studies in Medieval and Renaissance History* 15, ed. Joel Rosenthal and Paul Szarmach (forthcoming). For architectural parallels between the Bayeux Tapestry and manuscripts, see Lewis, *Archaeological Authority*, 151–53.

35 Owen-Crocker, "Embroidered Word," 50.

36 There are dissenting views: Michael Lewis feels the Canterbury influence/place of design might be exaggerated, suggesting it is a self-perpetuating theory, and notes that there is more evidence surviving from Canterbury than other places which have accordingly been overlooked; Lewis, "La Tapisserie de Bayeux et l'Art Anglo-Saxon," in Lemagnen, Brown, and Owen-Crocker, *L'Invention*, 229–45 (English summary at 245). Other scholars, for different reasons, have suggested French origins, notably Wolfgang Grape, *The Bayeux Tapestry: Monument to a Roman Triumph*, trans. David Britt (Munich: Prestel, 1994), who rejects Anglo-Saxon influence and argues for manufacture in Bayeux from comparison with continental manuscript images and sculpture; and George Beech, *Was the Bayeux Tapestry Made in France? The Case for Saint-Florent of Saumur* (New York: Palgrave Macmillan, 2005), who argues for manufacture in the Loire on the basis of evidence of a textile workshop at Saint-Florent, the fact that its Abbot William had been Lord of Dol, which features in the Brittany campaign in the Tapestry (Scenes 16–20), and some comparison with murals, sculptures, and manuscript art in the wider region. Beech does, however, attempt to reconcile his thesis with the acknowledged evidence of

The Bayeux Tapestry artist(s) may, on occasion, have copied images one-to-one, or possibly even traced them onto the preliminary cartoon.[37] Many more were probably simply remembered, by an artist/designer who knew the Canterbury libraries well and was accustomed to memorising text and to meditating upon it with the aid of mnemonic pictures.[38] Thus the designer, wishing to produce suitable images for the Tapestry on the topic of the building of the Norman fleet, used features of Noah's building of the Ark from the Old English illustrated Hexateuch (fig. 2.17) but did not copy the image in its entirety, instead using details from it in different places. The figure with the forked beard and full-skirted tunic is copied twice, once in reverse; his characteristic straddling position is reproduced,[39] and his distinctive woodworking tool is given to another carpenter working on another vessel, above (fig. 2.18). The

---

Canterbury design, suggesting either collaboration between Saint-Florent and St. Augustine's, or a product designed in Canterbury and made in Saint-Florent (96–99). Significantly, French art historian Maylis Baylé concludes her survey "The Bayeux Tapestry and Decoration in Northwestern Europe: Style and Composition," in Bouet, Levy, and Neveux, *Bayeux Tapestry*, 303–25, with the assertion that the Bayeux Tapestry was produced in England "and logically in the artistic surroundings of Canterbury," and was responsible for introducing Anglo-Norman (including Anglo-Scandinavian) elements to the Norman duchy (324–25). Sylvette Lemagnen, until recently curator of the Tapestry, concurs: "The Tapestry comprises too many images and written forms of Anglo-Saxon origin for us to give credit to its possible production on the Continent"; Lemagnen, *La Tapisserie de Bayeux: Une Découverte Pas à Pas / A Step-by-Step Discovery*, with translation by Heather Inglis (Bayeux, France: Orep Éditions, 2015), 13.

37 See note 8. Eleventh-century artists may have known how make a medium with which to trace by scraping and oiling animal skin to the point of it becoming transparent, or by making a transparent membrane from fish glue and leaf glue, methods described ca. 1400 by Cennino d'Andrea Cennini, *The Craftsman's Handbook: The Italian "Il Libro dell' Arte,"* trans. Daniel V. Thompson (1933; repr. New York: Dover Publications, 1960), 13–14. However, unlike tracing onto parchment, which can be done by means of pressing down on the tracing medium and then drawing over the resulting indentations, tracing onto linen would require some means of marking the material, such as leadpoint drawn on the back of the tracing medium, which would then be rubbed until the lead drawing offset onto the linen. This method has tentatively been suggested for transferring designs onto vellum in the Lindisfarne Gospels (BL MS Cotton Nero D.iv, ca. 700); Brown, *Lindisfarne Gospels*, 220. To create her own embroidery, Jan Messent drew the design on paper and then "traced through from the underside," noting that the design could easily be seen through fine linen. She then outlined the traced image with a fine brush and dark watercolour paint. She comments: "This method, far easier than the other [pricking and pouncing], might even have been used by the designer and his assistants, or they may have felt confident enough to draw freehand, straight onto the linen, copying preparatory sketches"; Messent, *Embroiderers' Story*, 73.

38 The technique of making mnemonic pictures was known in Antiquity and was evidently revived in the ninth century: The illustrations in the Utrecht Psalter are in this category, functioning in that case "to cue and trigger recollection of textual material that the reader already knows"; Mary Carruthers, *The Book of Memory: A Study of Memory in Medieval Culture*, 2nd ed. (Cambridge: Cambridge University Press, 2008), 281–85, quotation at 285.

39 This is awkward in both cases: The Hexateuch artist seems to have drawn the legs the wrong way round, making an impossible twisting of the body; the Tapestry artist has the figure impossibly straddling the whole ship; see further Owen-Crocker, "Stylistic Variation," 10.

Fig. 2.17: Noah building the ark in the Old English Hexateuch (London, British Library, MS Cotton Claudius B. iv), 13v, detail. Photo: Courtesy of the British Library Board.

artists' sketches were subsequently enlarged if necessary and laid out by the draftsman using templates and a square configuration.[40]

The St. Augustine's manuscript tradition received new blood in the form of Scollandus, the first Norman abbot of the monastery, who had arrived by at least 1072 and ruled until his death in 1087.[41] He was one of a number of monks sent to England after the Norman Conquest by Rollandus, abbot of Mont Saint-Michel, where Scollandus had been a scribe; his name is mentioned as one of six writers in a colophon in a surviving Mont Saint-Michel manuscript.[42] A large number of Mont Saint-Michel manuscripts survive in the municipal library of Avranches, a town in the Normandy area, having been, like collections from other religious houses, confiscated and nationalised during the French Revolution.[43] Eleventh-century manuscripts from Mont Saint-Michel, which Richard Gameson describes as "the most decoratively active Nor-

40 Owen-Crocker, "La Tapisserie de Bayeux."
41 Also known as Scolland or Scotland. His original name was Écoulant. The start of his abbacy is uncertain. It is dated variously in Pastan and White, *Bayeux Tapestry and Its Contexts*: ca. 1070 at p. 81, ca. 1072 at p. 121, and 1070 at p. 194.
42 J. J. G. Alexander, *Norman Illumination at Mont Saint-Michel, 966–1100* (Oxford: Clarendon, 1970), 16–18; Monique Dosdat, *L'Enluminure Romane au Mont-Saint-Michel, Xe–XIIe Siècle* (Rennes, France: Editions Ouest-France, Édilarge SA, 2006), 32–33. His name survives in Avranches, France, Bibliothèque Municipale, MS 103, 220v (Gregory's *Dialogues*).
43 Bibliothèque Virtuelle de Mont Saint-Michel, www.unicaen.fr/bvmsm (accessed Aug. 2, 2019).

Fig. 2.18: Building the Norman fleet. The design copies the Hexateuch but also uses templates. Photo: By special authorization of the City of Bayeux. Overdrawing: Maggie Kneen.

man scriptorium,"[44] offer compelling evidence for the repeated use of shapes, and some of these bear striking resemblance to details on the Bayeux Tapestry (fig. 2.19). It is likely that monks' scribal tools, templates, and stencils were brought at this time from Mont Saint-Michel, along with gifts of manuscripts which could be copied or traced. It was probably as much an acknowledgement of the Mont Saint-Michel presence at Canterbury as geographical veracity that led to the inclusion of a fairly detailed image of that monastery in the depiction of William's Brittany campaign in the Bayeux Tapestry (W19, Scene 16). The seated, pointing figure depicted in the upper border next to the monastery may well have depicted a specific person associated with Mont Saint-Michel, but it wears male, secular clothing and is impossible to identify as the abbot or anyone else. The probable significance of Scollandus with regard to the creation of the Tapestry was argued by Gameson.[45] The Norman abbot's influence on the

44 Richard Gameson, "The Origin, Art and Message of the Bayeux Tapestry," in Gameson, *Study of the Bayeux Tapestry*, 157–211, at 172.
45 Ibid.

Fig. 2.19: Comparison of elements from a Mont Saint-Michel manuscript and the Bayeux Tapestry. Top left: Decorative curlicue extracts from a single illuminated initial in Avranches, France, Bibliothèque Municipale, MS 103, 5r, scribes of which included Scollandus, who became abbot of St. Augustine's Abbey, Canterbury. Top right: A selection of repeated curled templates found throughout the length of the Bayeux Tapestry. Bottom left: A beast-head motif in a sketch from MS 103, 89v. Bottom right: A similar motif from a shield on W8, Scene 7, of the Tapestry. Drawing: Maggie Kneen.

Tapestry may have been even deeper: Elizabeth Pastan and Stephen White moved towards a position later more strongly suggested by Howard B. Clarke that Scollandus was the master-designer of the Tapestry.[46] Pastan and White have recently proposed that the Tapestry was designed to hang in the monks' choir of his new Romanesque abbey church, the building of which was begun ca. 1073.[47]

46 Elizabeth Carson Pastan and Stephen D. White, "Problematizing Patronage: Odo of Bayeux and the Bayeux Tapestry," in *The Bayeux Tapestry: New Interpretations*, ed. Martin K. Foys, Karen Eileen Overby, and Dan Terkla (Woodbridge, UK: Boydell, 2009), 1–24; Howard B. Clarke, "The Identity of the Designer of the Bayeux Tapestry," *Anglo-Norman Studies* 35 (2013): 119–39. Both retain the possibility that the benefactor/patron of the Tapestry was Odo, half-brother of William the Conqueror.

47 Pastan and White, *Bayeux Tapestry and Its Contexts*, esp. Stephen D. White, "Locating Harold's Oath and Tracing His Itinerary," 121–24; Pastan, "Representing Architecture," 194–95; and Pastan and White, "Conclusion," 288–92, at 290. Here the authors reject the theory of a celebrity patron, in favour of the conception of an artwork made both by and for the community of St. Augustine's. The jury remains out on Pastan and White's overall thesis. For many years the scholars' favourite candidate for patron of the Tapestry has been Odo, who was both Earl of

FROM PRELIMARY DESIGN TO FINAL CARTOON

One of the questions about the Bayeux Tapestry that has received little attention is that of how the design was transmitted to the linen which was to be embroidered. Desirée Koslin assumed that a cartoon was drawn on parchment, that this was enlarged and that the design was transferred to the linen by pricking and pouncing: making tiny holes in the lines on the pattern, then forcing powder, usually charcoal, through the holes,[48] a form of tracing described ca. 1400 by Cennini and certainly used by later medieval artists and embroidery workshops.[49] Embroiderer Jan Messent considered prick-and-pounce the most likely method of transferring the cartoons to the linen and illustrated the method but, perhaps significantly, chose not to do this in her own Bayeux Tapestry–type embroidery.[50] Carola Hicks, who considered the making of the embroidery at some length, was obviously influenced by Messent and Koslin but remained somewhat sceptical:

> Artists drew on parchment …. These drawings might have been scaled up by the de-signer and assistants [into cartoons]. … If cartoons had been used, the outlines would have been transferred to the linen by the technique of "pricking and pouncing" …. Then the dots were joined up by brush and ink to produce the original outlines …. However it is just as likely that the assistants did not use cartoons, but simply copied the original drawings onto the linen.[51]

The question of what form the enlarged cartoon took has not been satisfactorily an-swered. In the absence of commercially produced paper at this time,[52] the usual early medieval writing/drawing material for permanent works[53] was animal skin (parch-

---

Kent and Bishop of Bayeux, and the fact remains that the Tapestry was rediscovered in Bayeux Cathedral. Commentators also differ on whether the Tapestry was made for an ecclesiastical or secular place.

48 As part of the interesting suggestion that parts of the design were erroneously inverted as the pattern pieces were laid down; Desirée Koslin, "Turning Time in the Bayeux Tapestry," *Textile and Text* 13, no. 1 (1990): 28–45.

49 Cennini, *Craftsman's Handbook*, 87. Cennini recommends using charcoal dust wrapped in a piece of rag for pouncing onto white cloth. This method is rather tedious, but has the advantage that the pattern pieces can be used repeatedly, and both sides of them might be used as stencils for repeat shapes.

50 Messent, *Embroiderers' Story*, 49, but compare 73, discussed further above at note 37.

51 Carola Hicks, *The Bayeux Tapestry: The Life Story of a Masterpiece* (London: Chatto and Windus, 2006), chap. 3, "The Project," quotations from 44, 46. When explaining the pricking and pounc-ing method, Hicks mentions the possibility of cartoons being put on the wrong way round, which is Koslin's thesis.

52 Linen or hemp paper was only beginning to be manufactured in Europe, in the Iberian pen-insula, in the second half of the eleventh century. Craftsmen may already have been making it for their own use. Theophilus (probably Roger of Helmarshausen, a Benedictine monk of the first half of the twelfth century) refers to "pergamenam Graecam, quae fit ex lana lini" ("Greek parchment, which is made from linen rags") as preparation for making gold leaf; *Theophilus: De Diversis Artibus*, ed. and trans. C. R. Dodwell (Oxford: Clarendon, 1986), 20–21.

53 Small wax tablets could be used for temporary notes.

ment or vellum), but this was costly and time-consuming to prepare. To produce a cartoon the size of the Bayeux Tapestry on animal skins, which are relatively small, seems an improbable undertaking, especially since one can draw or write directly onto linen cloth in charcoal or with ink using a sharp quill pen, or possibly in plummet or silverpoint.[54] Howard Bloch appears to have considered plummet but is ambiguous about how the cartoon might have been made.[55] Cyril Hart favoured the method of direct drawing onto the linen with charcoal;[56] Clarke cautiously suggests it.[57] A recent assumption that the embroidery was worked with no under-drawing at all is surely untenable to anyone who has embroidered, except possibly for very small details such as border foliage, which is sometimes clumsy-looking.[58]

A piece of linen surviving in the treasury of Sens Cathedral, in north-central France, may provide a missing link to elucidate the method of creating an embroidery (fig. 2.20). A rectangle of cloth measuring 130 by 94 centimetres (51.2 by 37 inches)

54 Cennini, *Craftsman's Handbook*, 7, describes plummet as a stylus made of two parts lead to one part tin "beaten with a hammer." Clemens and Graham call plummet "the precursor of the modern pencil" and state that it was in regular use for ruling manuscripts and for under-drawing from the late eleventh century, adding that it left "a faint, grainy, greyish or reddish line on the page"; Raymond Clemens and Timothy Graham, *Introduction to Manuscript Studies* (Ithaca, NY: Cornell University Press, 2007), 133, 268. It was sometimes fitted into a handle; see the illustrations in Christopher de Hamel, *Scribes and Illuminators*, Medieval Craftsmen (London: British Museum Press, 1992), 23, where fig. 15 shows later medieval styli comprising fine metal points fitted into bone handles and fig. 16 a clumsier-looking stick of lead. The authors are grateful to Professor Timothy Graham for this reference. Detailed hardpoint drawings survive in unfinished eleventh- to twelfth-century manuscripts, showing it could be used for fine and intricate work, but it was normally inked over; Jonathan J. G. Alexander, *Medieval Illuminators and their Methods of Work* (New Haven, CT: Yale University Press, 1992), 38–39. Professor Michelle Brown assures the authors that either leadpoint or silverpoint could be used successfully to draw on linen; pers. comm., Sept. 5, 2019.

55 R. Howard Bloch, *A Needle in the Right Hand of God: The Norman Conquest of 1066 and the Making and Meaning of the Bayeux Tapestry* (New York: Random House, 2006). Bloch writes of a workshop equipped with "design sketches either on loose pieces of parchment or in set-scene pattern books, lead for drawing on linen" (87); but also says "the overall coherence of conception ... indicates that those who actually executed such a single vision must have worked either from a separate drawing or set of drawings or, alternatively, that the pattern for the Tapestry might have been drawn directly on the linen surface," conjecturing that washing has removed under-drawings "in lead or other material" (88). However he also confusingly speculates that the drawings were "traced directly upon the linen [but] it is hard to believe that whoever traced them could have worked without some version of a preliminary sketch" (89). Bloch is evidently not using the word "traced" in the technical sense of reproducing a drawing by means of a transparent medium as discussed above at note 37, in which a preliminary drawing is essential.

56 Hart, "Schools of Illumination," 124, suggesting all the scenes and the borders were drawn this way by a single St. Augustine's monk.

57 "The *scénariste* [as opposed to the *artiste*] may or may not have been responsible for drawing in charcoal or some other medium the actual cartoons in advance of the work of embroidery, although no trace now remains of this process"; Clarke, "Identity," 122.

58 "If no trace has ever been found it is safest to assume that it did not exist. ... [A]ny cartoon would have been worked on the linen base, which would certainly have left traces noticed over the years." Wright, *Decoding the Bayeux Tapestry*, 133–34.

Fig. 2.20: Eleventh-century linen embroidery cartoon from Sens Cathedral, with embroidered section at bottom left and centre. Photo: By permission of the Treasury of Sens Cathedral.

is divided into five horizontal zones, densely covered with ink-drawn images,[59] which were identified by Maurice Prou as a depiction of part of the biblical story of King David and his son Absalom (found in 2 Samuel 15–18).[60] The item was brought to

---

59 "dessinés à l'encre"; Monique King, "David et Absalon, une Tenture 'Brodée' d'Environ 1100 au Trésor de Sens," *CIETA-Bulletin* 75 (1998): 48–52, at 48. We are grateful to Frances Pritchard for bringing the object, and this article, to our attention.

60 M. Maurice Prou, "Brodée du XIe au XIIe Siècle au Trésor de la Cathédrale de Sens," in *Mélanges Offerts à M. Gustave Schlumberger*, vol. 2 (Paris: Librairie Orientaliste Paul Geuthner, 1924), 465–76.

the attention of the historic textile community in 1998 by Monique King. Like the Bayeux Tapestry, the linen includes buildings, trees, human figures and horsemen, figures in armour, weapons, kite-shaped shields, and pennants (figs. 2.21 and 2.22). On iconographic grounds the Sens cloth has been dated to the late eleventh to the early twelfth century and thus close in date to the Bayeux Tapestry.[61] A small part of it has been embroidered,[62] which has led scholars to assume that the piece of linen is the (final) cartoon for an embroidery. In fact the attempt to embroider it may be misleading: Though the images on the linen are quite tall—King compared their height to those of the main register of the Bayeux Tapestry[63]—they are tightly cramped together, and the divisions between the horizontal zones are roughly drawn, with buildings penetrating the boundaries into zones above them. King describes the effect as "une composition confuse et touffue" (a confused and dense composition), points out that the embroidery does not add to the legibility of the design, and suggests the enterprise was abandoned as ill-conceived.[64] It must, indeed, have been very awkward to embroider such crowded images; the Bayeux Tapestry is much more widely spaced, and its overlapping figures much more systematically organised. It is possible, perhaps, that the small area of embroidery is a red herring, and that what we have in the unique Sens cartoon is not a final cartoon but one panel of preliminary cartoon that was yet to be laid out width-wise and the zones neatly drawn by a draftsman/woman. This is of course speculation, but what the Sens cartoon certainly demonstrates is that artists did draw in ink directly on linen and that one person at least recognised this as a work to be embroidered, as modern scholars have done, even if that person abandoned the task.

This raises another possibility, however, one which, as far as these authors are aware, has not been suggested before: that the Bayeux artists might also have made their preliminary drawings, of individual images or episodes, in charcoal, leadpoint, silverpoint, or ink on small pieces of linen, rather than on precious parchment, and that these were used to make the final cartoon on the long lengths of linen, which was drawn with one or more of these writing materials, laid out according to geometric principles and with the aid of drawing tools. Some of the artists' preliminary images might have been used by the draftsmen more than once (for example, the bull in the lower border of W7, Scene 7, which reappears enlarged in the main register of W45,

---

61 King, "David et Absalon," 51.
62 Unlike the Bayeux Tapestry, which is stitched with wool, the Sens linen is embroidered in silk, in split stitch, in rather drab colours, two shades of beige and two of brown; King, "David et Absalon," 48. The embroidery is visible at the bottom left of fig. 2.20.
63 This is slightly excessive. The Sens piece has undecorated edges of 2.5 centimetres (1 inch) top and bottom, leaving a space of 125 centimetres (49.2 inches) for five zones, an average of 25 centimetres (9.8 inches) each (though the top register is wider than those below). The Bayeux Tapestry measures about 50 centimetres (19.7 inches), top to bottom, its borders about 8.4 centimetres (3.3 inches) each, leaving a main register of about 33.2 centimetres (13 inches), though of course most of the figures do not fill the full register.
64 King, "David et Absalon," 48.

Fig. 2.21: Detail of fig. 2.20 (second zone from top, at left), showing Absalom hanging by his hair and a battle. Photo: By permission of the Treasury of Sens Cathedral.

Fig. 2.22: Detail of fig. 2.20 (second zone from top, right of center), showing a battle and the city of Mahana. Photo: By permission of the Treasury of Sens Cathedral.

Scene 40). In other cases the charcoal or metalpoint might have been brushed off or erased, or ink drawings washed out, and the linen pieces re-used for more preliminary drawings.

CONCLUSIONS

The experiment with curves shows that shapes of the same proportions (but different sizes) recur throughout the Tapestry. The shapes are so accurately repetitive throughout this enormous work that it is impossible to believe that they could all have been drawn freehand; nor could artists working freehand make these shapes incrementally bigger or smaller in a way that corresponded to a predetermined sequence that was merely a mental construct. The research therefore demonstrates that the design workshop owned sets of templates enabling the artists to draw similar shapes in a range of different sizes. The curved shapes identified include arches and other symmetrical models probably derived from them (kite and bulbous shapes), and also asymmetrical shapes. The exercise shows that the same sets of templates were used on each of the nine sections of linen, in the main register, the borders above, below, and to the left-hand side of it, and also in the curved letters (particularly C's, D's and uncial E's) of the inscription. They appear on images that modern scholars have related to specific Canterbury manuscripts and also in designs they have not assigned to any source. Even in areas where graphic differences may suggest a different artist's hand, where the work is more angular and spread out and the usual squares/rectangles are not so apparent (as in fig. 2.5), curved templates which appear elsewhere in the Tapestry are used.

It is therefore evident that the cartoon on which the Bayeux Tapestry was embroidered was achieved in one place, in a single complex operation, and by one team of draftsmen using the same sets of curved tools. Quite how this is to be reconciled with the perception of different contributing artists who drew in different styles, sketched faces in different ways, and used different source material is not yet entirely clear.[65] Evidently different contributions were brought together to be professionally laid out; possibly some details, such as faces, were added later by hand. The extent of template use is perhaps surprising and we are not, at this stage, speculating about why the cartoon was so heavily dependent on tool-assisted composition rather than entirely freehand drawing: We are simply letting the research speak for itself. The whole cartoon, in its separate pieces, was probably sent to different workshops to be embroidered before

---

65   For different types of faces in the Bayeux Tapestry, see Owen-Crocker, "Faces and Places," and for the argument concerning a second artist drawing in a different style from the principal artist, in conjunction with different principles of laying out the work, see Owen-Crocker, "La Tapisserie de Bayeux." Further graphic differences within the Tapestry include the borders' use of images of Aesop's fables from an unidentified source, not used in the main register; and foliage in very different styles in different parts of the borders.

the sections were reunited again and stitched together at which time some additional embroidery was carried out on either side of, and across, joins.[66]

One further issue relating to the research question "How do our findings develop our understanding of how the Tapestry was designed?" seems clear: The St. Augustine's, Christ Church, and Mont Saint-Michel communities were monastic and male. The Bayeux artists took much of their original inspiration and impetus from the rich collections of illustrated manuscripts in the famed Canterbury libraries, and the draftsmen used details and methods of duplicating details related to techniques in manuscripts originating at Mont Saint-Michel as well as St. Augustine's and Christ Church. Anyone with detailed knowledge of the Canterbury libraries was almost certainly male, and so were the artists of eleventh-century Canterbury and Mont Saint-Michel. Whatever the roles of women at earlier and later stages of the making of the Tapestry may have been,[67] the initial drawing work and the wielding of the templates in laying out the cartoon were probably carried out by men.

Very little seems to have been drawn on the Tapestry without some utilisation of a template or templates. Apart from the insights and information to be gleaned as

---

66 Bédat and Girault-Kurtzeman, "The Technical Study," 97; Gale R. Owen-Crocker, "The Bayeux 'Tapestry': Invisible Seams and Visible Boundaries," *Anglo-Saxon England* 31 (2002): 257–73, at 259–64, reprinted as chapter 2 in Owen-Crocker, *Collected Papers*, 1–21, at 4–9; Alexandra Lester-Makin, "The Front Tells the Story, the Back Tells the History: A Technical Discussion of the Bayeux Tapestry," in *Making Sense of the Bayeux Tapestry: Readings and Reworkings*, ed. Anna C. Henderson with Gale R. Owen-Crocker (Manchester: Manchester University Press, 2016), 23–40, esp. 26–36.

67 Spinning and embroidering fall into the categories of traditional women's work: spindle whorls are found almost exclusively with female burials, not male, in the furnished graves of the early Anglo-Saxon period, and the phrase *spinl healfe*, "spindle side," was used by King Alfred in his will to designate his female relatives; see transcription S 1507 at The Electronic Sawyer: Online Catalogue of Anglo-Saxon Charters, https://esawyer.lib.cam.ac.uk/charter/1507.html, line 24 (accessed Nov. 23, 2019). Some women are indeed still called "spinsters" today. Spinning seems to have remained a predominantly female (and low-status/low-paid) occupation until the Industrial Revolution. All the documented embroiderers of Anglo-Saxon England are female, though all of them are specialists in gold work. Nothing is known about making the kind of wool embroidery in which the Tapestry is worked; Alexandra Lester-Makin, *The Lost Art of the Anglo-Saxon World: The Sacred and Secular Power of Embroidery* (Oxford: Oxbow, 2019), 113–121. Male embroiderers are documented from later in the medieval period; Kay Staniland, *Embroiderers*, Medieval Craftsmen (London, British Museum Press, 1991), 14, 49–50, and see, for example, for payments to male embroiderers in the mid-fourteenth century, Lisa Monnas, "Embroideries for Edward III," in *The Age of Opus Anglicanum*, ed. M. A. Michael (London: Harvey Miller, 2016), 37–73, at 46–67. Male embroiderers may well have existed in the eleventh century. However the recent contention that the Tapestry was embroidered (directly onto the linen) by secular men, ex-soldiers, and others with technical knowledge, is implausible; see Wright, *Decoding the Bayeux Tapestry*, summarised at 133–35.

Stitching the pieces together could have been done by either, or both, sexes since both men and women might sew: Ælfric lists both *sutor*, "seamer" a (grammatically masculine) tailor, and (the feminine equivalent) *sartrix*, "seamstre" in his late-tenth-century Latin/Old English glossary; Julius Zupitza, ed., *Ælfrics Grammatik und Glossar* (Berlin: Weidmann, 1880), 190.

The weaving of such long pieces of cloth must have been carried out on the relatively new horizontal treadle loom, initially male equipment, and so was probably done by men.

to how the design team worked together, which promises to bring us even closer to an understanding of the Tapestry as a whole, we are also set to consolidate, from the study of the Bayeux Tapestry, new and fundamental knowledge about the use of artists' tools in eleventh-century design that have been hiding in plain sight for almost a millennium.

Construction and Reconstruction of the Past:
The Medieval Nordic Textile Heritage of Hemp

Git Skoglund

Ever since cultural researchers in Scandinavia began collecting textile artifacts in the late nineteenth century, both the study of locally sourced raw materials and the study of textile production from peripheral regions have been marginalized, whereas the techniques used to make textile arts have enjoyed much greater scholarly attention. Museums have collected and stored textiles for their ability to reveal cultural practices of the past, but they have not documented the growth and production of textile fibers from plants that were grown locally by households in geographically isolated peripheral regions. This is especially true for textiles made of hemp (*Cannabis sativa* L.), although hemp was a common material in preindustrial home production throughout the world, and the result is that hemp textiles have often been invisible in historical contexts.[1] One reason for this neglect is that the examination of hemp textiles falls between two disciplines: cultural studies on the one hand, and natural science on the other. A number of researchers have studied the cultural aspects of Scandinavian plant-based textile artifacts, while natural scientists have taken less interest in studying the physical properties of the extant textiles.[2] Another reason is that hemp textiles are commonly recorded as "linen" or "flax" in most museum records without analysis of the plant fiber content. The problem in visually distinguishing between different plant fibers has not been sufficiently addressed, and there are few reports clearly demonstrating how these textile analyses have been conducted, which creates a gap in cultural and historical knowledge about medieval Scandinavians' use of natural resources. It

---

This article is based on my presentation during the DISTAFF session on "Aspects of Memory in Medieval Textiles and Garments" at the International Medieval Congress in Leeds, England, July 2, 2018.

1   There has been difficulty in distinguishing between hemp and other bast fibers due to methods that left uncertainty, but newer analytical methods have been useful in making this determination.

2   Git Skoglund, "Hampa i det Svenska Textilarvet: En Studie i Hur Historia om Textilföremål Arrangeras i Mellanrummet Mellan Natur och Kultur" (magister's thesis, University of Uppsala, Gotland Campus, 2012), 45–47, available online at http://uu.diva-portal.org/smash/get/diva2:620671/FULLTEXT01.pdf.

is notable that in recent decades, archaeology has shed new light on textiles made of plant fibers due to an increased number of finds in Europe which have also been well analyzed. What this article seeks to highlight is the importance of common terminology and interdisciplinary research that bridges the divide between botany and other disciplines dealing with historical textiles and plant materials.

The exclusion of plants, nature, people, and/or the environment in historical textile research has resulted in our overlooking key aspects: for example, textile production that has long been going on in geographically peripheral areas, such as mountainous areas, and women's knowledge of plant cultivation. We actually know very little about locally grown textile plants during the Middle Ages; there are no sources created by the people who actively carried out all the steps involved. Written sources are often used as historical references for both gardening and textile production, and these play an important role in the construction of textile heritages worldwide. However, there are no medieval texts written by the women who actually grew crops and processed them into textiles and who therefore could have given firsthand accounts from this period, and there are only scant references that date to the late preindustrial period.[3] In Scandinavia, from the Middle Ages until the nineteenth century, literacy was reserved for prominent men, such as royalty, priests, and landlords, and they viewed plant textiles as commodities. Therefore, both the processing from plant to textile and the processors themselves have been relegated to the peripheries of textile heritage.[4]

KITCHEN GARDENS AND GROWING TEXTILE-PRODUCING PLANTS

Before industrialization, in traditional hemp cultivation areas worldwide, textile plants were grown in small plots in gardens or near buildings (fig. 3.1). Early historical sources from Scandinavia indicate that hemp was grown near livestock barns and cabbage plots.[5] An eighteenth-century source shows the relationship between hemp and the kitchen garden: A land surveyor, called to investigate if the smell of hemp killed cabbage worms, confirmed that hemp was grown near a cabbage plot. His report asserts that the worms' deaths were not due to the smell but rather to birds who were attracted to the hemp seeds and then ate the worms.[6] Another eighteenth-century reference from northern Sweden illustrates the relationship between hemp and houses:

3 Although useful for knowledge about the use and prevalence of textile products, inventories and tax documents shed little light on the crop production that yielded the raw material for these items.
4 Git Skoglund, "Hampa, Textil och Historiska Trädgårdar: En Studie om Föreställningar och Konstruktioner av ett Nordiskt Textilarv" (master's thesis, University of Gothenburg, 2017), 63–69.
5 Karin Hallgren, "En Kåhltäppa eij at Räkna: Köksväxtodlingen i 1700-talets Jordbrukssystem" (Ph.D. diss., Swedish University of Agricultural Sciences, 2016), 181–83.
6 Olof Gerdes, *Förklaring Huru Vida Luckt af Hampa Födrifver Kålmask* (Stockholm: Kungliga Svenskavetenskaps-Akademins Handlingar, 1771), 89–90.

Fig. 3.1: Hemp plant in a garden environment in Transylvania. Photo: Git Skoglund.

Hemp is here to be sown in all times, [and] is well worth the effort for the farmer. They sow it in the fertile soil, mostly near the houses … hemp and hop should not stand [too] close to the house, because their smell is thought to be unhealthy for humans.[7]

The earliest Nordic archaeobotanical evidence of *Cannabis* pollen, seeds, and stems connected with a retting pond (indicating localized hemp textile production) was found in southern Sweden during excavations of a settlement dating from the second century.[8] This find was the first to prove that hemp was used for textile production in early settlements, and it increased the likelihood that other finds of hemp pollen and

---

7 Johan Otto Hagström, *Jemtlands Aeconomiska Beskrifning eller Känning, i Akt Tagen på en Resa om Sommaren 1749* (Stockholm: Tryckt hos J. Merckell, 1751), 14. All translations from Swedish are my own.

8 Mikael Larsson and Per Lagerås, "New Evidence on the Introduction, Cultivation and Processing of Hemp (*Cannabis sativa* L.) in Southern Sweden," *Journal of Environmental Archaeology* 20, no. 2 (2015): 111–19.

seeds from Norway, Sweden, and Finland[9] will also indicate that hemp was grown for fiber production early on (fig. 3.2 and table 3.1).[10]

In Norway, palaeobotanical finds from Trondheim (dating from a period before the eleventh century and into the twelfth century), Oslo (from the eleventh century), and Bergen (from the twelfth and thirteenth centuries) all show that hemp was grown in pre-urban environments.[11] However, interpretations of plant relics as indications of woven textile production are rare, and hemp remains are usually considered as evidence of rope making.[12] In addition to this, historical texts frequently describe hemp plants as being grown for medicinal use. For example, in 1736, a gardener described how cataract was treated with hemp seeds, how green winter hemp could be put on a snake bite to remove the poison, and how hemp seeds cure bowel pain.[13] Clearly the hemp plant was used to make medicine, rope, and textiles, and although medieval hemp remains are abundant, just as flax remains are, hemp receives less scholarly attention with respect to local textile weaving. One reason that plant finds of hemp are often identified as a raw material for rope production, and not for "finer" textiles, is that hemp for rope making was well documented during modern times by import lists and in state documents, which closely monitored shipbuilding. But less discussed is

9 Denmark has been excluded from this article because no known analyses have been carried out on Danish historical textiles for the purpose of distinguishing hemp and flax, but hemp may also have been grown for textile production in Denmark during prehistoric times.

10 Ulf Hafsten, "Jordbrukskulturens Historie i Oslo och Mjøstrakten Belyst ved Pollenanalytiske Undersøkelser," *Viking: Tidskrift for Norrøn Arkeologi* 21/22 (1958): 51–74, at 70, 71; Eli-Christine Soltvedt, *Makrofossilanalyse av Prøver fra Hustomt I, II, III og V, Valum, Hamar k., Hedmark* (assignment report, Arkeologisk Museum i Stavanger, 1994); Catherine Jessen and Frans-Arne Stylegar, "Ødegården Sosteli i Åseral fra Romertid til Vikingtid," *Viking: Norsk Arkeologisk Årbok* 75 (2012): 131–44, at 139; Jens Holmboe, "Nytteplanter og Ugraes i Osebergfundet," *Osebergsfundet* 5 (1921): 1–78, at 32; Ann-Marie Robertsson, "Vikingatida Hampodling," *Jämten: Länsmuseets och Heimbygdas Årsbok* 85 (1992): 183–88, at 187; Ingemar Påhlsson, *Västannortjärn: En Pollenanalytisk Undersökning* (Stockholm: Riksantikvarieämbetet och Statens Historiska Museer, 1981): 12; Urve Miller and Karin Hedin, *The Holocene Development of Landscape and Environment in the Southeast Mälaren Valley, with Special Reference to Helgö*, Excavations at Helgö 11 (Stockholm: Kungliga Vitterhets Historie och Antikvitets Akademien, 1988), 38; Irmeli Vuorela, T. Grönlund, and T. Lempiäinen, "A Reconstruction of the Environment of Rettig in the City of Turku, Finland on the Basis of Diatom, Pollen, Plant Macrofossil and Phytolith Analyses," *Bulletin of the Geological Society of Finland* 68, no. 2 (1996): 46–71, at 64.

11 Ingvild Øye, "Dyrkning i Norske Middelalderbyer: Tverrfaglig Belyst," in *Sources to the History of Gardening: Four Interdisciplinary Seminars 2010–2013 Arranged by the Nordic Network for the Archaeology and Archaeobotany of Gardening (NTAA)*, ed. Anna Andréasson, Elisabeth Gräslund Berg, Jens Heimdahl, Anna Jakobsson, Inger Larsson, and Erik Persson (Alnarp, Sweden: Sveriges Lantbruksuniversitet, 2014): 169–80, at 175.

12 There are several examples of this interpretation in archaeological research. Eva Andersson, "The Common Thread: Textile Production During the Late Iron Age to the Viking Age" (Ph.D. diss., Lund University, 1999), 36.

13 Håkan Tunón, ed., *En Fulständig Swensk Hus-hålds-bok af Reinerus Reineri Broocman: En Handbook i Gårds- Och Hushållsskötsel i Vid Mening från 1700-talets Första Hälft*, vol. 2 (Stockholm: Kungl. Skogs- och Lantbruksakademin, 2016): 692, 720, 1091, 1084.

Fig. 3.2: Map of Scandinavia showing locations of ancient hemp finds discussed in the text. See Table 3.1 for the remains excavated at each location. Map: Cath D'Alton.

Table 3.1. Scandinavian excavations of hemp plant remains

Location	Remains found	Dating of remains
Oslo Fjord area	seeds	350 BCE–450 CE
Rödön	pollen	100–200 CE
Lindängelund	pollen, seeds, and stem	100–200 CE
Hamar	pollen and seeds	400 CE
Åseral	pollen	650–800 CE
Oseberg	seeds	800 CE
Lake Mälaren	pollen and seeds	800–1050 CE
Lake Siljan	pollen, seeds, and fibers	800–1050 CE
Trondheim	paleobotanic material	1100–1200 CE
Bergen	paleobotanic material	1100–1200 CE
Oslo	paleobotanic material	1100 CE
Turku	seeds and pollen	1200–1700 CE

the fact that hemp fibers used for cordage were mostly not locally grown but rather imported from Russia.[14] Another reason is that many hemp textiles in museum collections are invisible because they are archived as linen or flax.

Flax (*Linum usitatissimum* L.), by contrast, has received very different scholarly treatment. One example of this is in the handling of archaeobotanical finds in monasteries in Norway: Seed capsules of flax were identified as materials for textile production, despite the fact that there were only seed capsules found, and no other plant remains that could be more closely associated with fiber production.[15] Flax has gained an accepted position as a historic textile plant because of many factors, but one is our knowledge of the rising trade and commercial cultivation of finer linen fabrics after the Middle Ages. Already by the end of the seventeenth century, flax linen use had increased in royal homes, made available through Russo-Swedish trade. Import lists show that flax cloth was of two kinds: Extra-fine linen was always imported from the Netherlands, with the exception of a small quantity of exclusive output from Moscow, and coarser linen fabric was imported from Russia.[16] However, the trade in imported plant textiles during the early modern period should not be equated with locally made plant textiles during the Middle Ages. Late medieval sources inform us that both hemp and flax were grown locally in royal gardens.[17] Later, in the eighteenth century, a household book describes a housewife's responsibilities in castles and mansions:

> She will work in particular the planting of flax and hemp, and when the plants mature she pulls up the stalks, retting, barking, hackling, and then together with the maids during long winter evenings make it into yarn.[18]

Even so, the linen trade came to be the center of Swedish textile heritage, and history tells us little about local plant textile production during the Middle Ages.

Both textile history and garden history use related methodologies and have much in common, often dealing with medieval textiles preserved in churches, as well as plant remains connected to castles, monasteries, and mansions throughout Scandinavia. In addition, excavations in urban areas, in garden soils, and near houses are shedding new light on medieval life.[19] There were different kinds of gardens in prehistoric times. Gardens have existed since the Iron Age in the form of leafy hedges, in which vegetables, trees, herbs, or medicinal plants were grown. Other forms of older, simple medieval gardens have been discovered at sites in Turku in western Finland,

---

14 Olle Wahlbeck, *Rep och Repslageri under Olika Tidsåldrar* (Linköping, Sweden: Samhall Klintland Grafiska, 1991).

15 Per Arvid Åsen, *Norske Klosterplanter: Levende Kulturminner fra Middelalderen* (Kristiansand, Norway: Portal, 2015), 165.

16 Agnes Geijer, *Oriental Textiles in Sweden* (Copenhagen: Rosenkilde and Bagger, 1951), 25.

17 Peter Lundberg, *Trädgårdspraxis år 1754*, ed. Hans Mårtensson (Kalmar, Sweden: Akantus, 2002), 17.

18 Tunón, *En Fulständig Swensk Hus-hålds-bok*, 81.

19 Jens Heimdahl, "Barbariska Trädgårdsmästare: Nya Perspektiv på Hortikulturen i Sverige Framtill 1200-talets Slut," *Fornvännen* 105, no. 4 (2010): 265–80, at 267.

along with finds of macrofossil seeds of hemp, hop, and flax.[20] During the late Middle Ages all types of gardens probably played important roles in textile production. Medieval garden types had different names such as "spice plot," "herb garden," or "cabbage plot."[21] Yet, there are no existing sources recording how the processing from crop to textile was performed.

ON THE PERIPHERY AND BETWEEN TWO FIELDS:
HEMP IN GARDEN AND TEXTILE HISTORY

Today's traditional hemp textile-producing regions share common environmental factors. They are most often situated in remote river valleys surrounded by mountains, with limestone soils and a temperate climate with summer rainfall.[22] Humans have lived for millennia in such natural surroundings, where they grew crops, fished in the rivers, and bred animals, a self-reliant community structure that was common in many parts of the world during the prehistoric period. Present-day hemp cultures also occupy the cultural periphery of dominant societies within a remote rural setting where many local traditions have survived.

Textile traditions are studied in geographically and culturally peripheral regions today by both textile and garden historians, and those two fields incorporate various disciplines, such as ethnology, archaeology, geology, agronomy, etc. Ancient hemp textile knowledge can be tracked in several directions. One way is to search in regions experiencing a slow transition to a market economy, where there exist memories of traditional textile making in the local context of settlement gardens. When the worldwide transition into industrialization took off in the nineteenth century, it advanced much faster in regions with closer relationships to economic and political power and much more slowly in geographically isolated and politically remote areas. In these peripheral regions, we find traces of ancient hemp processing along with modern-day producers themselves. For a modern example, in eastern Europe, there are rich hemp textile traditions in the Carpathian Mountain areas of western Ukraine and Transylvania in Romania, which have survived in the form of both knowledge and preserved household textiles.[23] In Asia, there remain many such culturally conservative regions, for instance, the Hmong culture along the border between China and Vietnam.[24] In

20 Terttu Lempiäinen, "Om Trädgårdskonstens och Trädgårdsodlingens Historia i Finland: Skriftliga, Språkliga och Arkeobotaniska Källor," in Andréasson et al., *Sources to the History of Gardening*, 251–58, at 256.
21 Lundberg, *Trädgårdspraxis år 1754*, 17.
22 The author has observed this phenomenon during field work in Scandinavia and in Transylvania and Vietnam.
23 Florica Zaharia, "Materials and Technology," in *Carpathian Echoes: Traditional Textile Materials and Technologies in the Carpathian Mountains of Romania and Ukraine*, ed. Melody Lawrence and Maria Rewakowicz (New York: Ukrainian Museum, 2016): 10–11.
24 Robert C. Clarke and Wenfeng Gu, "Survey of Hemp (*Cannabis sativa* L.) Use by the Hmong (Miao) of the China/Vietnam Border Region," *Journal of the International Hemp Association* 5, no. 1: 4–9, at 7.

both Transylvania and northern Vietnam, hemp textile traditions are still alive, and the women's processing of the hemp plant into finished fabric remains visible.

In the Middle Ages, almost all of Scandinavia was in Europe's periphery, compared to central Europe, and Scandinavian agriculture developed gradually. In the early medieval period, it was in southern Scandinavia that agriculture developed first, as is illustrated by church paintings that show agricultural tools, something we do not see in northern regions until later.[25] Scandinavian hemp textiles are preserved in northern and southwestern Sweden, eastern Norway,[26] and western Finland.[27]

Textile art history is another research path that leads to the discovery of fine medieval hemp textiles. Wool and plant-fiber wall hangings with rich decorative patterns and/or technically notable designs are highly valued and have been preserved in Swedish and Norwegian churches.[28] Previous researchers have identified the plant fibers in these fabrics as linen or flax.[29] More recently, this author and colleagues used polarized light microscope (PLM) fiber analysis at Bergen University in Norway to test ten medieval Scandinavian textiles that had been preserved in churches and found that four of them contained hemp in varying amounts.[30] The PLM method is based on the natural twist of cellulose molecules in plant fibers which can be seen in polarized light; flax fibers exhibit a counterclockwise S-twist, and hemp fibers exhibit a clockwise Z-twist (fig. 3.3).[31] Two pieces of a Swedish wall hanging (Överhogdal Ia and Ib) were found to contain both flax and hemp blended together in the warp yarns (figs. 3.4 and 3.5). The same fiber mix was found in the Marby textile border from Sweden, and the Lomen coverlet from Norway contained only hemp fibers in the linen ground weave (fig. 3.6).[32] A more recent PLM investigation of a medieval offering cloth conducted at the University of Helsinki in Finland showed that the fabric also contained hemp

25 Gösta Grotenfelt, "Landtbruket i Finland under Medeltiden," in *Finlands Kulturhistoria: Medeltiden*," ed. Poch Nordmann and Magnus Gottfrid Schybergson (Helsinki: Söderström, 1908), 45–76, at 48.
26 Git Skoglund, *Hampa det Vita Guldet: Textilväxten Cannabis Sativa* (Möklinta, Sweden: Gidlunds, 2016), 82–89.
27 Hjördis Dahl, *Högsäng och Klädbod: Ur Svenskbygdernas Textilhistoria* (Helsinki: Svenska Litteratursällskapet i Finland, 1987), 313–18.
28 Anne Marie Franzén and Margareta Nockert, *Bonaderna från Skog och Överhogdal: Och Andra Medeltida Väggbeklädnader* (Stockholm: Kungl. Vitterhets, Historie och Antikvitets Akademien, 1992), 113–25.
29 Ibid. (This source is an example; there are several investigations of these medieval textiles.)
30 Git Skoglund, Margareta Nockert, and Bodil Holst, "Viking and Early Middle Ages Northern Scandinavian Textiles Proven to be Made with Hemp," *Scientific Reports* 3 (2013), available online at www.nature.com/articles/srep02686.
31 The PLM technique is at present the only conclusive method to distinguish between hemp and flax fibers in textiles. We should note that PLM is a simple method to use for intact above-earth examples; however, when degraded fibers from archaeological excavations are investigated, PLM is more problematic, since only intact fibers give results in polarized light.
32 Ibid.

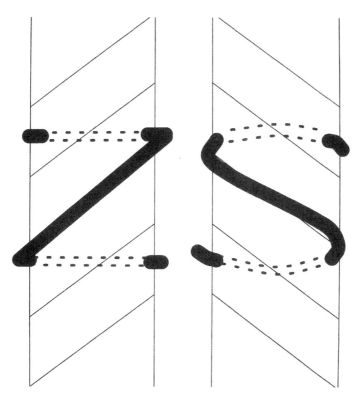

Fig. 3.3: Fibrillar orientations of bast fibers: Z-twist for hemp/hop on left, S-twist for flax/nettle on right. Drawing: From Git Skoglund, Margareta Nockert, and Bodil Holst, "Viking and Early Middle Ages Northern Scandinavian Textiles Proven to Be Made with Hemp," *Scientific Reports* 3 (2013), fig. 5.

fibers, but this object was probably not domestically manufactured.[33] Even so, these natural science investigations place hemp firmly within the Nordic textile heritage. Previous researchers have treated these medieval hemp relics from Norway and Sweden as woven art, based on their relationship to folk art. They were not manufactured by professional weavers in any of the professional studios that existed in the Middle Ages, the products of which are often referred to as "royal art."[34] The raw materials in these fabrics were most likely grown locally and probably in gardens. This relationship sheds new light on both medieval textile production and gardening.

33 The researchers place the cloth's origin with the Khanty and Mansi people of western Siberia, close to the Ural Mountains. Jenni A. Suomela, Krista Vajanto, and Riikka Räisänen, "Seeking Nettle Textiles: Utilizing a Combination of Microscopic Methods for Fibre Identification," *Studies in Conservation* 63, no. 7 (2018): 412–22, at 416.

34 Margareta Nockert and Göran Possnert, *Att Datera Textilier* (Hedemora, Sweden: Gidlund, 2002), 82.

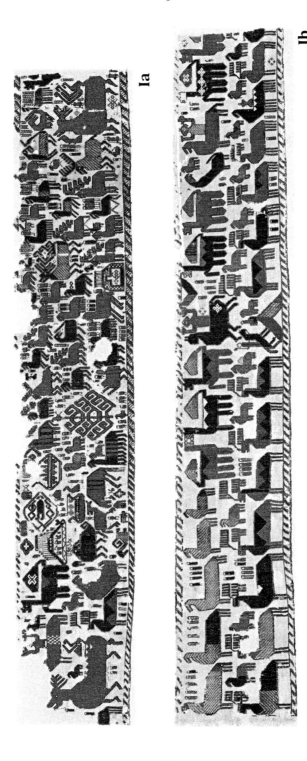

Fig. 3.4: Överhogdal wall hangings, dated 900–1000 (Östersund, Sweden, Jamtli Museum, inv. no. 8090). Ia (top): 164 centimeters (at top edge) by approximately 33 centimeters. Ib (bottom): 195 centimeters by approximately 34 centimeters. Both Ia and Ib are woven on the same warp, a mixture of hemp and flax. Photo: Jamtli Museum (Jamtlis fotosamlingar), by permission.

Fig. 3.5: Detail of Överhogdal wall hanging Ia from figure 3.4. Photo: Jamtli Museum (Jamtlis fotosamlingar), by permission.

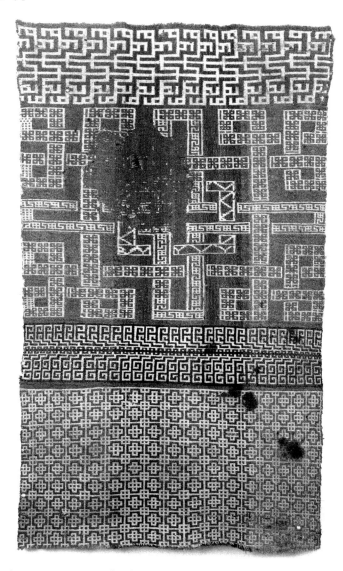

Fig. 3.6: Coverlet from Lomen, Norway, dated 1165–1260, 130 centimeters by 82 centimeters (Oslo, National Museum of Art, Architecture and Design, inv. no. 1217). Double weave with a wool layer and a linen layer that consists of hemp fibers. Photo: National Museum of Art, Architecture and Design, Oslo, by permission.

FINE MEDIEVAL HEMP TEXTILES

Medieval Scandinavian household fabrics that contain hemp fibers are of the same fineness, quality, and color as the same categories of flax textiles, and with the naked eye, it is not possible to distinguish a locally made medieval fabric of hemp from a flax fabric. The same situation applies to a collection of eighteenth- and nineteenth-century fabrics locally made in southern Sweden that use a weaving technique and design with roots in the Middle Ages and in which hemp fibers have been identified.[35] One is a plain-weave hemp fabric border with a knotted decorative edge (fig. 3.7). Another is decorated with blue and red designs, and the blue yarn and the ground weave both contain hemp fibers (fig. 3.8). An eighteenth-century coverlet with wool decorations that contains hemp fibers in the ground weave was found in an old cottage in Hallavara in Hallands County (fig. 3.9). In some of the medieval textiles (e.g., Överhogdal 1a and 1b) the hemp fibers were spun together with flax fibers, and the reasons for this remain unclear.

Nor do we know what tools the processors used to produce fine hemp yarn during the Middle Ages, or whether they used tools at all, although the majority of finds of ancient textile tools in Scandinavia contain what are considered "flax tools." In traditional Asian hemp cultures, very fine hemp textiles are produced without hackling, combing, or draft spinning tools, and their strategy of processing from plant into fabric differs from European preindustrial traditions. The fundamental difference is that Asian weavers splice finely split fiber strips together by hand to form a yarn,[36] and before that they often peel the fibrous bark directly from the fresh or dried stalks.[37] In contrast, medieval European weavers isolated individual fiber elements by hackling, combing, and draft spinning them from a distaff to form yarn as they did with wool. Moreover, in the European process, the stalks were retted in water to release the fibrous bark from the stalks, and most often rinsed before drying.[38]

We do not know how hemp was traditionally grown in Scandinavia, how tall it was, or what kind of hemp seeds were grown, so we must learn from more recent traditions of making fine hemp fabrics. For instance, in Transylvania, the textile plants are not very tall (1.5 to 2 meters), and the stalks are thin (less than 1 centimeter in diameter). Generally male plants called "summer hemp" are used for production of finer textile materials.[39]

---

35 The author has examined the textiles from southern Sweden using PLM fiber analysis to distinguish among the different types of bast fibers; see note 31 above. Skoglund, *Hampa det Vita Guldet*, 80–81.

36 Goro Nagano and Hiroi Nobuko, *Base to Tip: Bast-Fiber Weaving in Japan and Its Neighboring Countries*, trans. Monica Bethe (Kyoto: Sachio Yoshioka, 1999), 350–51.

37 Clarke and Gu, "Survey of Hemp," 7.

38 Florica Zaharia, *Textile Tradiționale din Transilvania: Tehnologie și Estetică* (Suceava, Romania: Accent Print, 2008), 288.

39 Ibid.

Fig. 3.7: Tapestry border with a knotted decorative edge, probably from the eighteenth or early nineteenth century (Halmstad, Sweden, Hallands Art Museum, inv. no. HM 992). Plain weave of hemp fibers. Photo: Jan Svensson, courtesy of Hallands Art Museum.

Fig. 3.8: Wall hanging with a decorative edge sewn in a knot pattern, probably from the eighteenth or nineteenth century (Halmstad, Sweden, Hallands Art Museum, inv. no. HM 10463). The ground weave contains hemp fibers, as does the blue-colored pattern. The red yarn has not yet been definitively identified. Photo: Jan Svensson, courtesy of Hallands Art Museum.

Fig. 3.9: Wall hanging, probably from the eighteenth or nineteenth century (Halmstad, Sweden, Hallands Art Museum, inv. no. HM 10430). The ground weave contains hemp fibers and the pattern yarn is wool. Photo: Jan Svensson, courtesy of Hallands Art Museum.

"LINEN" AS AN UMBRELLA TERM FOR BAST-FIBER TEXTILES

Textile terms that refer to fabric, tools, and raw materials contain linguistic elements that are expressed in different languages and dialects through written records. Today, "linen" (Swedish *linne*) is the common English word for a fabric woven of flax, but many historical sources indicate that the term "linen" should not be connected only to flax plants.[40] In Sweden, Norway, and Iceland before the 1800s, the old Nordic terms *lärft* or *lerreft* had been used since the Middle Ages.[41] Most likely *lärft* originates from the old German term *leinwandbindung*, which denotes a plain, tabby-weave cloth.[42] Generally, historical sources about *lärft* do not mention from which plant it is made. The situation is often the same in English, yet in older sources there are examples showing that the term "linen" was used to describe both hemp and flax fabrics. For instance, the author of a an early-seventeenth-century manual describes linen and its characteristics and writes that housewives must become proficient "in the making of all sorts of linen cloth, whether it be of hemp or flax, for from those two only is the most principal cloth derived, and made both in this, and in other nations."[43] *The Workwoman's Guide, by a Lady*, from 1838, describes the use of different plant fibers for linen weaving and says that "The Suffolk hemp is considered the best."[44] It is notable that this source was likely written by a woman (the author's name was not published at that time). Such sources are rare, since in preindustrial literature from this period it was primarily men who recorded household activities, creating a major knowledge gap in the recording of textile garden heritages.

Traditional use of the term "linen" has not yet been fully clarified, but in modern texts concerning ancient textile heritage in Scandinavia, the term is used when plant textiles are discussed. *Linne* is a relatively new term in Scandinavia and means a plain-weave fabric made of plant fibers, but the historical knowledge of locally made linen in Scandinavia is not extensive. Compared with animal fibers, plant fibers decompose quickly when buried under the soil, and only in exceptional circumstances have they been preserved in archaeological sites.[45] Finds from dry desert areas like Egypt—which

---

40 Agnes Geijer, *A History of Textile Art* (London: Pasold Research Fund in association with Sotheby Parke Bernet, 1979), 30–33.

41 Elisabeth Strömberg, Agnes Geijer, and Marta Hoffmann, *Nordisk Textilteknisk Terminologi: Förindustriell Vävnadsproduktion: Definitioner på Svenska och Synonymer på Danska, Isländska, Norska och Finska samt på Engelska, Franska och Tyska* (Oslo: Tanum, 1974).

42 Geijer, *History of Textile Art*, 44.

43 Gervase Markham, *The English Housewife: Containing the Inward and Outward Virtues Which Ought to Be in a Complete Woman; As Her Skill in Physic, Cookery, Banqueting-stuff, Distillation, Perfumes, Wool, Hemp, Flax, Dairies, Brewing, Baking, and All Other Things Belonging to a Household 1568–1637*, ed. Michael R. Best (Kingston, Ont.: McGill-Queen's University Press, 1986), 152.

44 Maria Wilson, *The Workwoman's Guide, Containing Instructions to the Inexperienced in Cutting Out and Completing Those Articles of Wearing Apparel, &C Which Are Usually Made at Home; Also, Explanations on Upholstery, Straw-Platting, Bonnet-Making, Knitting* (London: Simpkin, Marshall, and Co., 1840), 12, 142.

45 Margareta Nockert, "The Högom Find and Other Migration Period Textiles and Costumes in Scandinavia" (Ph.D. diss., University of Umeå, 1991), 66.

provide excellent conservation environments, especially in comparison to humid Scandinavia—show that in these regions flax fibers were by far the dominant textile material.[46] The Scandinavian importation of flax fabric from Egypt became common and was well documented during the seventeenth century; records from Norway show how much flax fabric and *lerreter* ("linen") was imported.[47] Therefore, we have more knowledge about flax linen goods than other linens, and "linen" has come to represent only flax rather than any bast (stem) fiber—flax, hemp, hop, or nettle.

Hemp and flax were the two most commonly used textile plants in medieval Scandinavia and continued to be grown into the early twentieth century. Hop (*Humulus lupulus* L.) and nettle (*Urtica dioeca* L.) are also mentioned in older sources. Hop belongs to the same family as hemp (*Cannabaceae*) and has strong and flexible fibers that could be processed into textiles in the same way as hemp,[48] but it was the hop cones from female plants that are commonly documented, in the context of beer making.[49] Norwegian sources from the eighteenth century show that all fabrics derived from bast-fiber plants were called *lin* ("flax") and could be woven of hemp, flax, hop, and/or nettle.[50] Another closely related Nordic word is *liina*—used in Finno-Ugric languages—which could mean nettle.[51] *Liina* probably derived from the Greek word *linteum*, meaning handkerchief or towel.[52] As Emelie von Walterstorff attests, other sources connect "linen" to the English word "lining," which also is seen in the Swedish verb *lina*, which means to line a garment.[53] Von Walterstorff further speculated about two common old Swedish words, *hampkrus* and *linningskrus* ("hemp-curl" and "lining-curl"). In a 1943 article, she concluded that the term *linning* ("lining") represents a reasonable transition into the term "linen" and cites a local textile term from Dalarna parish: *svartsärken* ("black dress") made of *leningsvävnad* ("lining weave").[54] Moreover, medieval sources show that Byzantium imported Bulgarian "linen" whose

46 Geijer, *History of Textile Art*, 18.
47 Helen Engelstad, *Refil, Bunad, Tjeld: Middelalderens Billedtepper i Norge* (Oslo: Gyldendal, 1952), 41.
48 Margrethe Hald, "The Nettle as a Culture Plant," *Folkliv: Acta Ethnologica Europaea* 6 (1942): 29–49.
49 Else-Marie K. Strese and Clas Tollin, *Humle: Det Gröna Guldet* (Stockholm: Nordiska Museet, 2015), 255–57.
50 Gerald Shøning, *Reise, Som Giennem en Deel af Norge i de Aar 1773, 1774, 1775 paa Hams Majestæt Kongens Bekostning*, ed. Karl Rygh (Trondheim, Norway: Adresseavisens Bogtrykkeri, 1910), 14.
51 Toini-Inkeri Kaukonen, *Pellavan ja Hampun Viljely ja Muokkaus Suomessa: Kansatieteellinen Tutkimus* (Helsinki: Kirjapaino-Osakeyhtiö Sana, 1946): 23, quoted in Suomela, Vajanto, and Räisänen, "Seeking Nettle Textiles," 413.
52 *Mediae Latinitatis Lexicon Minus*, ed. Jan Frederik Niermeyer, C. van de Kieft, and J. W. J. Burgers (Leiden: Brill, 2002).
53 Emelie von Walterstorff, "Om Hamp- och Linningskrus," *Rig: Tidskrift Utgiven av Föreningen för Svensk Kulturhistoria* 26 (1943): 27.
54 Ibid. Von Walterstorff has discussed the term "lining" with regard to plain weaves of coarse fabrics in older upper-class clothing, especially silk bodices in the Rococo style. She also noted that linings of peasant garments were similar.

quality was most likely a bit coarser and which was used especially for linings in certain tunics.[55] We do not know from which plant fibers it was woven.

There are many historical writings that illustrate how the term *linne* became common later in Scandinavia, especially during the nineteenth century as the global textile trade expanded. Materials could be mixed together, and both hemp and flax were listed as "linen" in customs documents.[56] By contrast, the term *linne* does not occur in older Swedish household inventories that describe homemade textiles. Instead, old Nordic words like *lärft* and *läruft* were used, together with common terms for fabrics such as *vävnader*, *lakan*, and *tyg* ("weaves," "sheets," and "cloth") and in some cases with the prefix *hampe-* ("hemp"): for example, *hampe-väv* ("hemp weave").[57] This shows that over time, the trade of linen products became centralized and the locally made textiles were pushed to the periphery. Today the term implies textiles made from flax plants rather than other bast-fiber plants.

Sometimes in modern texts the term "linen fibers" is used to describe flax fibers alone, but historical sources show that this usage is incorrect. The term "linen" is correctly used to describe a plain-weave fabric—one that is made of any bast fiber or a combination of them. Inconsistent descriptions and terms for textile and botanical materials can be misleading. As a further example of this confusion, some authors have used the term "hemp bast" instead of "hemp fibers," while at the same time referring to flax fibers as "linen fibers."[58] Both flax and hemp, together with other bast plants such as nettle and hop, extract fibers from the bast (the inner layer of the bark); therefore in these cases it is difficult to know whether the author is referring to the fibers or the bast itself, because hemp bast has been used to produce items such as hemp-bast sandals.[59]

CONCLUSION

Our understanding of traditional plant-based textile heritages emerges from two interdisciplinary fields: textile history and garden history. Both examine the traces left by textile plant cultivation with shared methodologies. However, researchers in each field often remain disconnected from the findings in the other field because of the tendency to focus on either textiles or the cultivation of plants. Therefore, it is important

55 Robert Sabatino Lopez, "Silk Industry in the Byzantine Empire," *Speculum* 20, no. 1 (Jan. 1945): 1–43, at 31.

56 Florence Montgomery, *Textiles in America 1650–1870* (New York: W. W. Norton, 2007), 278.

57 Carl-Martin Bergstrand, *Ur Västgötaprästers Bouppteckningar från Tiden före 1761* (Skövde, Sweden: Skövde Antikvariat, 1977), 145–53.

58 Johanna Banck-Burgess, "The Textiles from the Princely Burial at Eberdingen-Hochdorf, Germany," in *Textiles and Textile Production in Europe From Prehistory to AD 400*, ed. Margarita Gleba and Ulla Mannering (Oxford, UK: Oxbow Books. 2012): 139–50.

59 Robert Connell Clarke and Mark David Merlin, *Cannabis: Evolution and Ethnobotany* (Berkeley: University of California Press, 2013), 266.

to clarify how terms are used in discussions about textiles and botany. Plant textile materials should be studied in the contexts of the processing that the producers make visible. Laboratory and experimental research is also required to gain more knowledge of medieval plant textiles. Therefore, it is within these adjacent interdisciplinary fields that plant textile studies are located. Here, I have focused on garden history and textile history, but there are many more aspects of traditional textile cultures to explore.

Both plant material and textiles of hemp and flax occur in the medieval textile heritage and connect the past with the present. This connection is obvious in previous research, but interpretations of both the textiles and their plant sources differ. Flax holds a stable and obvious position as a traditional textile plant and product, but the position of hemp remains unclear. This is due in part to the modern usage of the term "linen" as applying only to flax. Therefore, it is important to identify plant fibers in historical textiles using an objective methodology which is free from the value judgments imposed by our contemporary mindset.

Sources show that the term "linen" likely originally described a cloth of plant fibers and possibly originated in the term for "lining" cloth. Not only have terms been important in centralizing flax plants in studies of the Middle Ages, but also large quantities of fine flax fabrics were imported into Scandinavia, pushing the historical knowledge of local textile plant production into the periphery, together with the now invisible people who processed these plants into textiles. Historical sources were predominantly written by men and most often concern what belonged within the masculine sphere, such as the use of hemp plants for medicines or the production of rope, while on the other hand flax plant cultivation was better documented because linen made of flax had a higher economic value and corresponding higher production levels.

Thus, hemp cultivation and the making of textiles continue in peripheral regions not simply because of the location of climates favorable to them. Hemp cultures survive today because economic, political, and environmental factors continue to operate through the active role of the processor. In such isolated regions, the processor remains of crucial importance, as it is she who processes plants into textiles and also controls and preserves local traditions.

Written sources serve as a starting point for what we know about household production and use of textile plants during earlier periods, but they do not give us the whole picture. Therefore, material culture and the objects preserved in museum collections will be important witnesses as research on prehistoric production progresses.

The search for historically preserved hemp textiles can be pursued in two different ways: by looking into the historical research area of textile art, largely within museums, and by observing plant fiber cultivation and textile production in peripheral regions that have preserved their textile traditions. Hemp fibers are found in all kinds of textiles, ranging from simple everyday clothing and home textiles to very fine interior textiles with rich patterns and designs. That these interior textiles have in previous research been categorically referred to as "flax" shows the importance of scientific methods that can distinguish between various plant fibers. Historical hemp textile artifacts connect garden, art, and textile history of the medieval period.

Historicizing the Allegorical Eye: Reading Lady Mede

John Slefinger

Allegory often presents readers with clear descriptions of characters whose appearance parallels their metaphorical role. *Readers* of allegory—especially scholars—are also trained to read clothing this way: to look for allegorical conventions as an explanation for physical descriptions. Thus, one might read the ambivalent description of Lady Fortune in John Skelton's *Bowge of Court*—featuring both alluring and dangerous attributes—and connect it to other depictions in Chaucer's *Book of the Duchess*. The general explanation is that the character looks the way he or she does because that is how that allegorical character traditionally appears: Fortune is good to some and terrible to others simply because that is how Fortune appears in allegory.

Ostensibly, William Langland's *Piers Plowman* follows the same trend, giving a garish, ostentatious robe—complete with a dozen lines of description—to Lady Mede, who is the personification of reward, recompense, or the desire for worldly gain.[1] When Will, the narrator, first meets Mede, he is told that her clothing shows her to be a liar and a seductress, an interpretation a modern reader may find all too intuitive.

I am interested in complicating this way of reading in a few ways. First, the reliance on literary convention has a way of insulating allegory from historical trends and changes in material culture. *Piers Plowman* was published in three different editions, so-called the A-, B-, and C-texts respectively.[2] As A. V. C. Schmidt's definitive introduction explains, the texts represent "three successive states of a single work by one man" working over twenty to twenty-five years. The A-text is but 2,540 lines, whereas the B is a complete revision of the earlier work and nearly three times as long. The C is yet a further revision of the B, but maintains a similar length. The three texts are estimated to have been produced from 1367 to the mid-1380s.[3] This timeline is important, as it covers the period when fashion was on the rise in Western Europe, which

---

1 All citations of *Piers Plowman* in this essay come from the B-text in William Langland, *Piers Plowman: A Parallel-Text Edition of the A, B, C and Z Versions*, ed. A. V. C. Schmidt (London: Longman, 1995), and are cited by passus (section) and line numbers.
2 There is a fourth text: X, although its authenticity is less certain.
3 Schmidt, *Piers Plowman*, xvii–xix.

in turn spurred radical disagreement as to the transformative potential of clothing. The first half of this article will show how Langland consistently provides enough nuanced characterization that the one-noted costumes begin to lose their ability to signify accurately. Thus, he appeals to allegorical descriptive techniques only to undercut their reliability in both literary and material contexts. The second will consider how fourteenth-century developments in fashion influenced Langland's verse. Langland responded to an increased focus on dress by imbuing his allegorical imagery with material details. More broadly, I mean to demonstrate how, rather than merely designating some timeless Concept for the reader, allegory is only able to signify through a shared window of discourse. It relies on convention, but that convention intersects with materiality and helps to construct new materialities.

LADY MEDE'S SPLENDOR

As Lavinia Griffiths has observed, personification is "the translation whereby things absent, abstract, inanimate, are made human and present."[4] This palpability is both helpful and deceptive for contemporary readers. It is helpful because personification reveals how notions of identity "permeate the conceptualising process. In narratives which make sustained use of processes of personification the meaning of 'abstract' nouns is often investigated through their embodiment in systems of socialised relations."[5] That is to say, personification exposes how authors conceive of the intersections between abstract ideas and external markers. It is nevertheless deceptive because the immediacy can suggest a finality of meaning when that meaning may be elusive or transient. One allegorical figure that exemplifies both phenomena is Lady Justice. While sculptures of her exist around the world, her appearance is demonstrably different depending on location. Even the telltale blindfold is inconsistent. In many post-fifteenth-century representations, she is blindfolded in part to emphasize her impartiality and reliance on pure reason. However, some sculptures, such as the one atop the Old Bailey in London, omit the blindfold. According to local brochures, her "maidenly form" was assumed to demonstrate enough impartiality, rendering the blindfold redundant. In fact, Justice first appeared blindfolded in Sebastian Brant's 1494 *Ship of Fools*, but that blindfold was intended to mock the ignorance and dishonesty of the courts.[6] So not only does her representation shift according to location, the meaning of those representations shifts as well. Like the concept of justice itself, for all of the

---

4 Lavinia Griffiths, *Personification in* Piers Plowman (Cambridge: D.S. Brewer, 1985), 1.
5 Colette Murphy, "Lady Holy Church and Meed the Maid: Re-Envisioning Female Personifications in *Piers Plowman*," in *Feminist Readings in Middle English Literature: The Wife of Bath and All Her Sect*, ed. Ruth Evans (New York: Routledge, 1994), 140–64, here 142. Murphy is interested in how personification provides insights into contemporary understandings of gender, but the same applies, as I will show, to materialities.
6 Gregory G. Colomb, *Designs on Truth: The Poetics of the Augustan Mock-Epic* (University Park: Pennsylvania State University Press, 1992), 50.

formal conventions surrounding Lady Justice, her figure is as much a product of historical conditions as it is an expression of an abstract idea, and viewers of the statue who assume that the blindfold is symbolically consistent end up missing the point.

In her 1975 book *Language of Allegory*, Maureen Quilligan argues that the genre is inevitably fixated on a negotiation of linguistic meaning. That is to say, the trajectory of any allegory is from expressive ambiguity towards precision. The text is never a straightforward statement that has been translated into narrative but rather an intricate series of puns that focuses on language's ability to signify precisely. Words in allegory thus "extend meaning" by remaining allusive throughout the narrative.[7] The wordplay essentially asks "How much confidence may a man put in his language, or in words themselves?"[8] The idea of this interrogation of signs is both to demonstrate how easily language can be misinterpreted by characters (the fluidity of signification) and to hint at the possibility of arriving at a true meaning. The goal of the narrative is to develop the characters' abilities to differentiate specious interpretations from correct ones, which often ends with what Quilligan calls "the redemption of language."[9] As Quilligan explains, "The result is that the reader will become conscious of the significance of these words—of the very process by which they do in fact signify."[10]

If we take Griffith's focus on immediacy and Quilligan's emphasis on slippery language, we can see that even though the imagery of *Piers Plowman* may be immediate (or referential, as Mede is of *Le Roman de la Rose*), readers should not expect the personification imagery to be immediately *clear*, or at least, they should take any early interpretations with skepticism. As we shall see in the Lady Mede encounter, Langland offers early specious understandings of the figure that are either clarified or dismissed by the end of the section. Langland understands that his imagery evokes all sorts of reactions, but over the course of the section, Langland uses that immediacy to deconstruct how to understand the idea of Mede and how his contemporaries read clothing. If we turn to Lady Mede and her ostentatious robe, we recall that she is the personification of reward, or the desire for worldly gain. As a broad concept, Mede has the potential to corrupt men through bribery and the profit motive, or she has the potential to allow appropriate recompense for services rendered.[11] She appears in *Piers Plowman* as a bride to be sought, and while supposed authorities (such as the character of Holy Church) will offer their definitions of her, the poem stages a courtly debate about whom she should marry. Over the course of the section, the text requires readers to wrestle with these conflicting potentialities, attempting to define her role as either productive or noxious, and no dispositive conclusion is reached. Still, even

---

7 Maureen Quilligan, *Language of Allegory* (Ithaca, NY: Cornell University Press, 1979), 98.

8 Ibid., 46.

9 Ibid., 79–85.

10 Ibid., 68.

11 In the fourteenth century, the "overt self-interest" of the feudal system and the complexity of financial obligations rendered Mede rather influential, and increasingly bewildering to moralists. See John A. Yunck, *The Lineage of Lady Meed: The Development of Mediaeval Venality Satire*, (Notre Dame, IN: University of Notre Dame Press, 1963), 130, 232–37.

as the debate seems to be making progress in terms of better defining Mede's role, the significance of her robe becomes more and more opaque.

Will encounters Lady Mede early in passus II, and is immediately "ravysshed" by her clothing:

> I loked on my left half as the Lady me taughte,
> And was war of a womman wonderliche yclothed—
> Purfiled with pelure, the pureste on erthe,
> Ycorouned with a coroune, the Kyng hath noon bettre.
> Fetisliche hire fyngres were fretted with gold wyr,
> And thereon rede rubies as rede as any gleede,
> And diamaundes of derrest pris and double manere saphires,
> Orientals and ewages envenymes to destroye.
> Hire robe was ful riche, of reed scarlet engreyned,
> With ribanes of reed gold and of riche stones (II:7–16)

> [I looked on my left as the Lady instructed
> And was aware of a woman wonderfully clothed
> Adorned with fur-trimmed garments, the purest on earth
> Crowned with a crown, the king has none better
> Fancifully her fingers were adorned with gold wire
> And bright rubies as hot as any coal
> And diamonds of dearest price and two different kinds of sapphires,
> Pearls and water-stones which could stop poison.
> Her robe was very rich, dyed with fine scarlet,
> With ribbons of red gold and rich stones][12]

Readers familiar with earlier medieval allegory will find Lady Mede's attire immediately familiar. As John Yunck observes, Mede's dress is quite similar to that of Richece in the thirteenth-century *Roman de la Rose*, with its lavish fabrics and rich, venom-repelling gems.[13] And similar to the scene in the *Rose*, Will turns to his left before first seeing Mede, suggesting that focusing on Mede herself involves turning from the righteous path or emphasizing material over spiritual goods. However, for as much as the description may be foreboding, Langland includes a couple of elements that build on and depart from Guillaume de Lorris's depiction of Richece. For one, the fretted "fyngres" are both original and remarkably imaginative. Its effect is to suggest that every bit of Mede is ornamental. Then there is the line about the "coroune," which according to our narrator "the Kyng hath noon better." E. Talbot Donaldson actually glosses "co-

---

12 II:7–16. Translation mine, informed by William Langland, *Piers Plowman: The Donaldson Translation, Middle English Text, Sources and Backgrounds, Criticism*, trans. E. Talbot Donaldson (New York: W.W. Norton, 2006).

13 Yunck, *Lineage*, 289. Yunck also describes how Mede's figure is descended from earlier French and French romance allegory.

roune" as "coronet,"[14] however, the C-text uses "crowned" and "crown," which seems to confirm that Mede is not only wearing a crown, but also—because crowns were traditionally reserved for monarchs—shaming a king with her splendor. Perhaps then Langland includes the line about the king, for which there is no analogue in the *Rose*, to highlight how Mede disrupts traditional understandings of authority. Or maybe Langland is merely presenting us with an exaggerated image of wealth.

The stones with which Mede's robe and fingers are covered remain fascinating but ambiguous. Precious stones were often believed to have a variety of healing powers, from closing scabs to multiplying livestock to reconciling husbands with their wives.[15] Along with being thought to repel venom, the "ewages" Langland mentions in line 14 have a particularly interesting mythos. An ewage is a precious stone with the color of seawater, and it is often translated as a sapphire. In medieval lapidaries, sapphires in particular are said to have a wide range of powers, including the ability to strengthen memory, bring joy, prevent poverty, engender wisdom, slow a quick temper, and most commonly, guard against poison.[16] Indeed, an extant inventory of Edward III's jewels confirms he kept stones near his person for that expressed reason.[17] However, as Joan Evans shows, the wide range of uses attributed to ewages and sapphires suggests some inconsistencies.[18] Since no one single lapidary contains all of those uses, Langland may have heard of some applications but not others, found some more convincing than others, or not believed in the stones at all. In either case, the language shows he was aware of at least some of the relevant folklore. In medieval English poetry, the only other extant medieval use of "ewage" appears in John Lydgate's *A Commendation on Our Lady*, in which the ewages represent truth and fidelity.[19] Lydgate comes back to them as a symbol over and over.[20] This raises the question of how a reader should understand the ewage. If it provides wisdom, should we take Mede to be wise? Or joyful? Or, if it is equated with fidelity, as at least Lydgate's usage suggests, how should Will reconcile some of the symbolism of Mede's outfit with Holy Church's suggestion that Mede was close friends with the character False (II:6)? We are left to wonder if we should interpret the stones as lies, as some reliance on folk over ecclesiastical wisdom,

14 Langland, *Donaldson Translation*, 25.
15 See for instance Leo J. Henkin, "The Pardoner's Sheep-Bone and Lapidary Lore," *Bulletin of the History of Medicine* 10, no. 3 (Oct. 1941): 504–12; and Howard R. Patch, "Precious Stones in the House of Fame," *Modern Language Notes* 50, no. 5 (May 1935): 312–17.
16 Joan Evans, *Magical Jewels of the Middle Ages and the Renaissance, Particularly in England* (New York: Dover, 1976), 11, 13, 144–47.
17 Francis Palgrave, *The Antient Kalendars and Inventories of the Treasury of His Majesty's Exchequer: Together with Other Documents Illustrating the History of That Repository* (London: G. Eyre and A. Spottiswoode, 1836), 3:175.
18 Evans, *Magical Jewels*, 148.
19 John Lydgate, "A Balade; In Commendation of Our Lady," in *The Complete Works of Geoffrey Chaucer*, vol. 7, *Supplement: Chaucerian and Other Pieces*, ed. Walter W. Skeat (Oxford: Clarendon, 1897), 275–80, here 278.
20 Vivian Jacobs and Wilhelmina Jacobs, "The Color Blue: Its Use as Metaphor and Symbol," *American Speech* 33, no. 1 (Feb. 1958): 29–46.

or as something else entirely. No doubt Langland's details are suggestive, but the ambiguity of the scene and Will's inability to understand what he sees allows the reader to understand Mede's outfit and the jewels that adorn it in multiple, conflicting ways.

The exact function of the attire has been debated by scholars for some time. For James Simpson and Anna P. Baldwin, Mede's attire is neither interesting nor specific.[21] It is simply the apparel of a noblewoman and therefore symbolic of powerful lords whose financial influence corrupts. My issue with their cursory take is twofold: First, Langland spends too long—ten full lines—on the clothing itself for it to be simply an estate marker, and, second, Mede's costume is far too lavish to be simply that of a noblewoman. In fact, her costume surpasses most of the historic queens' robes that Stella Mary Newton describes in detail.[22] The verses may ultimately mark her as upper class, but that is not their sole function.

In "Class, Gender, Medieval Criticism, and *Piers Plowman*," David Aers criticizes Simpson's and Baldwin's approaches for seeing Mede's gender as "transparent."[23] Simpson should have considered why a poet might represent as female the competitively masculine magnates of his society. For Aers, the neglect of gender corrupts the historical reading and reduces the complexities of the text. However, for as much as Aers attempts to analyze what had previously been taken for granted, he falls back onto old patterns with respect to Mede's dress, saying that she is dressed in "the figure of a courtly lady … [and] as the figure of the *common prostitute*."[24] What Aers fails to ask is, if clothes define identity, then how can Mede occupy such a morally ambiguous position without oscillating between outfits?

For those critics who wish to focus more on Mede's specific clothing, two possible options are available, one historical and the other allegorical. With respect to the former, Mede's appearance has often been likened to Alice Perrers, who scandalized the English court in the 1370s with lavish dress, ambitions to power, and a certain ability to manipulate the king.[25] The connection between Perrers and Mede is strong if a little reductive.[26] While Langland fashions Mede from contemporary accounts of

21 James Simpson, *Piers Plowman: An Introduction to the B-text* (London: Longman, 1990), 43–60; Anna P. Baldwin, *The Theme of Government in* Piers Plowman (Cambridge: D.S. Brewer, 1981), 20–40.
22 As discussed below, Newton's work partially focuses on the wardrobes of Edward III, which provide keen insight into the specific costume the king donned as well as the clothing he prescribed for others. See Stella Mary Newton, *Fashion in the Age of the Black Prince: A Study of the Years 1340–1365* (Woodbridge, UK: Boydell, 1999).
23 David Aers, "Class, Gender, Medieval Criticism, and *Piers Plowman*," in *Class and Gender in Early English Literature: Intersections*, ed. Britton J. Harwood and Gillian R. Overing (Bloomington: Indiana University Press, 1994), 59–75, here 66. For further reading see Clare Lees, "Gender and Exchange in *Piers Plowman*," in the same volume, 112–30.
24 Aers, "Class," 66.
25 For further reading see Stephanie Trigg, "The Traffic in Medieval Women: Alice Perrers, Feminist Criticism, and *Piers Plowman*," *The Yearbook of Langland Studies* 12 (1998): 5–29.
26 Indeed, Bernard F. Huppé used the robust historical parallels to date the A-text. See Huppé, "The A-Text of *Piers Plowman* and the Norman Wars," *PMLA* 54, no. 1 (March 1939): 37–64.

Perrers, Mede's rather extended narrative role and allegorical title ought to remind us that the historical parallel is but one layer of her character—perhaps a starting point rather than a universal marker. With respect to the latter, Mede has also been compared to the Whore of Babylon, who likewise dresses in scarlet and corrupts those around her.[27] While some critics have chosen one of these options, many have acknowledged the availability of both, while warning against leaning too heavily on one-to-one historicism.[28] In other words, there is a small consensus that Mede might *reflect* aspects of either Perrers's reputation or the Book of Revelation to Langland's audience, but that Mede is not Perrers just as she is not the Whore of Babylon. I agree with that position, and I think it is crucially important to realize that an intimately detailed set of clothes can mean so much so widely: Langland crafted the scene to give such ambivalence to the finery he spent so long describing. Both comparisons are available, which expands the range of meaning afforded to the clothing while resisting any reductive moves and imports material realities into the allegorical dream world. Langland is using real figures to wrestle with abstract ideas. If the verse is liminal, so too is Langland's reach. Real-world clothing can have allegorical significance, *and* allegorical clothing can have material concerns.

In other words, just as we meet her, it is hard to settle on an exact interpretation of Mede's ornamentation. Nevertheless, the details are tempting for the critic: their specificity and length seem to mean something, as does their rather specific allusion to *Le Roman de la Rose*. In response to her appearance, Will immediately seeks to place her and to frame what her clothing must mean. Allegorical meaning will eventually be built into the robes, but Will's inability to discern their significance suggests a measure of ambiguity here. All Will can definitively say is that the unnamed, unmatched woman is "worthily atired" (II:19). Even that is perhaps ironic in context, because the reader has to wonder *for whom* Mede is worthy.[29]

Holy Church quickly provides answers to Will's questions, but given the complex, interlaced allegorical lineage, Holy Church's reading of Mede's character and outfit is remarkably terse. Mede has "noyed" her "ful oft," is a "bastarde," and never tells the truth (II:20 and 25). In Holy Church's estimation, Mede's clothing therefore suggests a few particular, nefarious aspects about its owner. It suggests she is a liar, a seductress, and a corruptive agent. Holy Church does not reference the clothes or the jewelry specifically, but if we take her word for it, we can infer that Mede's clothing attracts men in order to corrupt them, and that by coveting Mede, their conscience is overcome. Gerald Morgan reads Mede's attire in this way, taking Holy Church's word for it and

---

27 See for instance John Burrow, who describes Mede as a "modern version of the Scarlet Woman." *English Poets in the Late Middle Ages: Chaucer, Langland and Others* (Boca Raton, FL: Taylor and Francis, 2018), 156.

28 Namely, Aers, "Class," 66; Lees, "Gender and Exchange," 112–30; and Malcolm Godden, *The Making of* Piers Plowman (London: Longman, 1990), 35–37.

29 While the allegorical reading of seeing Mede as another iteration of Richece remains available, in both *Piers Plowman* and *Le Roman de la Rose*, the tension is not necessarily with what the figure is but rather to whom the figure is bonded.

attaching any ambiguity to Will's failure to internalize her truths.[30] For Morgan, the text is clear: Mede is extravagant and Holy Church's word final.

Moreover, this cynical understanding of Mede reflects certain contemporary versions of her. In *The Lineage of Lady Meed*, Yunck describes many fourteenth-century venality satires that closely echo Holy Church's criticism.[31] The longest of them, "Apocalypse of Golias," attacks each estate in turn, accusing them all of only giving money a hearing. Doctors charge too much for little treatment, friars focus too much on silver, and officials escape military service through bribery. The cynicism of the text reflects Mede's initial pairing with False and the way Holy Church unequivocally condemns her. If fourteenth-century readers were familiar with any of the extant satires, they may have shared Holy Church's distrust. There were certainly enough reasons to be skeptical of a moneyed economy. For example, kings regularly requested payments in order to get litigation expedited.[32] They also levied amercements, or small fines not for crimes but for failing in public duty.[33] The problem, as A. L. Poole describes, was that the ambiguity of the charges made it difficult to distinguish between being amerced and being extorted. And yet, for as much as these secular changes motivated numerous critiques, a large portion of the diatribes targeted the Church most of all, focusing on papal gratuities. Thus, even as a late medieval reader of satire may have been wary of Langland's Mede, the same reader could have been confused that a representative of the Church was bent on financial reform.

The other issue is that such a simplified reading neglects the complicated debate that follows, as well as Langland's tendency to criticize ecclesiastical leaders. Also, depending on how a reader understood Mede's outfit before, especially taking into account the lineage of "ewages," Holy Church's conflation of the elaborate attire into the enemy of the Church may seem incomplete. The exact nature of Lady Mede and her role in this dream world will be debated over the next two passus. While a reader such as Morgan may be inclined to trust the judgment of such an unimpeachable authority as Holy Church, the very length of the debate after her speech suggests hers is not the last word.

Just as Holy Church's explanation failed to define Mede's clothing adequately, the former's diatribe against Mede also fails to fit the latter's behavior. Throughout passus II, Mede is very passive and speaks rarely—she does not do much corrupting. Many figures fight over her, but her potential suitors are False and Favel. It is not that they are

30 Gerald Morgan, "The Dignity of Langland's Meed," *Modern Language Review* 104, no. 3 (July 2009): 623–39.
31 Yunck, *Lineage*, 230–35.
32 Sir Percy Henry Winfield, *The Chief Sources of English Legal History* (Delanco, NJ: Legal Classics Library, 2002), 138–39. The legal term was *oblata in spem*, and as Winfield notes, royal treasurers often went out of their way to distinguish between *in spem* and bribery.
33 A. L. Poole, *Obligations of Society in the Twelfth and Thirteenth Centuries: Ford Lectures* (Oxford: Clarendon, 1949), 77.

corrupted by their desire; it is that they desire her because they are already corrupt.[34] When Theology objects to Mede's marriage, he refers to her femininity half a dozen times in a twenty-line speech while insisting that the fault is not with Mede—she has not deceived anyone—but in what Simony and Civil have *done* with Mede. There is the sense that her female qualities undercut her agency. As the passus develops, Mede is reduced to a grammatical object, as she is led to London, set on a foal,[35] overmastered with merry speech, and taken into custody. Indeed, one of the only times Mede acts as a subject is the final clause of the passus, where she "trembled for fere" (II:236).

When Mede finally does act in the king's court, she bribes, flatters, and condescends to the courtiers and friars. In other words, she fulfills many of Holy Church's predictions. She gains forgiveness from a confessor for a horse-load of wheat (III:40), a go-between for a "nobel" [coin] (III:45–46), and servants for gold and silver cups (III:22). While her behavior is clearly bribery, and her funds allow lords to exercise their lechery, her influence also provides for a new roof and cloister for the church and coats for clerks. The moral ambiguities are reflected in Mede's speech to the king, in which she describes her many uses to him, such as maintaining loyal subjects and paying for foreign mercenaries. She goes on to explain that she is also necessary for the Pope to command obedience, for the minstrel to eat, and for tutors to be paid. The argument is that Mede, however morally manipulative, makes "pees in londe" (III:221) [peace in the land] and that "no wighte, as [Mede] wene, withoute Mede may libbe" (III:226) [No person, as Mede thinks, can last without Mede].

It's worth noting at this point that the allegorical plot is developing in order to better define a rather complex word. First, Will asks who Mede is—in other words, what does Mede *signify*?—and the reader is met with one ostensibly dogmatic definition (Holy Church's) that is eventually complicated by the combination of Theology's and Mede's speeches. As such, the narrative moves us from an early, rash interpretation to a more encompassing understanding of the word. That is not to say that Holy Church's arguments are completely invalidated: Mede never once denies that she encourages small amounts of corruption or greed. She just claims that the depth of her corrosion is minimal—"For kulled I nevere no kynge ne conseilled therafter" (III:187) [For I have never killed a king nor counseled such an action to happen]—and that her presence is necessary in the material world. However, for as much as Will's understanding of language is getting more refined, the clothing remains static. Mede's appearance never once changes, even as her body and behavior are given more attributes. This would be sensible if her traits were complementary, but at this point in the poem, the robes have absorbed a number of contradictory meanings. With each new speech, their

34 In fact, as Godden has shown, one can read Mede as an otherwise neutral figure who is herself corrupted by False and Favel, rather than the other way around. See Godden, *Making*, 36.
35 The available comparison to Jesus on a donkey riding into Jerusalem heightens the sense of corruption and parody in this scene, but again, Mede is not acting so much as being acted upon.

ability to mean one thing or the other decreases, suggesting our ability to settle who or what Mede *is* may be frustrated.

In passus III, Conscience gives two speeches about Mede, the first of which echoes most of Holy Church's concerns. However, in the wake of Mede's speech about her own utility, the King is convinced, saying "Bi Christe, as me thynketh / Mede is wel worthi, me thynketh the maistrye to have" (III:228–29).[36] In response, Conscience is then forced to break Mede into two different kinds: spiritual and earthly. Again, the momentum of the Mede narrative had worked to undercut Holy Church's original interpretation before replacing it with Conscience's more refined language. Thus, Conscience's riposte provides an ostensible debate victory for himself and therefore a cohesive understanding of Mede. But, besides the lack of an explicit end to the debate (the king stops it before any winner can be determined), the text is even more confusing than before, as there are now *two* allegorical Medes to consider, each having multiple valences. The symbolism of the clothing is confused as well, as it is unclear which Mede is wearing the extravagant outfit. We might say that both Medes are clothed the same way, but then the dress becomes even more ambivalent, as it may symbolize sexual excess or corruption (Whore of Babylon), political expediency (Perrers), the necessary wealth needed to maintain a kingdom (as Mede's speech suggests), or some form of spiritual favor (as do the rich clothes of the daughter in *Pearl*). The multiple allegorical traditions do not cohere well.

To sum up, at the beginning of this episode, Holy Church offered us a classically allegorical way to view Mede and her costume. But with each new development, Holy Church's original description becomes less reliable, along with the significance of the clothes themselves. When Langland finally offers us a clear understanding of Mede via Conscience, the complexity of the solution undercuts any solid reading of the clothes. Mede is alluring and deceptive indeed, but like her name, she is dangerous and necessary, spiritual and material. When the meaning of her costume can only be implied—for all the talk on the definition of her name, Mede's supposedly definitive clothes are ignored—Mede's expanding definitions do not clear up the ambiguities present from the beginning. Langland has appropriated conventional allegorical imagery in order to demonstrate both how misleading it can be and also how difficult it is to fully parse. Similarly, the topical valences of Mede's dress muddy the significance of material clothing. Even if the link between Mede and Perrers is convincing, the expansive, ubiquitous formulation that Conscience and the King settle on does not clarify how to read Perrers or her fashion. It would be hard to read Perrers as a spiritual reward for the king, but it remains unclear if she is necessary for the kingdom or a corrupting influence or both. And if it is both, one must wonder what scarlet signifies, or indeed ewages.

---

36 This phrasing is a little difficult. The King essentially says, "By Christ, as I think, Mede has argued worthily, and, I think, has the upper hand." Again, the sense that she is "worthi" appears over and over alongside the various estimations of her worth.

Those questions lead to the more profound one of why Langland would both-
er with this ostentatious description if it is to become so riddled with contradiction.
Langland is trying to unsettle both how readers think about Mede and also how they
think about clothing generally. It is hard to imagine Mede without the description
of her adornment, as it is her most characteristic trait. She is therefore trapped by
it despite its vexed significance. Potential, divisive readings of the jewels and fabric
are available to the reader, but they are both shortsighted and reductive. Rather than
providing us with a clear and present understanding of Mede's outfit, then, the text
emphatically resists attempts to define her costume—in fact, it is more opaque at the
end of the section than it was at the beginning.

FASHION AND ITS ALLEGORICAL HOLD

Langland's interpretive angst reflects the vexed politics of clothing during the 1360s
and 70s in which he was writing, and it is helpful to diverge from the text a little in
order to fully describe what I mean. As readers of this journal may be familiar with,
there is broad support for the idea—even if "birth" is too strong a word—that fashion during the 1340s reached a critical mass.[37] If the previous centuries were characterized by slow alterations of standardized attire, the 1340s introduced a period of
rapid change and radical new fashion to boot. Around 1340, tunics and long gowns[38]
fell out of favor, and dress that fit more tightly to the body became popular, leading
men to don pourpoints and doublets that accentuated waistlines and women to wear
tighter bodices and plunging necklines. In other words, the clothing of this time got
shorter and more sexually definitive. The reversion to short clothing was not unique
to history or even to the Middle Ages, as both short and long clothing had been in
vogue at different times over the centuries[39]—with longer clothing having dominated
much of upper-class dress since the twelfth century. What made the fourteenth-century switch unique was that, contrary to earlier shifts that would last for centuries,

37 See either Margaret Scott, *Medieval Dress and Fashion* (London: British Library, 2007), who
    argues for fashion in the twelfth century, or Sarah-Grace Heller, *Fashion in Medieval France*
    (Cambridge: D.S. Brewer, 2007), who finds evidence of fashion in the thirteenth. Of course,
    early modernists put fashion's birth later. The next three authors claim that fashion starts in
    the fifteenth, sixteenth, and seventeenth century respectively: Ann Rosalind Jones and Peter
    Stallybrass, *Renaissance Clothing and the Materials of Memory* (Cambridge: Cambridge
    University Press, 2000); Carole Shammas, *The Preindustrial Consumer in England and America*
    (Oxford: Clarendon Press 1990); Lorna Weatherill, *Consumer Behavior and Material Culture in
    Britain 1660–1760* (London: Routledge, 1988).
38 "Garments that sweep up all the filth off the ground for no useful purpose." Cited in Susan
    Schibanoff, *Chaucer's Queer Poetics: Rereading the Dream Trio* (Toronto: University of Toronto
    Press, 2006), 37.
39 King Edgar, for instance, is shown in 966 wearing short clothing. Laurel Ann Wilson, "'De Novo
    Modo': The Birth of Fashion in the Middle Ages" (Ph.D. diss., Fordham University, 2012), 56,
    265.

the 1340s introduced a period of rapid change that was driven less by large societal and technical developments than by the capricious desires of those wealthy enough to afford new clothing.[40]

As Laurel Wilson's work demonstrates,[41] choice, while not unheard of in the Middle Ages, nevertheless increased significantly in the second half of the fourteenth century.[42] For much of the Middle Ages, the enormous cost of clothing severely restricted consumption of luxury fabrics. However, as the fourteenth century developed, trade of luxury goods expanded, lowering the costs and expanding circulation.[43] Dramatic, luxurious clothing was no longer the privilege of the wealthy gentry and above.[44] This trend is crucial for understanding fashion's influence, because it helped to establish a cycle that drove individuals of means to purchase ever more ornate dress. As nobles sought to distinguish themselves through dress, they demanded more luxury goods, which in turn enriched the merchants who provided them. With their new capital, those same merchants turned around and bought fancy clothes, which pushed the nobility into a very expensive game of one-upmanship. Part of fashion was about individual expression, but an equally important part of it was an attempt to maintain and define social difference in a newly mobile society.

Perhaps a definitive example of this attempt to define is described by Stella Mary Newton in *Fashion in the Age of the Black Prince* when she examines the Royal Wardrobe for the 1360 Christmas celebration.[45] The records provide a nearly exhaustive

40 Or, as Susan Crane has put it, "change itself [became] an object of consumption." Crane, *The Performance of Self: Ritual, Clothing, and Identity During the Hundred Years War* (Philadelphia: University of Pennsylvania Press, 2002), 14.

41 Wilson's whole project is predicated on locating fashion's birth in the fourteenth century as a product of both the buildup of the wool trade, a richer mobile middle class, and the standardization of clothing. Wilson, "De Novo Modo."

42 Ibid. I mention Wilson's criteria not because I am particularly interested in whether or not the fourteenth century constituted the birth of fashion. Instead, I want to highlight how this period changed patterns in dress.

43 Ibid., 132.

44 Working in estate records, Frederique Lachaud makes a compelling case for some wealthy burgesses' wearing clothing suited to the upper estate in thirteenth-century England. That the wealthiest merchants were dressing extravagantly should not surprise us, however, and does not threaten the line I am taking here. It's not that no wealthy townsperson had ever bought scarlet: It's that as trade increased and prices dropped, a much wider array of people began to afford better clothing in the fourteenth century. See Frederique Lachaud, "Dress and Social Status in England Before the Sumptuary Laws," in *Heraldry, Pageantry, and Social Display in Medieval England*, ed. Peter R. Coss and Maurice Keen (Woodbridge, UK: Boydell, 2002), 105–23.

45 Besides the incredible detail that Newton offers, I focus on Edward III for a couple of reasons: First, we have more detailed records of his Wardrobe than we do of Richard II's. In fact, information from Richard's wardrobe exists (see W. Paley Baildon, "XXII.—A Wardrobe Account of 16–17 Richard II, 1393–4," *Archaeologia* 62 [1911]: 497–514), but it is hard to find and less detailed, and Edward's accounts are better preserved. Kay Staniland's fantastic summary of fourteenth-century Wardrobes makes little mention of Richard as well; Staniland, "The Great Wardrobe Accounts as a Source for Historians of Fourteenth-Century Clothing and Textiles," *Textile History* 20 (1989): 275–81. Second, Edward III reigned until 1377, at which point the A-text of *Piers Plowman* is generally considered to have been completed, with the B-text

picture of the clothing provided to everyone in the court from the king to the min-strels. Edward III's outfit is laid out in exact detail, from the tightness of the fit (in accordance with the new fashion) to the gold ribbon trimming that differentiated his outfit from the attire of the rest of the attendees. We learn that Queen Philippa's outfit was nearly identical to that of Edward's sister, Joan, except for the extra and expen-sive ermine that Phillippa's tailor had to work with. We also learn that students from Cambridge[46] wore tan-colored shortcloth with *popellus*[47] and miniver, that the indoor servants wore shortcloth mi-parti, and that the stonemasons were given budge (lamb-skin dressed with the wool on). As Newton notes, everyone in the procession had a clear role exquisitely defined by the cloth provided them by the royal court. There was little ambiguity, and even a passing observer would have been able to distinguish the powerful from the powerless. From this we can gather two broad ideas: first, Edward III believed in and used the power of clothing to prop up his authority as king, and second, clothing here expressed one's role in a sharply defined, hierarchical manner. Indeed, Edward was willing to spend a great deal of money in order to reinforce that link between clothing and status. Moreover, the fabrics and accessories provided by the Royal Wardrobe suggest that this procession was less about individuals than sys-tems; that clothing was not an expression of the self but an expression of one's status. Everyone's clothes, from the Prince of Wales's down to the stonemason's, were coordi-nated to convey the impression that each person had a role in the administration, and that their clothing reflected their designated roles. In other words, while clothing has many uses (discretion, protection from elements, etc.), this clothing in this moment functioned primarily as a uniform (in the contemporary sense of a garment signifying membership in a group) for the owner—removing individuality by placing the wear-er on a continuum. In a sense, Edward's use of clothing is how Simpson and Baldwin read Mede's robe: as a uniform, signifying obvious, flat identity. However, this new use of fashion was not as accepted for others as it was by the king.

Medieval commentaries display a newfound focus on superficiality and a ten-sion around its use. The invectives against new fashion trends were diverse, accusing the styles of being too revealing, capricious, sexually ambiguous, disruptive, waste-

---

additions soon to follow. If Langland was meditating on official roles of clothing during that time, he would have been thinking of Edwardian reforms.

46   Newton, *Fashion*, 66. There is an ambiguity here in that Newton specifies that the students in 1361 are from Kings College, Cambridge, although that college would not be officially endowed until 1441. The specific record Newton cites from the 1361 Patent Roll describes "scholars supported by the king's alms in the university of Cambridge," but again, there is an ostensible 80-year discrepancy. As it turns out, early in his reign Edward III had sponsored twelve stu-dents to attend Cambridge as the "Society of the King's Scholars." In 1337, he further endowed this group, and they became the College of the King's Hall (which later became part of Trinity Hall). The students in Newton are therefore not part of King's College, but King's Hall. See Alan B. Cobban, *English University Life in the Middle Ages* (London: UCL Press, 1999), 15.

47   The summer fur of a squirrel; University of Manchester Lexis of Cloth and Clothing Project database, http://lexissearch.arts.manchester.ac.uk, s.v. "pople."

ful, or morally compromising.[48] There are numerous examples, but one from Jean de Venette, written in 1340, will do: "Men were now beginning to wear disfiguring costumes …. Men thus tricked were more likely to flee in the face of the enemy, as the event afterwards many times proved true."[49] And later, in 1356, he wrote, "Now they begin to disfigure themselves in a still more extravagant way. They wore pearls on their hoods … by night they devoted themselves immoderately to the pleasures of the flesh."[50] Here Jean connects the new style to cowardly and lascivious behavior, suggesting both a lack of morals and a lack of masculinity. I would like also to make three observations: (1) Jean's references to specific styles and ornamentation reflect a pattern documented by Danielle Queruel, who demonstrated that as the fourteenth century developed, both moralistic tracts and romances reflected a more specific, object-oriented performance of status. Earlier works focused on abstract visions of man's position in society, whereas later works (while not necessarily questioning the hierarchy) used detailed descriptions of clothing and jewelry to accomplish the same goal.[51] (2) Although his language fits the new fashion, writers like Jean de Venette participated in a long medieval tradition of connecting material clothing to character.[52] This discourse broadly positioned clothing as both a material good—that is, made up of physical objects with financial cost—and a spiritual referent. In other words, medieval clothes were symbols as much as they were fabric. (3) The kind of one-to-one certainty Jean maintains is akin to that of Holy Church, whose early judgments are both confident and ultimately insufficient. If writers like Jean made up the rhetorical climate of Langland's composition, perhaps then the Mede episode works to critique the reactionary diatribes Langland may have seen as shortsighted.

In short, Edwardian practice and contemporary social critics reflected broader tensions between shifting identities and a certain uncertainty with respect to how to maintain social structure. They betray a culture in flux, attempting to reconcile ideology with social practices and to provide order in "social organization where structure was ambivalent."[53] By this, I do not mean to suggest that no one thought seriously

---

48 Wilson summarizes the diatribes and makes the case that the critiques of clothing changed after the "birth" of fashion by their referring to specific aspects of an outfit, such as its dagged edges, in their rhetoric. In other words, pre-fourteenth century, most of the criticism of clothing was broader, and as fashion took hold, writers started referencing particular styles they disapproved of. Wilson, "De Novo Modo," 141–49.

49 Jean de Venette and Guillaume de Nangis, *The Chronicle of Jean de Venette*, trans. Jean Birdsall (New York: Columbia University Press, 1953), 34. Jean goes on, describing the cost of the noble's vanity, namely making the ruling elite seem effeminate and therefore inadequate.

50 Ibid., 63.

51 Danielle Queruel, "Attitudes and Social Positions in Courtly Romances: Hainault, Fourteenth and Fifteenth Centuries," in *Showing Status: Representations of Social Position*, ed. Willem Pieter Blockmans and A. Janse (Turnhout, Belgium: Brepols, 1999).

52 Social invectives relating to clothing cited the Book of Isaiah and can be traced back at least as early as the thirteenth century.

53 Diane Owen Hughes, "Sumptuary Law and Social Relations in Renaissance Italy," in *Disputes and Settlements: Law and Human Relations in the West*, ed. John Bossy (Cambridge: Cambridge University Press, 1983), 69–99, here 99.

about appearance before 1340. However, from fashion's increasing rate of change, its wider penetration of society, the royal processions channeling it, and the invectives railing against it, mid-fourteenth-century England was fashion-obsessed in a way that it had not been before, even though there was disagreement over what it all meant.

So far, this article has worked to demonstrate how the Mede episode in *Piers Plowman* evokes allegorical and ecclesiastical traditions before undercutting their ability to signify reliably. I have further argued that interest in and penetration of fashion spiked in the mid-to-late-fourteenth century, inspiring the spread of a discordant discourse around the links between costume and societal or spiritual status. It is remarkable that this kind of thinking is often limited to the literary. For example, Griffiths writes that "personification allegories set up equations which allow for a bridging of temporal textual and ontological gaps. They see abstract intellectual systems—cosmology, ethics, logic, history—in terms of human relations."[54] It is true those gaps are collapsed in *Piers*, but they are also collapsed in wardrobes and moralist tracts. That does not mean everyone agreed: Edward thought fashion could reinforce rigid societal hierarchies, whereas writers like Jean de Venette saw its penetration as disruptive. For both, however, everyday costume carried the allegorical potential as well. Likewise, Mede's clothing is both corporeal—and thus similar to actual clothing worn by actual people—and symbolic of various character traits, and we should read the ambiguity of her clothing as commenting on multiple conversations at once.

Most of the scholarship around Mede has attempted to fix her in place. I think this is partly because allegoresis often seeks a sort of key to unlock allegorical texts, but this critical practice is the natural result of personification allegory. Mede is a fixed figure with a fixed outfit, which generates a "powerful desire" to define.[55] However, even though Langland allows the debate to reach some sort of conclusion (Conscience's probable victory is interrupted by the king), the clothes remain profoundly ambivalent. As such, the text resists the critical need to fix clothes to attributes. Moreover, since the clothes are both allegorical and material, Langland is not only demonstrating the ambivalence of clothes in allegory—he is also expressing a deep skepticism concerning the power of material clothes to define.

Langland's exploration of abstract ideas is inextricably tied to questions about decorum, costume, and exterior expression. He is not asking just *what* Mede is but also how to attach character traits to material goods, and how we could ever do so with any confidence. Those ewages, with all of their supposed magical power, remain ambivalent. Either the verse obscures the meaning of the clothing and highlights the disparity between appearance and reality, or it discourages us from simply likening a character to her outfit. Regardless, she is crucially unable to change her outfit, even as her identity is constantly and discordantly being defined by the men who observe her. This discordance is crucial because it suggests that clothing can only provide

---

54 Griffiths, *Personification*, 106.
55 For Lees, this desire to define is partly the result of Mede's gender. See Lees, "Gender and Exchange," 114.

crude details about its wearer, those details are subject to public interpretation that is bound to mislead, and one's outfit cannot be modified to reflect change. These characters, then, are trapped in an imprecise semiotic system which arbitrarily favors the rich and powerful.[56]

Like his peers, Langland was worried about fashion. He worried not because it deprived men of masculinity as Jean de Venette claimed, nor because it bankrupted them, nor because it threatened social norms; he was worried about it because he knew in this fashion-obsessed era, clothing was constantly examined but nearly always misread. He understood that once status is commodified, "the self is to some degree for sale."[57] He would have agreed with one fourteenth-century homilist, who worried about clothing's ability to falsify status rather than merely reflect it: "For we may se now al day that, be it never so pouer a man, and a have on a gay gowne of selk … eny man is fain to make him cher and also for to be mek and lowliche to him."[58] That is why he imported material concerns into conventional imagery. As fashion rose in importance and galvanized a clumsy attempt to codify clothing and status, Langland decoupled his imagery from otherwise certain allegorical markers. He constantly made use of allegorical conventions only to undercut their reliability. In fact, Mede is not the only character whose clothing floats between the material and the allegorical: Langland employed some of the same techniques when describing the parade of deadly sins, the Doctor of Divinity, and Hawkin the Active Man. In each of these instances, Langland described a character's clothing specifically, had another character offer an initial read of that outfit, and then systematically undermined that interpretation. Part of this point here is to show how dress does not always fit someone's character. The more profound observation, however, is that even though clothing is by its nature ambiguous, viewers of that clothing—specifically, those with power—will nevertheless be tempted to derive some misguided insight from it. This is true for characters like Holy Church, whose early claims about Mede are shown to be incomplete, and it's also true for contemporary critics. When we read allegorical clothing looking for definitive, one-to-one signification, we fall prey to the same instincts that Langland was trying to critique.

56 In fact, the only time characters *do* change their garb is in passus II, when Liar and Guile sneak past the king's guards by donning friars' robes (lines 220–40). Clothing, it seems, is only malleable (and therefore extra deceitful) when it is used by the Church.

57 Claire Sponsler, *Drama and Resistance: Bodies, Goods, and Theatricality in Late Medieval England* (Minneapolis: University of Minnesota Press, 1997), 12.

58 Worcester, UK, Worcester Cathedral Library, MS F.10, 49b; quoted in Gerald Robert Owst, *Literature and Pulpit in Medieval England: A Neglected Chapter in the History of English Letters and of the English People* (Cambridge: Cambridge University Press, 1933), 410.

Sex, Lies, and *Verdugados:* Juana of Portugal and the Invention of Hoopskirts

Mark D. Johnston

Every reader of this journal knows hoopskirts, in their many styles, as iconic aristocratic fashions of late medieval and early modern Europe, depicted in numerous paintings from those eras. Many may also have read the story that Juana of Portugal, second wife of King Enrique IV of Castile, invented the garment to hide illicit pregnancies. Like any new fashion in the later Middle Ages, hoopskirts attracted criticism, especially from clerical moralists, who decried their extravagance, cost, peculiar appearance, incentives to lust, unhealthy side effects, and cumbersome use. Whether any women actually used hoopskirts to conceal pregnancy may remain forever impossible to know. However, the political opponents of Enrique IV did not hesitate to appropriate this claim as one of many slanderous accusations made against his queen, during the decades when they fought to replace him on the Castilian throne with his siblings Alfonso and Isabel.

This study reviews the earliest known textual and artistic evidence regarding the appearance of hoopskirts at the Castilian court in the mid- to late fifteenth century, including its enthusiastic adoption by Isabel as queen of Castile. It contrasts evidence of the new fashion's popularity with the often-cited denigration of hoopskirts by Isabel's official chronicler Alfonso de Palencia and by her confessor Hernando de Talavera. Their vilification of the new fashion became a commonplace in attacks on hoopskirts into the early modern era. This study concludes that the association of Juana of Portugal with immoral use of *verdugados*, disseminated during a period of intense partisan strife, was a fiction of political propaganda. Nonetheless, that fiction was so potent that it cemented the legend of the hoopskirt's ignoble invention as a topos for disparaging the fashion into modern times.[1]

This essay is dedicated to the memory of Nancy F. Marino, Distinguished Professor of Spanish at Michigan State University. Before her untimely death in 2018, she often shared with this author her expert knowledge of fifteenth-century Castilian court culture. *Forse altra avrebbe cantato con miglior plectro.* This contribution to *Medieval Clothing and Textiles* originated in a presentation to a DISTAFF session at the 2015 International Congress on Medieval Studies at Kalamazoo, Michigan; Robin Netherton subsequently encouraged me to revise it for publication.

1 Amanda Wunder, "Women's Fashions and Politics in Seventeenth-Century Spain: The Rise and Fall of the *Guardainfante*," *Renaissance Quarterly* 68 (2015): 133–86, describes the evolution and criticism of Spanish hoopskirts in early modern times.

As Carmen Bernis Madrazo explains in her comprehensive survey of Spanish fashions from this era, the original Spanish term for the new fashion was *verdugo* (green branch), because freshly cut wicker branches or canes were used to create hooped skirts.[2] Attached in concentric horizontal rings around a skirt, the bent canes created a billowing cone or bell shape. A skirt enlarged in this way was termed *verdugado* (caned). From this Spanish adjective was derived, with some phonological deformation, the English noun *farthingale*. Originally unadorned and sewn onto the outside of a skirt, the hoops were soon covered in decorative fabric, and eventually simply sewn inside a skirt. Francisco Martínez Botella, an expert recreator of Spanish historical dress, emphasizes that canes were applied to both full-length gowns as well as separate waist-high skirts. The full-length garment, as in an example recently recreated by Martínez Botella (fig. 5.1), extended from the bodice to the ground, and so could easily have prompted charges of concealing pregnancy.[3] The canes employed to enlarge skirts were also used in public whippings, so *verdugo* came by metonymy to mean executioner, as it still does in modern Spanish. Later critics of hoopskirts often exploited this lexical coincidence to mock them as punishing to their wearers.

CASTILIAN SEXUAL POLITICS IN THE MID-FIFTEENTH CENTURY

It is almost impossible to separate condemnation of *verdugados* from the tumultuous, even lurid, history of the Castilian crown in the mid-fifteenth century. The claim that hoopskirts served to disguise illicit pregnancies arose amidst the sexual politics involving the several offspring of King Juan II of Castile (1405–54). His first wife, Maria of Aragon (1403–45) bore him a son, the future Enrique IV (1425–74). His second wife, Isabel of Portugal (1428–96), bore him two children, Prince Alfonso (1453–68) and Enrique's eventual successor, Queen Isabel I (1451–1504).[4]

At the center of this dynastic melodrama was Enrique IV. Even the most sympathetic contemporary chroniclers offer an unflattering portrait of him: Unusually tall, overweight, and with an oddly shaped face, he was timid, socially awkward, and in-

2 Carmen Bernis Madrazo, *Trajes y Modas en la Época de los Reyes Católicos, I: Las Mujeres* (Madrid: Consejo Superior de Investigaciones Científicas, 1978), 38–42.
3 Personal correspondence with author, July 16–24, 2019. See examples on Martínez Botella's Facebook page, which documents his extensive work in recreating hoopskirts: www.facebook.com/sastrehistoricoytradicional. His post of June 23, 2018, includes various late medieval miniatures depicting the range of styles that used *verdugos*; www.facebook.com/sastrehistoricoytradicional/posts/1124014511069985 (accessed Dec. 3, 2019).
4 The extant documentation from fifteenth-century Castile, as for any Western European realm in this era, is vast. The modern scholarship is equally extensive. The following account of this period summarizes the interpretations provided by Marsilio Cassotti, *A Rainha Adúltera: Joana de Portugal e o Enigma da* Excelente Senhora, *Crónica de uma Difamaçao Anunciada*, trans. António Junior (Lisbon: A Esfera dos Livros, 2012); Manuel Fernández Álvarez, *Isabel la Católica* (Madrid: Espasa, 2003); Luis Suárez, *Enrique IV de Castilla: La Difamación como Arma Política* (Barcelona: Ariel, 2013); Luis Suárez, *Isabel I* (Barcelona: Ariel, 2012); and Óscar Villarroel González, *Juana la Beltraneja: La Construcción de una Ilegitimidad* (Madrid: Silex, 2014).

Fig. 5.1: A gown enlarged with *verdugos* (sewn inside), as recreated by Francisco Martínez Botella. Photo: By permission of Francisco Martínez Botella.

decisive. In 1440 he married his young cousin Blanca of Navarre (1424–64), but their union produced no offspring and so was annulled in 1453 for lack of consummation. Enrique's opponents nicknamed him "the Impotent," not simply for his failure to produce an heir, but also for his weak leadership of his realm.

Enrique succeeded his father as king of Castile in 1454, and soon married another cousin, the Portuguese princess Juana de Avis (1439–75), known today as Juana of Portugal. In 1455 the new queen arrived at the Castilian court with a retinue of young Portuguese noblewomen who served her for years to come.[5] Juana's attendants displayed provocative attire and promiscuous behavior, according to the chronicle of Alfonso de Palencia.[6] He mentions their stunning beauty, daring décolletage (allegedly extending below the navel), heavy perfumes, use of full-body white makeup, and constant flirtation with attentive suitors. Palencia concludes that their arrival initiated the moral decline of the Castilian court, but says nothing about *verdugados*.[7] Extravagant or unusual fashions—from Moorish-inspired apparel to gender-bending acts of cross-dressing—were certainly not unknown, and were regularly denounced, at the court of Castile in this era.[8] Palencia's often-quoted description of Juana's retinue, written some twenty years after the events that he describes, reflects perfectly the drumbeat of defamation that her husband's adversaries had already mounted against him and his second wife.

In February of 1462 Juana of Portugal bore a daughter, also named Juana. The birth of Princess Juana, along with her acclamation as heir to Enrique IV, was celebrated with all the customary public ceremony. Her aunt Isabel even served as godmother at her baptism. Nonetheless, Juana's birth hardened the partisan divisions between rival noble factions, one allied with Enrique and his daughter, the other with Alfonso

5 On Juana's household, see Francisco de Paula Cañas Gálvez, "Las Casas de Isabel y Juana de Portugal, Reinas de Castilla: Organización, Dinámica Institucional y Prosopografía (1447–1496)," in *Las Relaciones Discretas entre las Monarquías Hispana y Portuguesa: Las Casas de las Reinas (Siglos XV–XIX)*, ed. José Martínez Millán and Maria Paula Marçal Lourenço, 3 vols. (Madrid: Polifemo, 2008), 1:9–231.

6 Known today as the *Décadas* [Decades], for its decimal organization, or *Crónica de Enrique IV* [Chronicle of Enrique IV], because it is chiefly devoted to Enrique's reign. Modern editions include Brian Tate and Jeremy Lawrance, eds. and trans., *Gesta Hispaniensia ex Annalibus Suorum Dierum Collecta* (Madrid: Real Academia de la Historia, 1998–99); and Antonio Paz y Melia, trans., *Crónica de Enrique IV*, 4 vols. (Madrid: *Revista de Archivos*, 1904–08), republished as *Crónica de Enrique IV*, 3 vols., Biblioteca de Autores Españoles 257, 258, and 267 (Madrid: Atlas, 1973–75). The Latin edition by Tate and Lawrance comprises only the first "decade" of Palencia's opus, covering the years 1440–68; Paz y Melia translates the entire work, but occasionally omits lengthy documents cited in the Latin text. Citations in this article are to his 1904–08 four-volume edition.

7 *Décadas* 1.3.10, ed. Tate and Lawrance, 115–16; trans. Paz y Melia, 1:194–95.

8 See Nancy F. Marino, "How Portuguese Damas Scandalized the Court of Enrique IV of Castile," *Essays in Medieval Studies* 18 (2001): 43–52; Jeremy Lawrance, "Vestimenta y Opresión: El Caso del Verdugado a Finales de la Edad Media," *Cahiers d'Études Hispaniques Médiévales* 39 (2016): 111–36; and María del Cristo González Marrero, "Un Vestido para Cada Ocasión: La Indumentaria de la Realeza Bajomedieval como Instrumento para la Afirmación, la Imitación y el Boato. El Caso de Isabel I de Castilla," *Cuadernos del CEMYR* 22 (2015): 155–94.

and Isabel. In late 1464, the faction opposed to Enrique forced his assent to proclamation of Alfonso as heir to the throne. To support their position, Enrique's opponents circulated the claim that Princess Juana was actually begotten by the king's court favorite, Beltrán de la Cueva (1435?–92). They invented for her the notorious epithet "la Beltraneja," that is, the daughter of Beltrán.[9] Later chroniclers even suggested that Princess Juana was conceived through a process of artificial insemination.[10]

Prince Alfonso died in 1468, and his faction quickly proclaimed Isabel heir to the throne. By now, Juana of Portugal—actively seeking to ensure her daughter's inheritance and constantly maligned by Enrique's adversaries—had become a political liability to her husband. Enrique placated his opponents by agreeing to custody of Queen Juana by Alfonso de Fonseca I (1418–73), the powerful Archbishop of Seville. Fonseca brought Queen Juana to his castle of Alaejos in late 1468.[11] There, if not previously, she took as a lover one of her noble guards, the archbishop's nephew Pedro de Castilla (1439?–75). Queen Juana and Pedro eventually produced two children. It was these pregnancies that Palencia later cited to claim that she tried to hide her condition at Alaejos with hoopskirts. With assistance from her partisans, Juana soon escaped custody at Alaejos and began an itinerant life, housed in various locations by the noble Mendoza family, the most powerful allies of Enrique IV.[12] After 1468, she still attended some court functions, probably to witness acts necessary for advancing the political fortunes of her daughter. Meanwhile, she openly promoted and advanced Pedro de Castilla within her own household. After the Mendoza family defected to Isabel's faction in 1472, Juana of Portugal settled in Madrid, at the Convent of Saint Francis, where she died in 1475.

At the same time, after secret negotiations, Princess Isabel of Castile married Prince Ferdinand of Aragon (1452–1516) on October 19, 1469, an alliance with enduring consequences for European history. With their marriage, a full-fledged civil war began between their allies and the nobles who supported Enrique and his daughter Juana "la Beltraneja." Enrique IV died on December 11, 1474, and Isabel's adherents declared her queen of Castile. In response, on May 25, 1475, Enrique's faction betrothed Princess Juana, at age thirteen, to her older uncle King Alfonso V of Portugal (1432–81). For the next four years, Portuguese and Castilian forces fought, with foreign support on each side, for control of the Castilian throne. The Battle of Toro, in March of 1476, provided for Isabel and Ferdinand the decisive victory that ensured, in September of 1479, a treaty ending the War of Castilian Succession and over two decades of civil strife.

9 Villarroel González (*Juana la Beltraneja*, 65–66) analyzes in detail the partisan construction of Juana's reputation as illegitimate, which probably began at her birth.
10 See Emilio Maganto Pavón, "Enrique IV de Castilla (1454–1474): Un Singular Enfermo Urológico: Retrato Morfológico y de la Personalidad de Enrique IV 'El Impotente' en las Crónicas y Escritos Contemporáneos," *Archivos Españoles de Urología* 56 (2003): 211–20.
11 *Décadas* 1.10.5–6, ed. Tate and Lawrance, 463–65; trans. Paz y Melia, 2:118–22.
12 See Helen Nader, *The Mendoza Family in the Spanish Renaissance, 1350 to 1550* (New Brunswick, NJ: Rutgers University Press, 1979).

THE *VERDUGADO* AS ARISTOCRATIC FASHION

Amidst the turmoil of these years, what do we know about the new fashion of *verduga-dos* that Juana of Portugal allegedly adopted for illicit purposes in 1468? The origins and early evolution of the *verdugado* remain unknown. No contemporary documents or artwork confirm the popularization of hoopskirts during the 1450s and 1460s. As noted already, Palencia does not cite *verdugados* as one of the scandalous fashions introduced with the arrival of Juana of Portugal at the court of Castile in 1455. The first testimonies to their vogue instead date from the early 1470s.

Histories of fashion commonly identify the first known pictorial representation of hoopskirts as a panel from the altarpiece created by Aragonese artist Pedro García de Benabarre (active 1445–85) for the important church of St. John in Lérida. Alberto Velasco Gonzàlez has analyzed in detail the altarpiece and the circumstances of its creation, probably between 1473 and 1482.[13] The altarpiece illustrates the life of St. John the Baptist, along with the lives of other major saints. The panel cited as the first representation of hoopskirts depicts the "Banquet of Herod," at which Salome presents the severed head of John the Baptist. Modern reproductions of this panel usually show only its lower left quarter, which portrays Salome and two attendants wearing *verdugados*. The entire panel in fact illustrates a lavish court banquet (fig. 5.2), in which Velasco Gonzàlez notes various elements, from musicians to furniture, considered typical of the extravagance and luxury of courtly life.[14] Panels representing the birth of Saint John and his decapitation also portray women wearing *verdugados*.[15]

Benabarre's depiction of *verdugados* confirms their popularity as courtly fashion, but how did he know of its stylishness? Benabarre apparently never worked outside Aragon; from 1452 to 1460 he was active in Barcelona, the nominal home of the Aragonese court (resident in Naples during these years) and of an urban patriciate that eagerly imitated aristocratic styles. Perhaps he or the assistants in his large workshop had seen the new fashion there; or perhaps they simply copied it from the work of other artists. Whatever the source of their knowledge of the *verdugado*, its depiction in a large public work, that is, the altarpiece for a major provincial church, assumed that viewers in Lérida would readily recognize the *verdugado* as typical of aristocratic life.

His assumption was certainly justified by the example of Queen Isabel, who embraced the new fashion. While still princess, in 1473, she wore a hoopskirt to host receptions for Burgundian ambassadors, according to a document known only from an 1821 monograph by historian Diego Clemencín.[16] The document describes in de-

---

13 Alberto Velasco Gonzàlez, *Fragments d'un Passat: Pere Garcia de Benavarri i el Retaule de l'Església de Sant Joan de Lleida* (Lérida, Spain: Museu de Lleida Diocesà i Comarcal, 2012), 50.

14 Now in the National Art Museum of Catalonia, and viewable online at www.museunacional.cat.

15 Both now in the Museum of Lérida, and viewable online at www.museunacional.cat.

16 "Relacion de las Fiestas de Alcalá en Obséquio de los Embajadores de Borgoña," in Diego Clemencín, *Elógio de la Réina Católica Doña Isabel, al Que Siguen Várias Ilustraciones sobre Su Reinado* (Madrid: Real Academia de la Historia, 1821), 326–30. Clemencín lists his source as a certain *Repertório de Algunos Actos y Cosas Singulares que en Estos Réinos de Castilla Acaecieron,* from a manuscript in the royal library, but cited from a copy at the now ruined Hieronymite

Fig. 5.2: The "Banquet of Herod," by Pedro García de Benabarre, from the altarpiece of the church of St. John of the Market (Lerida, Spain), ca. 1473–82. Photo: Courtesy of the Museu Nacional d'Art de Catalunya de Barcelona.

tail the lavish ceremonial of the receptions. For the second day of these events, Isabel appeared "vestida de un brial de brocado carmesí verdugado de cetí verde"[17] [wearing a dress of crimson brocade with green sateen hoops].

The earliest known artistic depiction of Isabel also portrays her wearing a *verdugado*. This image is an illuminated initial from the so-called *Libros Blancos* [White Books] created in late 1477 or early 1478 and held today at the Cathedral of Seville.[18] During 1477 and 1478, Isabel and Ferdinand toured Andalusia, which had been in constant turmoil during the War of Castilian Succession, in order to demonstrate their control of the province.[19] Artists employed by Isabel likely illustrated the *Libros Blancos* to serve as royal propaganda.[20] The illuminated initial introduces the text of Isabel's endowment of an annual Mass in Seville, commemorating the monarchs' victory at the Battle of Toro.[21] In her detailed analysis of this illustration, Ana Isabel Carrasco Manchado notes that it features only Isabel, kneeling before the Virgin Mary and child Jesus, giving thanks for the divine favor of her succession to the Castilian throne, symbolized by her crown at the foot of the miniature. Carrasco Manchado concludes that both the event and the illustration exemplify how Isabel and Ferdinand used liturgical celebrations to make "visible lo invisible y verídico lo real"[22] [the invisible visible, and to legitimate reality].

Beginning in the 1480s, there is no doubt about Isabel's enthusiasm for *verdugados*. Her household accounts, extant from 1482, record her purchase of several dresses already fitted with *verdugos* as well as supplies of the canes used to cre-

---

monastery of Fresdelval, referencing "G.5, fól. 66." As Clemencín explains (*Elógio*, 326), this document dates the embassy in 1478, but it surely occurred in 1473, as González Marrero confirms ("Un Vestido para Cada Ocasión," 181, n. 126).

17 Clemencín, *Elógio*, 327.

18 Archivo de la Catedral de Sevilla, *Libros Blancos*, vol. 1, fol. 148. Described by José Gestoso y Pérez, *Los Reyes Católicos en Sevilla (1477-1478)* (Seville: Revista de Tribunales, 1891), 25–29. A low-resolution digital reproduction of the image is viewable online at www.icolombina.es/catedral/blanco.htm.

19 As recounted by Palencia, who accompanied the monarchs: *Décadas* 3.8.1–3.10.10; trans. Paz y Melia, 4:313–490.

20 Javier Docampo, "La Iluminación de Manuscritos Durante el Reinado de Isabel la Católica: Nuevas Consideraciones," in *La Miniatura y el Grabado de la Baja Edad Media en los Archivos Españoles*, ed. María del Carmen Lacarra Ducay (Saragossa, Spain: Institución "Fernando el Católico," 2012), 225–74, at 230–31. Ana Isabel Carrasco Manchado exhaustively surveys Isabeline propaganda in "Discurso Político y Propaganda en la Corte de los Reyes Católicos (1474-1482)" (Ph.D. thesis, Universidad Complutense de Madrid, 2000), summarized in "Discurso Político y Propaganda en la Corte de los Reyes Católicos: Resultados de una Primera Investigación (1474-1482)," *En la España Medieval* 25 (2002): 299–379, and in *Isabel I de Castilla y la Sombra de la Ilegitimidad: Propaganda y Representación en el Conflicto Sucesorio (1474-1482)* (Madrid: Sílex, 2006).

21 Gestoso y Pérez (*Reyes Católicos en Sevilla*, 28–29) provides the text of the document. His description of the illuminated initial is somewhat confusing, apparently not recognizing the dress depicted as a *verdugado*.

22 Carrasco Manchado, "Discurso Político y Propaganda" [thesis], 461–63 and 586–89, at 462.

ate hoops.[23] The queen's fondness for the *verdugado* surely explains other artistic representations of her wearing this fashion. For example, the lavishly illustrated manuscripts of the *Rimado de la Conquista de Granada* [Poem of the Conquest of Granada] of Pedro Marcuello, created during the decade after the surrender of the Moorish kingdom in 1492, include full-page portraits of the royal family. In these illustrations, both Isabel and her daughter, the ill-fated princess Juana "the Mad" (1479–1555), wear *verdugados*, some waist-high skirts and some full-length gowns.[24]

ALFONSO DE PALENCIA: THE *VERDUGADO* IN POLITICAL PROPAGANDA

The examples cited should leave no doubt about the popularity of the *verdugado* at the Castilian royal court, from the early 1470s and for decades afterwards. Clearly, the claim that *verdugados* concealed illicit pregnancies did not deter Queen Isabel, or any other noblewoman, from embracing the new fashion. Its vogue in fact made it an easy target for any critic of court life, including Isabel's own chronicler, Alfonso de Palencia (1423–92).[25] Palencia came from a family of *conversos* (converted Jews) and was one of many *letrados* (educated men) of non-aristocratic origins who became prominent in government during this era. Often despised by the nobility as parvenus, most *letrados* determined their loyalties by their employment. Palencia first entered royal service in 1456 as official chronicler for Enrique IV, but by 1464 changed his allegiance to the league of nobles opposing Enrique. During 1468 and 1469, he helped lead the diplomatic negotiations to arrange the marriage of Ferdinand and Isabel. She appointed him as her royal chronicler, but dismissed him in 1480, apparently for refusing to submit drafts of his work for review by her advisers. Palencia retired to Seville, with a royal pension, still professing loyalty to the queen. He died there in 1492, having completed only the first three "decades" of his chronicle, covering events from the 1440s to late 1477.

Today Palencia enjoys a reputation as one of the most accomplished Humanist authors of fifteenth-century Spain. In his *Décadas*, frequently quoted by modern historians, Palencia claims to follow Humanist historiographical ideals, confecting his work from existing chronicles (which he often derides as inaccurate), official documents (some from his own hand), and eyewitness testimony (including his own experience).

23 Bernis Madrazo, *Trajes y Modas*, 40–41. For Isabel's account books, see Antonio de la Torre, ed., *Cuentas de Gonzalo de Baeza, Tesorero de Isabel la Católica*, vol. 1: *1477–1491* (Madrid: Consejo Superior de Investigaciones Científicas, 1955), 292. Detailed analysis of the ledgers from Isabel's later reign is available in María del Cristo González Marrero, "Las Mujeres de la Casa de Isabel la Católica," in Martínez Millán and Marçal Lourenço, *Relaciones Discretas*, 2:841–85.

24 Estrella Ruiz-Gálvez Priego, ed., *Rimado de la Conquista de Granada: Edición Facsímil Integra del Manuscrito 604 (1339) XIV-D-14 de la Biblioteca del Museo-Condé, Castillo de Chantilly (Francia)* (Madrid: Edilan, 1995). On this work, see Barbara F. Weissberger, "Patronage and Politics in the Court of the Catholic Monarchs: The *Cancionero de Pedro Marcuello*," *Studies in Iconography* 26 (2005): 175–204.

25 The following paragraphs summarize the introduction to Palencia's *Décadas*, ed. Tate and Lawrance, 1:xxxv–lxxv, the best critical account of the chronicler's life and work.

He also recorded whatever gossip, innuendo, or rumor served his partisan loyalty. Palencia presumably began gathering source materials for the *Décadas* during his initial service as chronicler to Enrique IV. However, he probably began serious work on his opus only in late 1467, using papers confiscated at Segovia by Isabel's forces from the king's new historian, Diego Enríquez del Castillo (1443–1503?).[26] Palencia's *Décadas* offer, in elegant Latin style, detailed, often mordant, descriptions of his contemporaries and their deeds or misdeeds. In his chronicle, he habitually applies derogatory epithets to every opponent of Isabel and Ferdinand and exploits any opportunity to deride the character of Juana of Portugal. Even Queen Isabel does not escape his censure: Describing one of her decisions during the tour of Andalusia in 1477–78, Palencia observes that she acted with a resolve "impropia de su sexo" [inappropriate to her sex].[27]

Palencia's typically censorious perspective is patent in the famous passage where he claims that Juana of Portugal used hoopskirts to conceal illegitimate pregnancy during her confinement at Alaejos in 1468:

> Nunc … reginae Iohannae diverticula resumenda curabo. Permanserat diu in arce Ala-hegii sub praesidio archiepiscopi Hispalensis; nec potuerat se continere quin solitis stimulis amatoriis pungeretur pulcherrima mulier in aetate florenti iamdudum a corrivalibus falsi coniugis oppugnata atque expugnata. … Potuissetque, quamvis aegre, simulare pudorem et cum futura moderatione saltem obturare partem aliquam diruptae integritatis, sed assiduus colloquiorum consensus et proni ad libidinem mores aliud crimen induxerunt. Gravida enim quum esset, potuit aliquandiu tegere ventris tumorem cum vestibus quibus ex industria dudum utebatur, et ad exemplum ipsius omnes nobiles in Hispania mulieres induebantur pariformiter, tunicis amplissimis protensione implicabili circumtexentibus membra feminarum cum circulis multis durissimis panno subductis et consutis, ita ut corpora omnium mulierum tenuissimarum viderentur crassa atque tumida, neque erat aliqua mulier illa amicta veste quae pregnans proximaque partui non iudicaretur. Sed omnis haec preparatio dissimulandi conceptionem non valuit in illa mansione arcta fallere contuentes quin pregnantem reginam susurrarent; et quamvis Henricus aliquotiens eam visitavisset, neque regina promebat se gravidam ex Henrico coniuge, neque fuisset quis ex omnibus huic pronus credulitati. Duos tamen notabant corrivales, neque tunc satis constabat utri eorum facinus attribuerent, vel archiepiscopo vel sobrino ex sorore archiepiscopi Petro.[28]

> [Now … I must try to summarize the misdeeds of Queen Juana. She remained a while at the castle of Alaejos, in custody of the Archbishop of Seville; yet she could not control herself, a most beautiful woman in the prime of life prompted by the usual amorous urges, for so long courted and conquered by rivals to her so-called husband. … She was able,

26 Enríquez del Castillo later wrote, probably after 1481, his own chronicle of Enrique's reign, defending the legitimacy of Juana "la Beltraneja." See Cayetano Rosell, ed., *Crónica del Rey Don Enrique el Cuarto*, in *Crónicas de los Reyes de Castilla*, vol. 3, Biblioteca de Autores Españoles 70 (Madrid: Rivadeneyra, 1878), 96–222, and Aurelio Sánchez Martín, ed., *Crónica de Enrique IV* (Valladolid, Spain: Universidad de Valladolid, 1994). On the propaganda of Enrique's adherents, see Shima Ohara, "La Propaganda Política en Torno al Conflicto Sucesorio de Enrique IV (1457–1474)" (Ph.D. thesis, Universidad de Valladolid, 2004).
27 *Décadas* 3.10.8, trans. Paz y Melia, 4:479.
28 *Décadas* 2.1.3; Latin text cited from Lawrance, "Vestimenta y Opresión," 115–16; trans. Paz y Melia, 2:171–72. The English translation is mine.

though with difficulty, to feign modesty and future restraint, at least partially protecting her damaged reputation, but her constant assent to assignations and her inclination to lust led to another crime. She became pregnant, but was able for a while to hide her swelling belly with clothing that she had deliberately used for some time, and which all Spanish noblewomen wore in imitation of her example, wide dresses stretched rigidly to cover ladies' limbs with many very stiff rings sewn into the fabric, so that even the bodies of the thinnest women appeared thick and swollen, and there was no woman wearing this garb who would not be considered pregnant and soon to give birth. But all these precautions to hide her condition in that small household could not deceive observers who instead gossiped about the pregnant queen; and although Enrique sometimes had visited her, neither did the queen acknowledge being pregnant by her husband Enrique, nor was there anyone inclined to believe her. Instead they mentioned two co-rivals, although it was not evident to which they might rightly attribute the misdeed, whether to the archbishop or to the archbishop's nephew Pedro.]

Diego Enríquez del Castillo of course mentions none of these salacious details. In a very short chapter, he notes only that Juana was very unhappy at confinement by the Archbishop of Seville, and so escaped from his castle with the assistance of her supporters.[29]

Several phrases from Palencia's account deserve particular attention for their implications about the history of hoopskirts:

1. "ex industria dudum utebatur": suggests that Juana had employed this ruse deliberately (ex industria) and for some time (dudum)
2. "ad exemplum ipsius": assumes the role of monarchs in setting standards of fashion and decorum for their subjects
3. "omnes nobiles in Hispania mulieres induebantur pariformiter": acknowledges that the *verdugado* was popular among noblewomen of the era
4. "iudicaretur," "susurrarent," "notabant," "attribuerent": all these verbs reflect Palencia's reliance on gossip, rumor, and innuendo
5. "Sed omnis haec preparatio dissimulandi conceptionem non valuit": acknowledges that Juana's efforts were unsuccessful and that the *verdugado* did not hide her illicit pregnancy

Most importantly, and contrary to so many modern citations of this passage, Palencia does not say that Juana of Portugal invented the *verdugado*. Instead, he castigates Juana for setting a bad example by employing a popular fashion to hide immoral behavior. We have no record of the style of *verdugado* worn by Queen Juana. Lawrance deems "absurd" the claim that the apparel described by Palencia could conceal pregnancy.[30] Couched within citations of gossip, rumor, and innuendo, Palencia's association of this claim with Juana's extramarital affairs confirms that the accusation of concealing pregnancy with *verdugados* was "not news." It was instead already an established

---

29 Cayetano Rosell, *Crónica del Rey*, chap. 117, 178–79; Sánchez Martín, *Crónica de Enrique IV*, 309.
30 Lawrance, "Vestimenta y Opresión," 118.

trope in criticism of this female aristocratic fashion. Palencia merely exploited this commonplace as another partisan slur against Juana of Portugal.

HERNANDO DE TALAVERA: THE *VERDUGADO* IN MORAL THEOLOGY

In 1477, the last year chronicled in Palencia's *Décadas*, Isabel's newly appointed confessor, the Hieronymite friar Hernando de Talavera (1428?–1507), wrote his treatise *Contra la demasía de vestir y de calçar y de comer y de beuer* [Against excess in dress, footwear, eating, and drinking].[31] Like Palencia, Talavera was a *converso* and *letrado*.[32] Originally a professor of moral theology at the University of Salamanca, he abandoned academic life to join the Hieronymite order in 1470, becoming prior of the order's major convent of Santa María del Prado in Valladolid.[33] Once Isabel adopted this city as home for her court, Talavera's talents as a clerical reformer and preacher attracted her notice and she selected him as her confessor. For the next two decades he served as one of her chief advisers and political operatives.[34] Isabel rewarded Talavera's loyalty in 1492 by appointing him as the first archbishop of Granada,[35] but his departure

31 Teresa de Castro, "El Tratado Sobre el Vestir, Calzar y Comer del Arzobispo Hernando de Talavera," *Espacio, Tiempo y Forma*, ser. 3, *Historia Medieval* 14 (2001): 11–92. Talavera's text survives in: (1) a manuscript copy from 1477, Biblioteca del Monasterio de El Escorial, MS b.IV.26; and (2) a revised version printed in *Breue & muy prouechosa doctrina de lo que deue saber todo christiano, con otros tractados muy prouechosos conpuestos por el Arçobispo de Granada* (Granada, Spain: Johann Pegnitzer and Meinhard Ungut, 1496), 314–414. All quotations are from the 1477 manuscript (hereafter cited as Escorial MS b.IV.26 with folio numbers). Cross-references to the 1496 printing (hereafter cited as ed. 1496) refer to pagination in the exemplar held by the Real Academia de la Historia in Madrid (cataloged as Inc. 132), available online in a digital reproduction through the Biblioteca Virtual del Patrimonio Bibliográfico, http://bvpb.mcu.es.
32 Reliable summaries of Talavera's career, adapted here, are the introductions to Hernando de Talavera, *Dos Escritos Destinados a la Reina Isabel: Colación Muy Provechosa, Tratado de Loores de San Juan Evangelista*, ed. Carmen Parrilla García (Valencia, Spain: Universitat de València, 2014), 11–43; and María Julieta Vega García-Ferrer, *Fray Hernando de Talavera y Granada* (Granada, Spain: Universidad de Granada, 2004), 19–63. See also Francisco Javier Martínez Medina and Martin Biersack, *Fray Hernando de Talavera, Primer Arzobispo de Granada: Hombre de Iglesia, Estado y Letras* (Granada, Spain: Universidad de Granada, 2011). Because Talavera led such a long and active career, and because most of his extensive administrative correspondence remains unedited in Spanish archives, no complete, critical account of his life and work exists. Most biographies of Talavera still rely on early modern accounts, such as the quasi-hagiographical *vita* composed by his former aide, Alonso Fernández de Madrid, *Vida de Fray Fernando de Talavera, Primer Arzobispo de Granada*, ed. Francisco Javier Martínez Medina [facsimile reprint of 1931 edition by F. G. Olmedo] (Granada, Spain: Universidad de Granada, 1992).
33 See Luis Resines Llorente, *Hernando de Talavera, Prior del Monasterio de Prado* (Salamanca, Spain: Consejería de Educación de la Junta de Castilla y León, 1993).
34 See Jesús Suberbiola Martínez, *El Arzobispo Talavera, la Iglesia y el Estado Moderno, 1486–1516* (Granada, Spain: Caja de Ahorros y Monte de Piedad de Granada, 1985). This work, the most detailed for any phase of Talavera's career, documents how he labored during the 1480s to ensure that the Castilian Crown would control future ecclesiastical administration of Granada (as the so-called *Real Patronato*).
35 On this phase of Talavera's career, see Miguel Ángel Ladero Quesada, "Fray Hernando de Talavera en 1492: De la Corte a la Misión," *Chronica Nova* 34 (2008): 249–75.

from the royal court also diminished his influence. The zealous Cardinal Francisco Jiménez de Cisneros, primate of Spain, replaced Talavera as Isabel's confessor. From 1499–1502, Cisneros outmaneuvered the archbishop to force conversion of Granada's Muslims, whom Talavera had sought to evangelize through pacific means. It is likely that Talavera made many enemies during his years as a royal counselor and influential prelate. Once Isabel died in 1504, these adversaries unleashed an Inquisition investigation of his household, alleging "judaizing."[36] The archbishop died in 1507, probably before learning that a papal review had exonerated his staff of all charges.

As a clerical reformer, Talavera embraced the new technology of printing: He established one of the first presses in Spain at Valladolid while serving as prior of Santa María del Prado. In 1496 he recruited from Seville two German printers currently working there in order to publish at Granada a compendium of his writings, as a guide to pastoral care for the clergy of his new archdiocese.[37] This volume included a revised version of *Contra la demasía*.

Talavera originally composed *Contra la demasía* as a defense of sumptuary laws proposed by the city of Valladolid in 1477. No record of this municipal legislation is known to survive,[38] but Talavera describes it thus:

> en la muy noble villa de Valladolid: fue ordenado por los venerables prouisores y por otros uenerables padres y honorables señores para ello deputados que, so pena de excommunion y de otras penas pecuniarias y de destierro. no traxiessen los varones ni las mugeres cierto traje deshonesto: los varones camisones con cabeçones labrados; ni las mugeres grandes ni pequeñas casadas ni donzellas hiziessen verdugos de nueuo ni traxiessen aquella demasia que agora usan de caderas. y a los sastres que no lo hiziessen de alli adelante so essas mesmas penas. Agora dubdaron algunas personas que en el junco buscan nudo: y lo claro hazen obscuro si se pudo esto uedar. e si aquellos señores que lo uedaron: touieron para ello auctoridad. y especialmente si se pudo poner sentencia de excommunión en las personas que lo vno y lo al se atreuiessen traspassar.[39]

> [in the very noble town of Valladolid, it was decreed by the venerable provosts and by other venerable fathers and honorable men supervising such matters that, under pain of excom-

---

36 Talavera was one of several *letrados* of *converso* origin who served Isabel and Ferdinand and were subject to persecution; see María del Pilar Rábade Obradó, "El Entorno Judeo-Converso de la Casa y Corte de Isabel la Católica," in Martínez Millán and Marçal Lourenço, *Relaciones Discretas*, 2:887–919.

37 On the contents, organization, and likely audiences of this compendium, see Mark D. Johnston, "Hernando de Talavera's Treatise on Gossip and Slander (1496): Introduction, Text, and Translation" (Alicante, Spain: Biblioteca Virtual Cervantes, 2018), 6–14, available online at www.cervantesvirtual.com. On Talavera's use of printing as an instrument of evangelization, see Felipe Pereda, *Las Imágenes de la Discordia: Política y Poética de la Imagen Sagrada en la España del Cuatrocientos* (Madrid: Marcial Pons, 2007), 263–79.

38 The municipal records of this era were apparently lost in a later fire. I thank colleague Adeline Rucquoi for confirming this information: email message to author, Jan. 25, 2019. Extant records from 1497 to 1499, including sumptuary legislation, are available in Fernando Pino Rebolledo, ed., *Libro de Actos del Ayuntamiento de Valladolid* [title varies], 3 vols. (Valladolid, Spain: Ayuntamiento de Valladolid, 1990–93).

39 Escorial MS b.IV.26, 38v–39r; ed. 1496, 324–25; Castro, "Tratado," 27. The English translation is mine.

munication, other monetary penalties, and exile, neither men nor women should wear certain indecent attire: the men, tunics with embroidered collars; the women, neither greater nor lesser, married or unmarried, should no longer make *verdugados* nor wear that extravagance of *caderas* [hip padding] that they now use; and that tailors should henceforth not create them, under the very same penalties. Now some people, seeking to twist the straight, and to make white black, doubt whether this can be prohibited, and whether those leaders who prohibited it had the authority to do so, and especially if one could place a sentence of excommunication on those persons who might dare to contravene one or the other.]

Historians of fashion should note that Talavera already mentions the *caderas* (hip pads) that became a common element in the apparatus of wide hoopskirts in later centuries. He also claims that more women than men opposed these decrees, but without identifying their class or status. Instead he cites the natural propensity of women, since Eve, for disobedience and curiosity.[40]

Talavera often invokes similarly broad misogynistic tropes to justify gendered differences in dress, but the women complaining at Valladolid were surely of high social rank. In the fifteenth century, the Castilian crown allowed local authorities to define noble status, while reserving for itself the right to adjudicate disputes about those claims. Disputes inevitably arose when individuals sought to transfer their privileges from one locale to another.[41] As home to Isabel's court, Valladolid attracted courtiers from throughout Castile and Aragon, all eager to assert their privileges, and to affirm their status through their dress and consumption. Valladolid already had deeply entrenched class divisions, so newcomers to the city encountered an environment ripe for fostering "town vs. crown" conflicts.[42] The Castilian crown first issued sumptuary regulations in the thirteenth century, and in the next century Iberian municipalities began producing similar legislation.[43] The decrees of 1477 from Valladolid, defended by Talavera, are a typical example.

Talavera's best vernacular writings are admired today for their careful argumentation and a lively style that reflects his Humanist training;[44] a translation of Petrarch

---

40 Escorial MS b.IV.26, 39r–39v; ed. 1496, 325; Castro, "Tratado," 27.
41 See Michael J. Crawford, *The Fight for Status and Privilege in Late Medieval and Early Modern Castile, 1465–1598* (University Park: Pennsylvania State University Press, 2014).
42 Analyzed in detail by Adeline Rucquoi, *Valladolid en la Edad Media*, 2 vols. (Valladolid, Spain: Junta de Castilla y León, Consejería de Educación y Cultura, 1987).
43 See Juan Vicente García Marsilla, "El Lujo Cambiante: El Vestido y la Difusión de las Modas en la Corona de Aragón (Siglos XIII–XV)," *Anales de Historia del Arte* 24 (2014): 227–44, at 241. The most comprehensive study of Castilian royal sumptuary legislation remains José Damián González Arce, *Apariencia y Poder: La Legislación Suntuaria Castellana en los Siglos XIII y XV* (Jaén, Spain: Universidad de Jaén, 1998). On the kingdom of Valencia, see Juan Vicente García Marsilla, "Ordenando el Lujo: Ideología y Normativa Suntuaria en las Ciudades Valencianas (Siglos XIV y XV)," in *Mercats del Luxe, Mercats de l'Art: La Corona d'Aragó i la Mediterrània en els Segles XIV i XV*, ed. S. Boruquet and J. V. García Marsilla (Valencia, Spain: Universitat de València, 2015), 561–91.
44 See Giovanni Maria Bertini, "Hernando de Talavera, Escritor Espiritual (Siglo XV)," in *Actas del Cuarto Congreso Internacional de Hispanistas (1971)*, ed. Eugenio Bustos Tovar, 2 vols. (Salamanca, Spain: Universidad de Salamanca, 1982), 1:173–90. Talavera's most admired work today remains *Cathólica Impugnación*, ed. Francisco Márquez Villanueva (Barcelona:

is among his earliest known works.[45] Unfortunately, *Contra la demasía* is not one of his best works, perhaps because of the ambitious task that Talavera set for himself: laboring to deliver a comprehensive defense of sumptuary legislation, based on principles of moral theology, medicine, hygiene, and legal theory. The argumentation of Talavera's treatise is too complex to review here, but it is an excellent example of how late medieval moral theologians adapted received doctrines to specific circumstances for lay audiences.[46]

Talavera begins *Contra la demasía* with a vigorous justification of the obligation of subjects to obey their rulers. He next offers a lengthy analysis of what is natural, necessary, and reasonable in human apparel, frequently citing distinctions of gender and class. Although we may quip today that "the Devil wears Prada," medieval moral theology did not explicitly define extravagance in fashion as sinful. To overcome this difficulty, Talavera borrows the principle of "excess" from Scholastic definitions of the sin of gluttony, in order to make excessive eating and drinking a paradigm for extravagance in fashion. The familiar Scholastic list of "five daughters of gluttony" then provides him with a scheme for his analysis of sinful dress.[47]

In the original 1477 text of *Contra la demasía*, Talavera digresses when explicating the third "daughter of gluttony," *nimis* [too much], to praise Enrique IV as an exemplar of good customs. Talavera instead blames Enrique's subjects, both men and women of all social classes, for the dissolution of mores during his reign.[48] The printed edition of 1496 suppresses this digression, substituting the general rule that:

> Mucho e mas que mucho deuria mirar en esto el príncipe. Rey e Reyna de qualquier reyno. Porque es regla general que no puede faltar: que qual el rey e qual la reyna, en lo malo y en lo bueno: tal es todo el reyno assi en esto como en todo lo al.[49]

> [Greatly and more than greatly should every prince, king, or queen of any realm observe this. For it is a general and infallible rule, that as the king or queen goes, in both good and evil, so goes the entire kingdom in this and in all else.]

Juan Flors, 1961), a polemical intervention in contemporary disputes about the treatment of *conversos*. On Talavera's role in these disputes, see Carolyn Salomons, "A Church United in Itself: Hernando de Talavera and the Religious Culture of Fifteenth-Century Castile," *Catholic Historical Review* 103 (2017): 639–62.

45 I. Scoma, ed., *Invectivas o Reprehensiones Contra el Médico Rudo y Parlero* (Messina, Italy: Edizioni Di Nicolò, 2000).

46 See Mark D. Johnston, "Gluttony and *Convivencia*: Hernando de Talavera's Warning to the Muslims of Granada in 1496," *eHumanista* 25 (2013): 107–26.

47 Cf. Aquinas, *Summa Theologiae* 2a.2ae.148,a.6 and the most popular confessional manual of Talavera's era, Guido de Monte Rochen's *Manipulus curatorum*; Anne T. Thayer and Katharine J. Lualdi, eds. and trans., *Handbook for Curates: A Late Medieval Manual on Pastoral Ministry* (Washington, D.C.: Catholic University of America Press, 2011), 225–26. The five modes of gluttony, neatly summarized in the Latin mnemonic "Prae-propere, laute, nimis, ardenter, studiose" ("too soon, too expensively, too much, too eagerly, too daintily"), still appear in modern compendia of Catholic moral theology; e.g. http://en.wikisource.org/wiki/Catholic_Encyclopedia_(1913)/Gluttony.

48 Escorial MS b.IV.26, 63v–64r; Castro, "Tratado," 47.

49 Ed. 1496, 360; Castro, "Tratado," 47. The English translation is mine.

It is tempting to interpret this passage as an oblique criticism of the failure of Enrique IV and Queen Juana to provide models of moral conduct for their realm. Whatever might have been Talavera's intention, he clearly articulates the principle, shared by Alfonso de Palencia, that monarchs must lead their subjects by example.

After explicating at length his fivefold paradigm of extravagance in dress, Talavera finally returns, in the last chapters of *Contra la demasía*, to analyzing the specific fashions banned at Valladolid in 1477. He lists twelve reasons why *caderas* and *verdugados* are physically or morally harmful.[50] His detailed explanation of each reason is too lengthy to quote here; a summary is sufficient to appreciate their miscellaneous argumentation. According to Talavera, the new fashions

1. are dangerous, causing spontaneous abortions or difficult births; unmarried or older women therefore should not wear these garments because they set a bad example for women of childbearing age;
2. induce sin, because so much warm, soft fabric provokes lust in women, an error as grave as spicing dishes which are already spicy or adding fire to fire;
3. hide from view evidence of adulterous pregnancies, which induces suspicions of fornication;
4. too easily expose legs and ankles that should remain hidden, for the sake of decency;
5. tempt men to invite women into situations for revealing their legs;
6. may warm the thighs (in the case of *caderas*), but leave (in the case of *verdugados*) all else below exposed to cold airs, so are contradictory;
7. can cause gynecological problems, from too much warm air in summer and from too much cold air in winter;
8. are very costly fashions, requiring extensive fabric;
9. create expenses that unnecessarily aggravate husbands (even if they do not admit it);
10. are often of low social origins, like the *faldetas* (apron skirts) invented for serving girls who clean homes;
11. make women look more like men and so monstrously deform women's natural appearance; and
12. constitute a fiction and so a form of mendacity, like makeup, that leads to many other sins.

The third reason cited obviously echoes the charge made by Alfonso de Palencia against Juana of Portugal. However, Talavera alludes only vaguely to this historical circumstance:

> Lo tercero es a la honrra y fama muy contrario porque comunmente. se que fue inuentado para encobrir los fornicarios e adulterinos preñados, por manera que todas las que los

---

50 Escorial MS b.IV.26, 83v–93v; ed. 1496, 387–412; Castro, "Tratado," 62–70.

trahen buenas e malas. son auidas por sospechosas & infamadas. y avnque no sea assi la verdad. pero ciertamente la qualidad y manera del dicho hábito lo haze assi sospechar.[51]

[Thirdly, it is very contrary to honor and reputation because commonly I know that it was invented to hide fornication and adulterous pregnancies, so that all those who wear it, good or bad, are considered suspect and disreputable. And even if this is not true, surely the quality and manner of this apparel incite this suspicion.]

Explaining his tenth objection to hoopskirts, their low social origins, Talavera again alludes to the allegedly scandalous circumstances of their invention. He notes that this fashion is "en alguna manera habito muy vil. y de su condicion e primera inuencion a uiles usos deputado" [in some ways a very vile garment, and from its nature and first invention intended for vile uses].[52] Martínez Botella doubts Talavera's claim about the low social origins of these fashions, considering it instead simply another excuse to denigrate the new fashion.[53] As Juan Vicente García Marsilla notes, the great courts were typically the "engines" of innovation in fashion.[54]

Overall, Talavera's twelve objections to *caderas* and *verdugados* are a hodgepodge of moral, medical, hygienic, social, and economic arguments, few supported with citations of scripture or other authorities. Assessing Talavera's arguments, Lawrance deems them comically incoherent, replete with inconsistencies that perhaps betray fantasies of Freudian "wish-fulfillment." Ultimately, Lawrance concludes, Talavera's conflicting arguments exemplify the inherent contradiction of "narcissism vs. submission" in all female fashion, as argued by Simone de Beauvoir.[55] A separate study could certainly identify the theological, medical, and legal sources of Talavera's twelve objections to *verdugados*, but such an exercise would not necessarily render Talavera's arguments more coherent. His arguments embrace broadly the three general objectives of Castilian sumptuary legislation, as identified by José Damián González Arce: (1) restraining economic excess; (2) affirming social segregation; and (3) sustaining basic political or moral principles, such as the authority of ruling elites and distinctions in gender.[56]

Despite the confused and digressive argumentation of Talavera's treatise, the immediate circumstances of its composition are obvious. *Verdugados* were among many popular fashions that local authorities sought to regulate through sumptuary laws. In his conclusion to *Contra la demasía*, Talavera reminds his readers that Valladolid is now home to the royal court. Therefore, all its residents and institutions must set an example of moral probity for the rest of the realm.[57] Carrasco Manchado has aptly

---

51 Escorial MS b.IV.26, 85v; ed. 1496, 390–91; Castro, "Tratado," 63. The copy of the 1496 edition in the Real Academia de la Historia misnumbers page 391 as 400. The English translation is mine.
52 Escorial MS b.IV.26, 87r; ed. 1496, 402; Castro, "Tratado," 65. The Escorial manuscript clearly reads "se que" [I know that] but the 1496 edition emends this to "se cree que" [it is believed that].
53 Personal correspondence with author, July 18, 2019.
54 García Marsilla, "El Lujo Cambiante," 239.
55 Lawrance, "Vestimenta y Opresión," 127–35, citing Simone de Beauvoir, *Le Deuxième Sexe*, 2 vols. (Paris: Gallimard, 1949), 1:151 and 2:345.
56 González Arce, *Apariencia y Poder*, 24; cf. García Marsilla, "El Lujo Cambiante," 241–43.
57 Escorial MS b.IV.26, 93v–95r; ed. 1496, 412–14; Castro, "Tratado," 70–71.

observed that Isabeline propaganda sought to render the invisible visible, and to legitimate reality.[58] Talavera's treatise likewise sought to render social customs and political institutions natural, necessary, and reasonable.

THE LEGACY OF A LEGEND

All the objections to *verdugados* cited by Hernando de Talavera in 1477 became clichés in diatribes against hoopskirts during later centuries. Meanwhile, the hoopskirt became identified as a Spanish national costume in the eyes of other Europeans.

The German Christoph Weiditz, in his famous illustrated manuscript *Trachtenbuch* (1530–40?), provides numerous illustrations of Spanish women's dress, many apparently styles of hoopskirts.[59] His illustrations were based on his firsthand observations during a tour of Spanish territories with the Emperor Charles V from 1529 to 1532.[60]

A watercolor sketch of 1540, perhaps based on Weiditz, offers intriguing, if somewhat incongruous, testimony to the association of Spanish hoopskirts with pregnancy. Preserved today at the Museo Stibbert in Florence in an eighteenth-century English collection of fashion illustrations, the sketch depicts Spanish women wearing *verdugados* and the platform shoes known as *chopines* [pattens].[61] One of the women depicted wears a hoopskirt, while patting an apparently swollen belly (fig. 5.3).

The Italian Cesare Vecellio, in his popular *Habiti Antichi* (1590) cites a date of 1440 for his illustration of a full-length Spanish hoopskirt, which he considers *antico* [antiquated], but still in use in some places.[62]

A subsequent Spanish innovation in hoopskirts from the 1630s, the famous *guardainfante*, portrayed in many paintings by Diego Velázquez, became the subject of intense criticism at the court of Spanish King Philip IV (1605–65). The innovation was ultimately banned by royal decree in 1639.[63] The name *guardainfante* is not unambiguous: In Old Spanish it could have meant simply "protects the noble heir," but

58 See note 22 above.
59 Nuremberg, Germanisches Nationalmuseum, HS 22474, e.g. fols. 15, 23, 57, 143, or 151. A full digital facsimile of Weiditz's manuscript is available online through the museum's website at http://dlib.gnm.de/item/Hs22474/html.
60 On Weiditz's tour, see Andrea McKenzie Satterfield, "The Assimilation of the Marvelous Other: Reading Christoph Weiditz's *Trachtenbuch* (1529) as an Ethnographic Document" (M.A. thesis, University of South Florida, 2007).
61 Cataloged as Anonymous (German), "Thus go the Ladies in Spain upon their Pattens," no. 12 in the series *Costumes of the time of Charles V Emperor of the Holy Roman Empire and King of Spain of all nations of the world, circa 1540*, bound in Museo Stibbert Library, no. 1938-1. I thank Simona Di Marco, vice-director of the Museo Stibbert, for identifying this material.
62 Cesare Vecellio, *Habiti antichi, ouero raccolta di figure delineate dal gran Titiano, e da Cesare Vecellio suo fratello, diligentemente intagliate, conforme alle nationi del mondo* (1590; repr. Venice: G. G. Hertz, 1664), 211.
63 See Rafael González Cañal, "El Lujo y la Ociosidad Durante la Privanza de Olivares: Bartolomé Jiménez Patón y la Polémica Sobre el Guardainfante y las Guedejas," *Criticón* 53 (1991): 71–96; cf. Wunder, "Women's Fashions," 139.

Fig. 5.3: Watercolor illustration of Spanish women wearing verdugados and pattens, c. 1540, illustration 12 from *Costumes of the time of Charles V Emperor of the Holy Roman Empire and King of Spain of all nations of the world, circa 1540, bound in A series of prints and drawings serving to illustrate the modes and fashions of ancient and modern dresses in different parts of the world* (Newport, UK: 1792), Museo Stibbert Library, no. 1938-1. Photo: By permission of the Museo Stibbert, Florence.

critics of the fashion interpreted it as "hides the infant." Major contributors to this polemic were Alonso Carranza (active 1620–40), Arias Gonzalo (active c. 1636), and Bartolomé Jiménez Patón (1569–1640). Their writings are typical of numerous treatises called *arbitrios* ("decisions" or "solutions"), produced in this era by independent authors (the eponymous *arbitristas*) who advocated reforms in Spanish society and economy.[64] Carranza, Gonzalo, and Jiménez Patón all cite economic considerations, a common rationale in any sumptuary legislation.[65] As it happens, neither Carranza, Gonzalo, nor Jiménez Patón cites the legend that Juana of Portugal used the *verdugado* to hide illicit pregnancy.

In 1636 Carranza denounced the *guardainfante* in his *Rogación en detestación de los grandes abusos en los traxes y adornos nuevamente introducidos en España* [A plea loathing the great abuses in dress and fashion recently introduced in Spain].[66] His treatise is a grandly Baroque display of erudition: It offers a nearly complete history of dress and fashion, copiously documented with biblical, classical, and modern authorities. Almost every one of Carranza's objections to the *guardainfante* has a precedent in the twelve reasons offered by Hernando de Talavera, whom Carranza nowhere cites. Carranza repeatedly claims that the disreputable fashions of his era came from France, asserting that the *guardainfante* originated there,

> Donde es tradicion (segun dizen los naturales de aquella tierra) que auiendose hecho preñada fuera de matrimonio vna donzella de gran porte y suerte, dio principio á este trage para encubrir su miseria, y que con esto se le dio el nombre de *Guard, enfant*, por el efeto.[67]

> [Where it is a tradition (according to natives of that country) that a maiden of great standing and fortune, having become pregnant outside wedlock, originated this apparel in order to hide her misfortune, and from this arose the name of "hides infant" as a result]

Could this French "tradition" echo the slander against Juana of Portugal, recorded by Alfonso de Palencia 150 years earlier? Given the established reputation of hoopskirts as disguises for pregnancy, perhaps it was an autochthonous French application of this trope. Or perhaps Carranza simply appropriated it as another example of the pernicious customs that had originated in France, Spain's great enemy at this time.

In response to Carranza's treatise, the otherwise obscure author Arias Gonzalo composed his brief *Memorial en defensa de las mujeres de España y de los trajes y ador-*

---

64 See Sina Rauschenbach and Christian Windler, eds., *Reforming Early Modern Monarchies: The Castilian* Arbitristas *in Comparative European Perspectives* (Wiesbaden, Germany: Harrassowitz, 2016).

65 See Giorgio Riello and Ulinka Rublack, eds., *The Right to Dress: Sumptuary Laws in a Global Perspective, c. 1200–1800* (Cambridge: Cambridge University Press, 2019). On the Spanish legislation of the 1630s, see González Cañal, "El Lujo," 93–95; and Wunder, "Women's Fashions," 154–59.

66 Alonso Carranza, *Rogacion en detestacion de los grandes abusos en los traxes y adornos nuevamente introducidos en España* (Madrid: María de Quiñones, 1636); Enrique Suárez Figaredo, ed., "Alonso Carranza, *Discurso contra los malos trajes y adornos lascivos*; [and] Ldo. Arias Gonzalo, *Memorial en defensa de las mujeres de España y de los trajes y adornos de que usan*," *Lemir* 15 (2011): 69–166, at 73–126. On Carranza's career, see Manuel Jesús García Martínez, "¿Transición o Crisis Profesional? La Alegación de don Alonso Carranza en Defensa de las Parteras (Siglo XVII)," *Híades: Revista de Historia de la Enfermería* 8 (2001): 299–309.

67 Carranza, *Rogacion*, 22r; ed. Suarez Figaredo, "*Discurso; Memorial*," 109. The English translation is mine.

nos [Memorandum in defense of Spanish women and of dress and fashion].[68] Gonzalo defends the right of women to follow prevailing fashions, and rebuts the claim that hoopskirts hide pregnancy, with a reminder of scriptural examples of forgiveness for fallen women, such as Mary Magdalene.[69]

Finally, in 1638, Jiménez Patón published excerpts from Talavera's *Contra la demasía*, with his own commentary, under the title *Reforma de trages: Doctrina de frai Hernando de Talavera, primer Arçobispo de Granada* [The reform of dress: Instruction from Friar Hernando de Talavera, first archbishop of Granada].[70] Although today Talavera's 1496 compendium survives in only fourteen copies, it was clearly well known to Jiménez Patón, a prolific Humanist author and teacher.[71] In his prologue, Jiménez Patón apologizes for publishing yet another treatise on *guardainfantes*, since Carranza had already done this, but complains that delayed publication of his work resulted from difficulties with his printers.[72] He nonetheless justifies his duplication of Carranza's effort by promising to offer the wise counsel of Hernando de Talavera, where Carranza offered simply his own opinions.[73] Like Carranza, Jiménez Patón cites numerous biblical, classical, and modern authorities to buttress his commentary. He follows in his text the overall structure of *Contra la demasía*. He also notes that Talavera cited few authorities, because the archbishop was writing for women, so Jiménez Patón promises to add relevant documentation. But when he comes to the claim that *verdugados* hide illegitimate pregnancies, he offers no references. Instead, he obliquely argues that it is better to abort an illegitimate pregnancy than to conceal it with deceitful apparel.[74]

Clearly, for these polemicists of the 1630s, the historical reference to Juana of Portugal no longer mattered, perhaps from deference to royal history or simply from ignorance of the accusations made in Palencia's *Décadas*. Wunder concludes:

> While there were many different reasons why a woman might have worn a *guardainfante*, hiding a belly swollen with child does not appear to have been among them: there is no historical evidence to corroborate the long-standing assertion that women used *guardainfantes* to conceal illegitimate pregnancies. Claims that they did are pure fiction and polemic.[75]

As fiction, the persistence of these claims probably reflects the dynastic anxiety endemic to European aristocratic society in the late medieval and early modern eras,

---

68 Arias Gonzalo, *Memorial en defensa de las mujeres de España y de los trajes y adornos* (Lisbon: Antonio Alvarez, 1636); Suárez Figaredo, "*Discurso; Memorial*," 127–66.

69 Gonzalo, *Memorial*, 53r–53v; Suárez Figaredo, "*Discurso; Memorial*," 162.

70 Bartolome Jimenez Paton, *Reforma de trages: Doctrina de frai Hernando de Talavera, primer Arçobispo de Granada* (Baeça, Spain: Juan de la Cuesta, 1638).

71 See Abraham Madroñal Durán, *Humanismo y Filología en el Siglo de Oro: En Torno a la Obra de Bartolomé Jiménez Patón* (Madrid: Iberoamericana, 2009).

72 Jimenez Paton, *Reforma*, prelim. fol. v (s.n.).

73 Ibid., prelim. fols. v–vi (s.n.).

74 Ibid., 45r.

75 Wunder, "Women's Fashions," 179.

when ruling families struggled to ensure legitimate lines of succession. As polemic, it aptly illustrates the potency of propaganda, confected like today's Internet memes from "alternative facts" and created to fuel the confirmation biases of partisan audiences, no less in 1477 or the 1630s than in the early twenty-first century.

Still, the claim that hoopskirts served to hide illegitimate pregnancies survived, freed from its original historical context, as a durable trope for castigating this apparel in Spain, France, and England until the eighteenth century.[76] Even after hoopskirts disappeared from European fashion in the early nineteenth century, the etymology of *guardainfante* as "hides the infant" remained in Spanish dictionaries.[77] Once modern historians and philologists recovered the text of Palencia's *Décadas*, his work re-acquainted today's readers with the accusation that Juana of Portugal adopted hoopskirts to hide illicit pregnancies.

CONCLUSION

From the chronology of events described in this study, historians of fashion should note several salient facts. First, the *verdugados* were already popular at the Castilian court by 1468. Second, the claim that hoopskirts could hide pregnancy had surely become a topos for criticizing the new fashion by that time. Third, Juana of Portugal did not invent the *verdugado* as a device to conceal her illicit pregnancy at Alaejos in 1468. Fourth, Alfonso de Palencia merely appropriated this topos to denigrate Juana in his *Décadas*, written years later. Fifth and last, Hernando de Talavera's *Contra la demasía* of 1477 helped to ensure for centuries to come the perpetuation of this platitude in polemics about hoopskirts as a female aristocratic fashion.

Ultimately, we are left to marvel that a fashion with such a lurid reputation became so popular so quickly and for so long. And we might wonder if, were it not for the viciously polemicized role of Juana of Portugal in the War of Castilian Succession, would this reputation have attained such durability in critiques of female aristocratic fashion? Would less celebrated female apparel, not identified with courtly culture, like the *faldeta* (apron skirt) mentioned by Talavera, ever have attained such an ignominious reputation for so many centuries? The persistent scandalous repute of the *verdugado* usefully reminds us that all artifacts of material culture, including the noblest or humblest fashions, always develop an identity, circulate as symbols, and struggle for status within the contested social and political discourses of their successive historical moments.

---

76 Ibid., 144–45.
77 Lawrance, "Vestimenta y Opresión," 134.

Fashion and Material Culture in the *Tabletop of the Seven Deadly Sins* Attributed to Hieronymus Bosch

John Block Friedman and Melanie Schuessler Bond

A tabletop painted about 1505–10 and signed with the name Hieronymus Bosch (ca. 1450–1516)[1] vividly depicts the seven deadly sins as they might play out in everyday life.[2] These are arranged in wedges or sections within a circle (fig. 6.1). Three of these failings—Envy, Pride, and Lust—are associated more than the other four shown in the painting with fashionable clothing and high-status material culture in late medieval moralizing literature and art. Thus, close and historically grounded study of these three sections can reveal how the artist skillfully presented certain clothing styles (and forms of decor) as eagerly desired by those wishing to present themselves as of high status,[3] but outmoded and ultimately understood as valueless by wiser beholders who recognize the fickleness of fashion. Though past treatments of the tabletop have seen there a general

We are indebted for information, visual materials, and fruitful discussions to Roberta Smith Favis, Kristen Figg, Laura Gelfand, Jacqueline Leclercq-Marx, Gary Schwartz, Larry Silver, Alison G. Stewart, Baudouin van den Abeele, and Theresa Zischkin. The librarians of the Ohio State University Library were especially helpful and gracious in getting us access to foreign-language books and periodicals relating to this study. A version of this paper was read in May 2019 for a DISTAFF session at the International Congress of Medieval Studies in Kalamazoo, Michigan.

1 Madrid, Museo Nacional del Prado, inv. no. 2822. The digitized painting and some discussion accepting it as by Bosch can be seen on the Prado's website, www.museodelprado.es/en, by searching the collection for the title "Table of the Seven Deadly Sins."

2 Of particular use for the understanding of the tabletop are Laura Gelfand, "Social Status and Sin: Reading Bosch's Prado Seven Deadly Sins and Four Last Things," in *The Seven Deadly Sins: From Communities to Individuals*, ed. Richard Newhauser (Leiden: Brill, 2007), 229–56, and the same author's "Class, Gender, and the Influence of Penitential Literature in Bosch's Depictions of Sin," in *Jheronimus Bosch: His Sources: Second International Jheronimus Bosch Conference, May 22–25, 2007*, ed. A. M. Koldeweij and Eric De Bruyn ('s-Hertogenbosch, Netherlands: Jheronimus Bosch Art Center, 2010), 158–73; Walter S. Gibson, "Hieronymus Bosch and the Mirror of Man: The Authorship and Iconography of the 'Tabletop of the Seven Deadly Sins,'" *Oud Holland* 87, no. 4 (1973): 205–26, and his *Hieronymus Bosch* (London: Thames & Hudson, 1973), 33–48; Larry Silver, "God in the Details: Bosch and Judgment(s)," *Art Bulletin* 83, no. 4 (Dec. 2001): 626–50, and his *Hieronymus Bosch* (New York: Abbe, 2006), 305–18.

3 Raymond van Uytven, "Showing Off One's Rank in the Middle Ages," in *Showing Status: Representations of Social Positions in the Late Middle Ages*, ed. Wim Blockmans and Antheun

John Block Friedman and Melanie Schuessler Bond

Fig. 6.1: *Tabletop of the Seven Deadly Sins*, school of Hieronymus Bosch (Madrid, Museo Nacional del Prado, inv. no. 2822), ca. 1505–10. Photo: Courtesy Museo Nacional del Prado.

striving for status,[4] revisiting its clothing and settings in a more comparative way, with a detailed analysis of the clothing, will unlock additional meaning in the tabletop by giving modern viewers a chance to see it with more of its original context intact. This context is crucial, because the artist examines the wages of Envy, Pride, and Lust among the upper classes through contemporary *kleider-kritik*[5] rather than with eschatological regard to the fires of hell, though such infernal punishment is vividly shown in one of the four corner medallions, with individual sins labeled and punished appropriately.[6]

The few definite facts known about the Dutch artist Hieronymus Bosch's life and career largely relate to the tensions in social class and mobility in Northern European society particularly associated with the three sins just mentioned. Like the Flemish manuscript miniaturist Simon Bening, Bosch married upward; his wife, Aleid van de Meervenne, was somewhat better off financially and higher socially than Bosch's family.[7] Through this marriage and his artistic commissions he acquired rental property and could be counted among the well-to-do burghers and successful artisans in 's-Hertogenbosch, a small city in the southern Netherlands near the modern Dutch-Belgian border which was then a vibrant center of commerce and manufacturing.

By 1488 he was a "sworn brother" of a confraternity—the Brotherhood of Our Blessed Lady—whose members (most of similar or higher station) included many of 's-Hertogenbosch's commercial, artistic, and ecclesiastical elite. By this connection Bosch also acquired social rank.[8] Bosch seems, as well as being upwardly mobile, to have been extremely pious, not at all unusual in this milieu, given the intense spiritual climate of the *Devotio Moderna*. This Northern European movement for religious reform, emphasizing meditation, often for extended periods, on Christ's last days, was widespread from the late fourteenth century through the early Reformation. It characterized communities, whether loose or official, of believers, and one out of every nineteen persons in Bosch's social milieu belonged to some religious order to which the phrase *Devotio Moderna* could pertain.[9] Both Latin and vernacular Passion tracts and paintings portraying the brutality and intensity of scriptural events from the Ar-

---

Janse (Turnhout, Belgium: Brepols, 1999), 19–34, esp. 29–34, and Laurel Ann Wilson, "Status," in *A Cultural History of Dress and Fashion in the Medieval Age*, ed. Sarah-Grace Heller (London: Bloomsbury Academic, 2017), 2:107–24.

4   For example, see Gelfand, "Social Status," who treats the clothing in Pride and Lust rather generally.

5   There is no English equivalent for this German phrase, but this roughly translates to "social criticism through clothing."

6   The Four Last Things rondels, which are in the four corners of the tabletop, can be conveniently examined in high resolution on the Prado website, note 1 above.

7   G. C. M. van Dijck, "Hieronymus van Aken / Hieronymus Bosch: His Life and 'Portraits,'" in *Hieronymus Bosch: New Insights into His Life and Work*, ed. Jos Koldeweij, Bernard Vermet, and Barbera van Kooij (Rotterdam, Netherlands: Museum Boijmans Van Beuningen, NAi, 2001), 9–16, here 11, and Matthijs Ilsink, Jos Koldeweij, Ron Spronk, Luuk Hoogstede, Robert G. Erdmann, Rik Klein Gotink, Hanneke Nap, and Daan Veldhuizen, *Catalogue Raisonné: Hieronymus Bosch: Painter and Draughtsman* (Brussels: Mercatorfonds, 2016), 16–24.

8   Gibson, *Hieronymus Bosch*, 14.

9   Ibid., 15.

rest through the Crucifixion aided these believers to mentally recreate the Passion, usually by including many concrete details drawn from extracanonical sources such as the Apocryphal Gospels. Bosch's paintings and those of his followers show some of the techniques and images, such as the spiked wood block beneath Christ's feet on the road to Calvary, common to works in the sphere of *Devotio Moderna*.[10]

Thus the tabletop of poplar wood[11] fits well within Hieronymus Bosch's known world whatever its exact authorship and domestic purpose. Although the painting was from its creation associated with Bosch and even copied as his by contemporary artists such as Pieter Bruegel the Elder,[12] there is considerable scholarly disagreement as to Bosch's role in its creation and even whether or not it was intended as a tabletop. Recent opinion ranges from that of the compilers of the authoritative *Catalogue Raisonné*, who, rejecting any association between Bosch and the painting, argue that "the available data for *The Seven Deadly Sins* … raises serious doubts regarding its execution by Bosch or even by his workshop,"[13] to Laurinda Dixon, who claims that it is

> possible that the painting is a workshop product. Bosch himself may have been responsible only for the original design, the iconographical programme and certain landscape and figural elements that display especially sensitive modeling and atmospheric effects, leaving the rest to assistants. Furthermore, some of the costume details point to a date earlier than the 1490s, well within Bosch's lifetime. All things considered, most scholars include [it] … among Bosch's "authentic" works.[14]

As to the form and purpose of the painting, moreover, there is similar controversy, with some scholars such as Dixon suggesting that it was not intended as a tabletop

10 See James H. Marrow, *Passion Iconography in Northern European Art of the Late Middle Ages and Early Renaissance* (Courtrai, Belgium: Van Ghemmert, 1979) and the same author's "Inventing the Passion in the Late Middle Ages," in *The Passion Story: From Visual Representation to Social Drama*, ed. Marcia Kupfer (University Park: Pennsylvania State University Press, 2008), 23–52.

11 As most panel painters including Bosch used Baltic oak supports, the cheaper poplar is a possible reason for doubting Bosch's connection with the Prado painting. See Ilsink et al., *Catalogue Raisonné*, item 57, 471–73.

12 See, for example, on how the Prado tabletop influenced Pieter Bruegel the Elder in two series of prints of "The Seven Deadly Sins, or Vices" (1556–1558) made probably for commercial reasons to cash in on Bosch's popularity; Jürgen Müller, "Pieter Bruegel the Elder and Pieter van der Heyden after Pieter Bruegel the Elder: The Seven Deadly Sins, or The Vices, 1556–58" in *Pieter Bruegel the Elder: Drawings and Prints*, ed. Nadine M. Orenstein (New Haven, CT: Yale University Press, 2001), 144–45.

13 Ilsink et al., *Catalogue Raisonné*, item 34, 468–74, here 472; the authors claim that "Without more substantial evidence, it is not possible to draw any secure conclusion as to whether or not this tabletop/painting should be placed in the group of paintings attributable to Bosch (or his workshop)," 474.

14 Laurinda Dixon, *Bosch* (London: Phaidon, 2003), 42–51, here 44. Ludwig von Baldass, *Hieronymus Bosch* (New York: Abrams, 1960), 15, said of this panel "the invention in every case, down to the smallest detail, is unquestionably to be attributed to Bosch himself." Silver (*Hieronymus Bosch*, 305) believes "there is good reason to see the tabletop as an authentic Bosch design, with some lesser workshop execution of individual figures or scenes, from the period when his studio's output was comprised of works of uneven quality."

but rather as a panel to be hung on a wall where its central Eye of God looked directly outward at the beholder, and others[15] pointing to wear to the paint consistent with use as a tabletop, claiming that it was intended for that purpose. In this orientation, it would be viewed from above.

However unsettled these issues of the Prado panel's purpose and authenticity as by Bosch may be—and they cannot be decided within the scope of the present article—they do not affect the way in which the work reflects a cultural universe very similar to that of Bosch and to that of the contemporary owners of his paintings.[16] Accordingly, we will skirt the vexed question of "authorship" by referring throughout to the creator of the tabletop as the "Tabletop Artist," a person active in Hieronymus Bosch's lifetime, and we focus on this artist as someone fully participating in the life and values of Bosch's time and place.

CONVENTIONALITY OF THE TABLETOP'S STRUCTURE AND IMAGERY

Though we tend to think of Bosch's authentic work as highly individual, phantasmagoric, and often dreamlike—a precursor to Surrealism—in fact much of the imagery in his known paintings, such as the Yale Art Gallery's *Allegory of Intemperance* fragment, is quite traditional, appearing in earlier and contemporary paintings, woodcuts,[17] and engravings, where it had widely accepted moral meanings. And the same claim can be made of the tabletop. The dogs of Envy, the mirror and domestic utensils of Pride, and the tent and the fool of Lust have such close parallels in the moralizing art and literature of the era as to suggest actual derivation and show the constant interplay between the Tabletop Artist's imagination and the artists working just before and around him. These topoi must be analyzed with reference to contemporary moralizing art—both painterly and graphic—and to the didactic writing associated with it. Thus, just as the clothing and decor depicted in the tabletop need to be revisited from the perspectives of fashion criticism and of social class, so should the work's organization and imagery—and the postures of figures within it—be recognized as more conventional than usually supposed.

Conventional as well is the less apparent subtext of the tabletop's view of fashion. Its engagement with the very idea of the fickleness of fashion in the outmoded

15 Jens Kremb, "Bemalte Tischplatten im Kontext Profaner Raumausstattungen des Späten Mittelalters" (Ph.D. diss., Rheinischen Friedrich Wilhelms Universität, Bonn, 2013), and Ilsink et al., *Catalogue Raisonné*, 473.
16 See Eric De Bruyn, "Jheronimus Bosch: His Patrons and His Public: What We Know and Would Like to Know," in *Jheronimus Bosch, His Patrons and His Public: Third International Jheronimus Bosch Conference, September 16–18, 2012*, ed. Jo Timmermans ('s-Hertogenbosch, Netherlands: Jheronimus Bosch Art Center, 2014), 14–29, here 19.
17 See Glenn F. Benge, "On the Closed Wings of the Garden of Earthly Delights Triptych," in Timmermans, *Jheronimus Bosch*, 46–67. Benge also observes (55) that "in creating his visual prompts, Bosch uses woodcut source images cited from the early printed books …."

clothing of all the figures illustrating the sins is an example of the *varietas vestium* or diversity of dress trope. This has been the focus of a recent study of later medieval English fashion culture,[18] but it was also a concern of European moralists generally, who in the main favored stasis rather than change.[19] The Tabletop Artist no doubt held such a view as well. With the rise of a money economy, flux in social mobility, and the increasing availability of dyestuffs, fabrics of remarkable fineness and hand such as scarlet and velvets, others mixing precious metals with fiber, and novel cuts involving application, contrast, slashing, and changes in length and fit, there was a philosophical concern with change and the "novelty" underlying fashion expressed through the amount and character of clothing to which the bourgeoisie and elites had access. Such change was, in Susan Crane's words, "an aspect of consumption."[20] So, too, Chaucer's *Parson's Tale* of about 1390 ties rapidly changing fashion involving excess fabric in garments such as the houppelande and the bag or bombard sleeve to social waste and to the sin of Pride, illustrating the point with a remarkably technical roll call of cuts and types of ornamentation,[21] while the fifteenth-century continuator of Ranulph Higden's *Polychronicon* (1330–1340) connects it to another of the sins we examine here: Envy. Though the *Polychronicon* is discussing the instability of dress with regard to the imagined fourteenth-century English national character in speaking of those who "pettishly despise their own things, and commend those belonging to others,"[22] the broader issue of *varietas vestium* seems to have concerned the Northern European artist of the tabletop in its extended treatment of the instability of fashion examined through the prism of Pride, Envy, and Lust.

The Tabletop Artist could also have seen visual representations of the *varietas vestium* topos. Artists tied variable fashion to Fortune in various ways. For example, a French Wheel of Fortune miniature illustrating Boethius' *Consolation of Philosophy* from 1410 illustrates the variety of the latest fashions and their folly for those in the grip of Fortune. A man in a red slashed doublet and red and green *mi-parti* hose ascends the wheel at three o'clock. A king at the top in the twelve o'clock position wears a houppelande and red hose, and in the nine o'clock position going downward is a figure in white slashed doublet and *mi-parti* hose. Finally, at the bottom of the wheel is a corpse, naked.[23]

18 See Andrea Denny-Brown, *Fashioning Change: The Trope of Clothing in High- and Late-Medieval England* (Columbus: Ohio State University Press, 2012).

19 For a general overview of the interplay between morality and dress in this period, see Aileen Ribiero, *Dress and Morality* (Oxford: Berg, 2003), 55–65.

20 Susan Crane, *The Performance of Self: Ritual, Clothing, and Identity During the Hundred Years War* (Philadelphia: University of Pennsylvania Press, 2002), 13.

21 Larry D. Benson, ed., *The Riverside Chaucer* (Boston: Houghton Mifflin, 1987), *The Parson's Tale*, part III, lines 415–430, pp. 300–01.

22 "þese men despiseþ hir owne, and preiseþ oþer menis"; *Polychronicon Ranulphi Higden Monachi Cestrensis*, ed. Churchill Babington (London: Longman, Green, 1869), vol. 2, book 1, chap. 60, 169–75, here 169.

23 This miniature is Cambridge, Trinity Hall, MS 12, 3r, printed in color as plate 1 of Denny-Brown, *Fashioning Change*.

In short, the panel through its depiction of material culture,[24] outmoded clothing fashion,[25] and sensual and psychological pleasure[26] comments on a broad spectrum of Netherlandish society, and the Tabletop Artist does not differ from the moralists and satirists of his age (Brant and Erasmus for example) or the engravers, woodcut makers, and painters of topics such as Unequal Couples[27] in criticizing the love of display, amatory folly, and fashion excess associated with Northern European material culture. Indeed, the economic prosperity and vibrant trading patterns of the region and the age created the necessary environment for fashion, since for some garments to be "fashionable" others must be much less so, and this disparity can only exist in a context of diverse material culture where commodities are easily enough accessible to consumers at all social levels to allow for conscious imitation of higher-class fashion by some of those lower on the social scale. Inherent in the *varietas vestium* trope is, of course, a criticism of the shallowness of fashion itself.

ENVY

The artist seems to understand envy[28] in an uncharacteristically psychological rather than allegorical way as unsatisfied desire (figs. 6.2 and 6.3), showing us the sin "in action," so to speak, and illustrating aspects of it through the clothing fashion and accessories of the several figures in the register, as well as through the presence of the dogs quarrelling over a bone prominently in the foreground.

24 See Joseph Koerner, "Bosch's Equipment," in *Things that Talk: Object Lessons from Art and Science*, ed. Lorraine Daston (New York: Zone, 2004), 27–65, as well as the same author's "Impossible Objects: Bosch's Realism," *RES: Anthropology and Aesthetics* 46 (Autumn 2004): 73–97; and "Bosch's Enmity," in *Tributes in Honor of James H. Marrow: Studies in Painting and Manuscript Illumination of the Late Middle Ages and Northern Renaissance*, ed. Jeffrey F. Hamburger and Anne S. Korteweg (London: Harvey Miller, 2006), 285–300.
25 As an example of how fine distinctions in fashion can become blurred in general discussions of this tabletop, Gelfand ("Social Status," 339–40) observes that "the social status of these three groups [peasants, bourgeoisie, elites] is made recognizable by Bosch thanks to the ways in which he dresses his figures …. Those intended to represent members of the upper classes are dressed in up-to-date, expensive fashions …." Gibson (*Hieronymus Bosch*, 34) is similarly broad in noting that "certainly details of costume … reflect styles which did not come into fashion until around 1490."
26 On sensual and sensuous pleasure in this period, see Richard Newhauser, ed., *Pleasure and Danger in Perception: The Senses in the Middle Ages and Renaissance* (Oxford: Berg, 2010).
27 The "unequal couple" was a pictorial topic common in this era and usually treated an older man paired with a much younger woman, though older women with younger men also appeared. Alison G. Stewart, *Unequal Lovers: The Study of Unequal Couples in Northern Art* (New York: Abaris, 1978). See also Keith Moxey, "Master E. S. and the Folly of Love," *Simiolus* 11 (1980): 125–48.
28 On this and the other sins discussed below, see Morton Bloomfield, *The Seven Deadly Sins* (East Lansing: Michigan State University Press, 1952), and more recently the introduction to and essays in Richard Newhauser, ed., *The Seven Deadly Sins: From Communities to Individuals* (Leiden: Brill, 2007), and Richard Newhauser and Susan J. Ridyard, *Sin in Medieval and Early Modern Culture: The Tradition of the Seven Deadly Sins* (York, UK: York Medieval Press, 2012).

Fig. 6.2: Courting couple in Envy scene, detail of figure 6.1.
Photo: Courtesy Museo Nacional del Prado.

Fig. 6.3: Older couple, man with falcon, and laborer in Envy scene, detail of figure 6.1. Photo: Courtesy Museo Nacional del Prado.

The scene is possibly that of a corner of a town which could be 's-Hertogenbosch where stands a bourgeois dwelling, in environs of exactly the sort in which Bosch, his patrons, and many of the members of the Brotherhood of our Blessed Lady might have lived. Perhaps it is a counting, mercantile, or customs house—showing diamond-pane windows with chevron-like heraldic motifs, which helps to localize the sin as one of well-to-do people or those with the desire to be seen as such.

All of the figures as well as the animals illustrate the anguish of unsatisfied desire. A young man courts a girl in the house who seems receptive but unavailable, and an older couple (probably the girl's parents) gaze at the man holding a falcon, envying him the youth they cannot have and, for the old man, the high-fashion garments—or so he imagines—which would be unsuitable to him by reason of age. A heavily burdened laborer trudges away from a scene designed to show off the wealth that he lacks. Even the dogs in the foreground envy the bone in the old man's hand that seems tastier than those larger bones on the ground before them.[29]

The young man who unsuccessfully courts the well-dressed young woman inside the house is physically and symbolically separated from her by barred windows and by late medieval fashion customs relating to sexual and marital availability. For one thing, a linen veil covers her hair. This may indicate that she is married or engaged, serving as a sign of her submission to God and to her husband or husband-to-be;[30] thus the man eagerly but vainly presses his flower and suit on her, though the prominent purse at his waist shows that he would probably be a good catch from a financial point of view. She is also represented as well-to-do; what can be seen of her gown reflects the fashion worn by other women of the mercantile class of this time,[31] and the sheer border next to her face suggests a second layer of much finer and more expensive veiling. She holds a carnation, a sign of high status as well as of courtship and betrothal in

---

29 On connections between envy and dogs in medieval encyclopediae, see M. C. Seymour, ed., *On the Properties of Things: John of Trevisa's Translation of Bartholomaeus Anglicus De Proprietatibus Rerum* (Oxford: Clarendon, 1975), vol. 2, book 18, chap. 27, 1170. See also A. Smets, "L'Image Ambigüe du Chien à Travers la Littérature Didactique Latine et Français (XII–XIV Siècles)," *Reinardus* 14 (2001): 243–53, and more recently, John Block Friedman, "Dogs in the Identity Formation and Moral Teaching Offered in Some Fifteenth-Century Flemish Manuscript Miniatures," in *Our Dogs, Our Selves: Dogs in Medieval and Early Modern Art, Literature, and Society*, ed. Laura Gelfand (Leiden: Brill, 2016), 325–62.

30 See Stewart, *Unequal Lovers*, 94: "around 1500, the practice seems … for married women in Germany … to wear their hair covered with a 'Frauenbinde,' a veil or bonnet …." While it is probably generally true that married women covered their hair and that uncovered hair might have indicated availability, there seems to be little scholarship on this particular subject and none that would confirm it for the time and place of the tabletop.

31 See, for example, the portrait of Cornelia Cnoop in the upper-right-hand corner of Gérard David's *The Virgin Among the Virgins* (Rouen, France, Musée des Beaux-Arts, ca. 1509; online at the museum's website, https://mbarouen.fr/en/oeuvres/the-virgin-among-the-virgins), and a portrait of a donor on the right-hand wing of *Triptych with Lamentation over Christ with Donors and Saints* by an unknown artist (Baltimore, Walters Art Museum, ca. 1490; online at https://art.thewalters.org/detail/25349/triptych-with-lamentation-over-christ-with-donors-and-saints).

the Netherlands,[32] perhaps signaling that she too desires to pursue a liaison with the suitor, though she is barred from it by an existing commitment.

The clothing of Envy's suitor reflects expense but not cutting-edge fashion, for his full-length pleated, fur-lined gown, defined rather generally by Anne van Buren as "a formal suit of long garments,"[33] would have been the province of older, conservative men. Young men tended towards short doublets and hose topped with a coat or a short gown, the gown often worn open to show off the tight-fitting garments beneath. Many images of the time show variations on this youthful fashion and how it contrasted with the longer, closed gowns of older men (fig. 6.4).[34]

Instead of fashionable garments displaying his figure, Envy's suitor wears a long gown, belted at the waist, with slightly widened sleeves. Although faint contrasting edges may indicate a fur lining, it does not have the fur lapels and collar seen on so many men's gowns of the time.[35] What it most resembles is the conservative style worn by a gray-haired bourgeois man in blue from the *Prayer Book of Maximilian of Austria* produced in Bruges in 1493.[36] Like the suitor, this worthy wears a belt and purse, though his sleeves are cut in an older style than the would-be lover's.

The suitor's robe may indicate that he wishes to present himself as a sober, mature person, but he is not completely without fashionable touches. For example, he seems to have the means and taste for a *carmignolle*, or little cap, probably of velvet,

32 For the carnation in the Netherlands, see John Block Friedman, "Dürer's Rhinoceros and What He or She Was Wearing: Carnations, Luxury Gardens, Identity Formation, and Urban Splendor, 1460–1550," *Journal of Material Culture* 20, no. 2 (Sept. 2015): 273–97. Gelfand ("Social Status," 253) identifies the flower with betrothal.

33 Anne H. van Buren and Roger S. Wieck, *Illuminating Fashion: Dress in the Art of Medieval France and the Netherlands 1325–1515* (New York: Morgan Library and Museum, 2011), 315.

34 Gerard David, in *The Skinning of Sisamnes* (the second panel of *The Judgment of Cambyses*, Bruges, Groeningemuseum, 1498; online at the museum's website, https://zoeken.erfgoed-brugge.be/detail.php?id=942553621), shows a scene in the upper right corner featuring both young gallants—one in visible doublet and hose under an open calf-length gown, and the other in doublet, striped hose, and a short coat—and older counselors in long closed gowns (which also would have been worn over doublet and hose, but these would not have been visible). The relatively youthful man sitting in the chair is also dressed in this younger style, but he has his open gown draped across his lap. A step or two up the social scale, an image from a version of the *Roman de la Rose* produced ca. 1490 (London, British Library, Harley MS 4425, 14v) shows a scene full of courtiers wearing elegant and sometimes fanciful versions of this style; see reproduction in Margaret Scott, *Medieval Dress and Fashion* (London: British Library, 2007), fig. 100. The contrast between fashions of younger and older men extended to other countries as well. For an example from Augsburg, Germany, see Ulinka Rublack and Maria Hayward, eds., *The First Book of Fashion: The Books of Clothes of Matthäus and Veit Konrad Schwarz of Augsburg* (London: Bloomsbury, 2015), 31.

35 For example, see *Wedding of Hercules and Alise* (Olivier de la Marche, *Mémoires*; Paris, Bibliothèque Nationale de France, MS fr. 2868, 18r, 1494–5) in Van Buren and Wieck, *Illuminating Fashion*, 261, fig. B.91, and *House of Delights and Amusements* (Berlin, Staatliche Museen Preussischer Kulturbesitz, Kupferstichkabinett, MS 78 D 5, 58r, 1497) in Van Buren and Wieck, *Illuminating Fashion*, 267, fig. B.94.

36 *The People Adore Christ the Savior* (*Prayer Book of Maximilian of Austria*; London, British Library, Additional MS 25698, 8v, 1493) in Van Buren and Wieck, *Illuminating Fashion*, 257, fig. B.89.

Fig. 6.4: Mature and youthful male clothing styles. Detail of *The Skinning of Sisamnes*, right panel of *The Judgment of Cambyses* diptych, by Gerard David (Bruges, Groeningemuseum), 1488. Photo: Public domain, via Wikimedia Commons.

with three-quarters of the brim turned up and often held by laces on the crown.[37] This was becoming increasingly fashionable on young dandies from the 1460s onward, and indeed, one of the striking features of the art of this period—Italianate in inspiration—is the profusion of bonnet-like hats, of the sort we see here. The ambiguous

---

37 Defined as "a man's barret or toque with a divided brim held up by laces tied on the crown in a tuft" by Van Buren and Wieck (*Illuminating Fashion*, 298), who also include quotations with examples.

drape around his neck may be another instance of this trend. It is most likely to be a vestigial tippet, originally part of the older *chaperon* (see below), but in this period attached to a fuzzy, round-crowned hat which, in addition to being worn on the head, might also be worn dangling from its tippet. The courtier in the striped hose in the *Roman de la Rose*[38] wears his in just this way as a fashionable complement to his very tiny *carmignolle*. *The Skinning of Sisamnes*[39] features two men standing just beyond the red-turbanned skinner in the foreground, one with the round-crowned hat on his head with its tippet wrapped around his neck and the other with what looks like a tippet draped across his shoulders in addition to the *carmignolle* on his head. The companion painting, *The Arrest of Sisamnes*,[40] shows that the *carmignolle* was worn with long gowns as well as with younger fashions, so it was not a ridiculous combination, but there is likely to be some mockery in the tabletop's depiction of a young would-be gallant wearing an older man's gown. Perhaps the artist wished to suggest that the lover suffers envy not only in the matter of the lady, but also that he envies the position and wealth garnered by older men in the community.

Contrasting with the aspiring lover in fashion is the old man standing next to his wife inside the building in the street-front half-doorway, who gazes not on the courtship just described, but instead on the younger man with the falcon at the right. The old man's clothing, a conservative fur-lined gown with sleeves that are full around the elbow and narrower at the wrist, is in an even older style than the young suitor's. Even further out of style is his *chaperon*—a type of headdress worn only by older men of his class at this time—the unfashionably long tippet of which wraps around his arm. The antiquated clothing and the man's lined and aged face present him as far from yet still desirous of the youth, vitality, and fashion of the man holding the falcon. Both the pose and the object of the gaze remind us of Ages of Man iconography, as he seems to envy what he takes to be the newest fashion on the younger man.[41]

The older woman inside the house, probably the wife of the older man, wears an old-fashioned linen headcovering wrapped wimple-style around her throat, the "veil, worn by matrons [and] old women;"[42] her dark gown is possibly fur-lined. The artist has been at some pains to fit her in, but her purpose in the composition is a bit obscure. Her gaze seems directed towards the man with the falcon, so it is possible that she is thinking longingly of the dashing men of her youth. Alternatively, if there is a contrast being made between the bourgeois residents of the house and the aris-

---

38 See note 34.

39 See note 34.

40 Gerard David, *The Arrest of Sisamnes*, the first panel of *The Judgment of Cambyses*; see note 34.

41 See for example the use of a similar apparently envious older observer counting money on the ledge of a French door who watches a young man holding a falcon ride away on a fine horse. This scene is in a miniature for the Ages of Man in Bartholomaeus Anglicus, *De proprietatibus rerum* (Paris, Bibliothèque Nationale de France, MS fr. 9141, 98r, first quarter of the fifteenth century), reproduced in Elizabeth Sears, *The Ages of Man: Medieval Interpretations of the Life Cycle* (Princeton, NJ: Princeton University Press, 1986), fig. 68.

42 On the wimple or *guimpe*, see Van Buren and Wieck, *Illuminating Fashion*, 320, for a list of examples in manuscript painting.

tocratic and leisured hunter, she may wish for the higher social status that the man with the falcon represents.

Also dramatically opposed to the falcon holder in clothing style is a laborer at the viewer's right, in a drab doublet with several patches and red hose with points (some unlaced) intended to hold them to his doublet. He bears a large, heavy sack, and part of his face is visible in the crook of his elbow. Though Larry Silver believes the sack-bearer is the falcon man's employee, "carrying a large bag of staples off to his walled urban estate in the background,"[43] he seems to be moving away from the manor house in the composition; thus his positioning may simply comment on the leisure of the main actors in the drama as comic yet enviable. His path takes him away from their obviously greater wealth and status, but his partially visible expression secures his place as an envying actor in this drama rather than a mere prop intended to provide contrast. His presence, the facial expression masked, leaves a strange and disruptive impression and is dramatically similar to the appearance of the fool—also seemingly unrelated to but commenting on the main action—in the section depicting Lust discussed below.

The type of the "man with falcon" comes largely from Labors of the Months calendar miniatures,[44] which often show a young gallant in a spring landscape holding a hawk, though usually without the minutiae of falconry as here. Such a gallant in moral contexts is sometimes surrounded by the toys of idleness: musical instruments, hunting dogs, as well as a hawk.[45]

Though some of the tabletop's commentators have called this man a "falconer" it is clear from his clothing that he is to be understood not as by occupation a huntsman in charge of maintaining birds,[46] but rather as a wealthy person exercising his social prerogative of hunting with a falcon. Though Larry Silver has called the bag at his belt a game bag with prey,[47] this is actually a hawking accessory that holds a "tiring" or desiccated chicken or dove's leg for the falcon used to keep it calm by giving it something on which to gnaw (fig. 6.5).[48] One need only examine a near-contemporary Labors of the Months *bas-de-page* (fig. 6.6) to see the contrast in fashion and status

43 See Silver, "God in the Details," 628; the quotation is from his *Hieronymus Bosch*, 317. By contrast, Gelfand ("Social Status," 255) believes the laborer is stealing the falcon man's grain.

44 On Labors of the Months scenes with falcons, see Bridget Ann Henisch, *The Medieval Calendar Year* (University Park: Pennsylvania State University Press, 1999), figures 3.5, 6.16.

45 See, for example, Peter Rolfe Monks, ed. and trans., *The Brussels Horloge de Sapience: Iconography and Text of Brussels, Bibliothèque Royale MS IV.iii*, Litterae Textuales (Leiden: Brill, 1990), 141.

46 For example, Gelfand, "Social Status," 255, and Dixon, *Bosch*, 51, so identify him.

47 Silver, *Hieronymus Bosch*, 317. For the quotation, see note 50 below.

48 On medieval falconry, see Baudouin van den Abeele, *La Fauconnrie au Moyen Âge: Connaissance, Affaitage et Médicine des Oiseaux de Chasse d'après les Traités Latines* (Paris: Klincksieck, 1994). On the "tiring" see Baudouin van den Abeele, "Le Faucon sur la Main: Un Parcours Iconographique Médiéval," in *La Chasse au Moyen Age: Société, Traités, Symboles*, ed. Agostino Paravicini Bagliani and Baudouin van den Abeele (Florence: Edizioni del Galluzzo, 2000), 89.

between an actual bird keeper and the nobles who hunt with falcons, riding through the gate just ahead of him.[49]

The man with the falcon has somewhat coarse, slightly caricatured features with a hint of beard stubble on the jaws and lank—not aristocratically curled—nape-length hair.[50] By features, then, he is unsuited to his rich, pleated houppelande, with extremely full bag sleeves and a high collar. Van Buren defines this as "a full outer garment, worn by men and women, the man's with gores inserted in the skirt made full-, calf-, or 'bastard' length, and very short."[51] The falcon man is wearing the calf-length version of the houppelande. Such a garment would in this period be anachronistic, as this particular style was out of fashion by the late 1430s.[52] In addition, as noted above in the discussion of Envy's would-be lover, younger men in the late fifteenth and early sixteenth centuries wore doublet and hose, especially while engaged in a field sport such as falconry, where they needed greater freedom of movement. The falcon man's outfit matches quite well with that worn by younger men at the first flush of the style's popularity, as is evident from the garb of three minor nobles in a Flemish miniature from ca. 1414.[53] Moreover, his hat, unlike that on the courting man, is also anachronistic and out of fashion in the later fifteenth and very early sixteenth centuries. It appears to be what has been called a "fish" *chaperon*;[54] these hats had long been replaced in youthful wardrobes by a great variety of novel flat caps and hats stylistically unrelated to the hood-*chaperon*, as is clear from the *carmignolle* just discussed.

If his clothing and accessories were merely fashions of the past, the man with the falcon might be explained as simply a representation of the youth of the older couple which they cannot now recapture. However, he also wears pattens, "a two-heeled

---

49 *The Hours of Albrecht of Brandenburg*, formerly at Bibliotheca Philosophica Hermetica, Amsterdam, was sold by Sotheby's in 2001 and its present whereabouts are unknown.

50 Most men of rank at this time are depicted with fairly careful coiffures. See John Block Friedman, "Hair and Social Class" in *A Cultural History of Hair*, ed. Roberta Milliken (London: Bloomsbury, 2018), 137–51, 198–202. These features and hair would be enough to call into question Silver's claim (*Hieronymus Bosch*, 317) that "a more complex depiction of envy makes class differences explicit. In a town house's street-front half-door opening, a middle-class man and his wife look covetously at the stylishly clad nobleman standing before them while holding a falcon in his hand and carrying its prey at his belt." The "prey" is actually the "tiring" leg used to calm the bird as discussed above.

51 See Van Buren and Wieck, *Illuminating Fashion*, 307. For discussion and examples of this garment, see their index, s.v. "houpeland."

52 For later versions of the style with smaller sleeves and varied collars, see *Jacquemart Makès and His Wife Adore the Crucified Christ* (Estinnes-au-Val, Belgium, Church of St. Martin, ca. 1431), in Van Buren and Wieck, *Illuminating Fashion*, 155, fig. B.37, and the mage on the right in Jacques Daret's *Adoration of the Magi* (Berlin, Staatliche Museen Preussischer Kulturbesitz, Gemäldegalerie, 1433–34), in Van Buren and Wieck, *Illuminating Fashion*, 157, fig. B.39.

53 *Salmon Is Questioned by the King* (Pierre Salmon, *Dialogues*; Geneva, Bibliothèque de Genève, MS fr. 165, 7r, ca. 1414) in Van Buren and Wieck, *Illuminating Fashion*, 131, F.82.

54 See Van Buren and Wieck, *Illuminating Fashion*, 110, in reference to *Demipho Arrives as Phormio Promises Geta to Defend Antipho's Marriage* (Terence, *Comedies*, "Phormio"; Paris, Bibliothèque Nationale de France, MS lat. 7907A, 125r, 1407), reproduced at 112, fig. F.64.

Fig. 6.5: Falconer with "tiring" leg. Marginal image from Breviary of Louis de Male (Brussels, Bibliothèque Royale MS 9427, folio 62v), after 1380. Photo: Courtesy Bibliothèque Royale.

clog of wood or cork, held to the foot by straps,"[55] which were a popular subject for artists from the later fifteenth century, initially as a fashion novelty and later to signal moral weakness and fashion obsolescence. Both Bosch and the Tabletop Artist seem to have viewed them with suspicion and distaste.[56] They appear in 1434 as elite accouterments in Jan van Eyck's slightly anachronistic *Arnolfini Marriage*,[57] but by

55 See Van Buren and Wieck, *Illuminating Fashion*, 312–13.
56 Hans Janssen, Olaf Goubitz, and Jaap Kottman, "Everyday Objects in the Paintings of Hieronymus Bosch," in Koldeweij, Vermet, and Van Kooij, *New Insights*, 171–92, who say "Pattens may indicate lewdness …" (190). The authors are undoubtedly thinking of the Dutch proverb for copulation watched by a pimp, literally "to guard the pattens" kicked off by an amorous couple, discussed in Dirk Bax, *Hieronymus Bosch: His Picture-Writing Deciphered*, trans. M. A. Bax-Botha (Rotterdam, Netherlands: A. A. Balkema, 1979), 280.
57 Much has been written about the social and cultural aspects of this work, but see Carola Hicks, *Girl in a Green Gown: The History and Mystery of the Arnolfini Portrait* (London: Random

Fig. 6.6: Hunters and falconer. Detail of calendar scene for May (8v) in the Hours of Albrecht of Brandenburg, by Simon Bening (formerly Oxford, Bodleian Library, Astor Deposit; present whereabouts unknown), 1530. Photo: John Block Friedman.

1493 they are associated with folly in the Frankfort Master's *Festival of Archers* (figs. 6.7 and 6.8), where a fool wears them.[58] A woodcut of 1517 places them on the old, ill-dressed, and sexually foolish husband of an ill-assorted couple,[59] and they appear in the foreground of the fight in the tabletop's portrayal of the sin of Anger. Moreover,

---

House, 2011). For comments on the anachronistic character of the woman's gown and the use of outmoded fashions for formal wear, see Van Buren and Wieck, *Illuminating Fashion*, 27–28.

58 This painting by the Frankfurt Master of ca. 1490–1500 (he was probably from Antwerp and has been connected with Hendrik van Wueluwe) is now in the Museum of Fine Arts, Antwerp, inv. no. 529, and is viewable online at https://lukasweb.be/en/artwork/festival-ar-chers. See Stephen H. Goddard, *The Master of Frankfurt and His Shop* (Brussels: Koninklijke Academie voor Wetenschappen, Letteren en Schone Kunsten, 1984); the same author's "Master of Frankfurt," Grove Art Online (www.oxfordartonline.com/groveart); and Kate Challis, "Master of Frankfurt," in *The Oxford Companion to Western Art*, ed. Hugh Brigstocke (Oxford: Oxford University Press, 2001). For the painting in question, see Roberta Smith Favis, "The Garden of Love in Fifteenth Century Netherlandish and German Engravings: Some Studies in Secular Iconography in the Late Middle Ages and Early Renaissance" (Ph.D. diss., University of Pennsylvania, 1974), 222–23 and fig. 103.

59 See Stewart, *Unequal Lovers*, 29, fig. 3.

Fig. 6.7: *Festival of the Archers*, by Master of Frankfort (Antwerp, Museum of Fine Arts, inv. no. 529), ca. 1480. Photo: Public domain, via Wikimedia Commons.

in Bosch's authentic work, the morally ambiguous Simon of Cyrene failing to carry the cross in *Christ Carrying the Cross* wears them prominently.[60]

However leisured he may appear, then, the man holding the falcon wears quite outdated and morally suspect finery, calling into ironical question the envious glance directed towards him by the man in the doorway, just as much as the smaller bone held by the man in the house is preferred by the dogs to the larger ones on the ground

60 Hieronymus Bosch, *Christ Carrying the Cross* (Vienna, Kunsthistorisches Museum, Gemäldegalerie, ca. 1490–1510) in Ilsink et al., *Catalogue Raisonné*, 239. We are grateful to Theresa Zischkin for a high-resolution photograph of this detail.

Fig. 6.8: Fool with pattens, detail of figure 6.7. Photo: Public domain, via Wikimedia Commons.

in front of them. In short, this unfashionable but costly attire points to the arrogance and vanity of the wearer and underscores the absurdity of misplaced social pretense. To a contemporary observer, the cultural weight of such an old-fashioned yet expensive outfit would have been instantly clear.

PRIDE

In the section depicting Pride (fig. 6.9), an upper-middle-class woman in the interior of a fine stone townhouse similar to the house in Envy stands before an ornate armoire arranging her headdress (perhaps in a parody of the conventionally negative siren-holding-a-mirror pose)[61] and regarding herself in a convex mirror[62] offered to her by a devil wearing identical headgear. In a side room a man with longish hair and calf-length robe repeats her gesture by regarding himself in another mirror.[63] Around the central figure are various finely portrayed objects illustrating the material culture found in many Netherlandish domestic interiors, which aided in identity formation among the emergent bourgeoisie at this period.[64] Thus, as with Envy, material culture and the variability of fashion play key roles in the sin of Pride, for the high-status decor and displayed fashion question the woman's taste and identify her as a *parvenue*.

The room is full of objects, natural and manufactured, that are exotic to the Netherlands; most of the manufactured ones were highly fashionable in previous decades but much less so at the moment of the tabletop's creation. On a small side table is a bouquet of flowers including three prominent stems of high-status carnations not native to Northern Europe but probably originally an import from the Ottoman Empire.[65] These flowers, whose role in courtship and betrothal scenes is also evident in the sections on Envy and Lust, had an even more important function as an indicator of social status in the *trompe l'œil* decoration of the margins and in the calendar scenes of many Netherlandish Books of Hours that Robert Calkins has called "bravura exercises in illusionism."[66] That the flowers should appear in three of the tabletop's sections depicting upwardly mobile people gives some idea of their close association with social class. Yet the socially competitive craze for growing and exhibiting carnations from the 1460s onward in the Netherlands would have been in decline by the period of the tabletop; thus the Tabletop Artist is calling attention to a now obsolescent fashion. Probably, then, contemporary viewers would have understood carnations to be both associated with social climbing and also *passé*.[67]

The bouquet of mixed flowers stands in a majolica vase, a high-status container of Italian origin. Its significance in Netherlandish material culture is echoed by that

---

61 See John Block Friedman, "L'Iconographie de Vénus et de Son Miroir à la Fin du Moyen Âge," in *L'Erotisme au Moyen Âge*, ed. Bruno Roy (Montreal: Aurore, 1977), 53–82.

62 See Dixon, *Bosch*, 45–46, Gelfand, "Social Status," 233. Janssen, Goubitz, and Kottman, "Everyday Objects," 172, and on 188: "until the sixteenth century the possession of a mirror was probably still unusual and appears to have been reserved for the well-to-do …."

63 Presumably, Gelfand ("Social Status," 240) is taking this person for a servant when she comments that the "woman looking in the mirror in *Superbia* is setting a bad example for the servants." She also identifies the figure in the smaller room as female (244) despite the shoulder-length hair and calf-length garment, which in this period would both indicate that the figure was male.

64 Robert Calkins, "Secular Objects and Their Implications in Early Netherlandish Painting," in *Art into Life: Collected Papers from the Kresge Art Museum Symposium*, ed. Carol Garrett Fisher and Kathleen L. Scott (East Lansing: Michigan State University Press, 1995), 183–211.

65 See note 32 above.

66 Robert Calkins, "Sacred Image and Illusion in Late Flemish Manuscripts," *Essays in Medieval Studies* 6 (1989): 1–16, here 4.

67 See Anne Goldgar, "The Use and Misuse of Flowers: Tulipmania and the Concept of Luxury," in *Luxury in the Low Countries: Miscellaneous Reflections on Netherlandish Material Culture, 1500 to the Present*, ed. Rengenier Rittersma (Brussels: Pharo, 2010), 69–84.

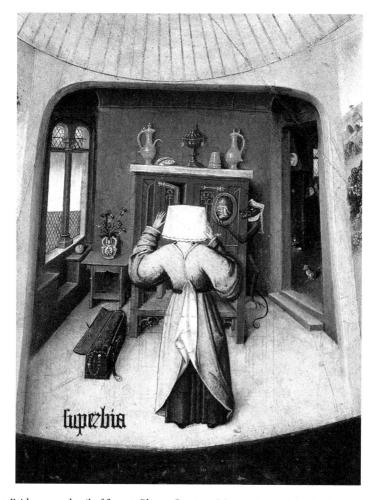

Fig. 6.9: Pride scene, detail of fig. 6.1. Photo: Courtesy Museo Nacional del Prado.

of the three Venetian *cristallo* (ripple glass) cups stacked atop the armoire next to the more local ceramics.[68] The appearance of both carnations and ripple glass in the miniatures of works such as *The Hours of Mary of Burgundy*[69] indicates their long-established position in high culture in the 1470s; moreover, majolica and carnations are very frequently paired by manuscript miniaturists intending to show the elevated status and good taste of the commissioners. Indeed, majolica was so sought after that by the late

68 See generally on this fashionable and expensive material, David Whitehouse, *Medieval Glass for Popes, Princes, and Peasants* (Corning, NY: Corning Museum of Glass, 2010).

69 Otto Pächt, *The Master of Mary of Burgundy* (London: Faber and Faber, 1948), figs. 12 and 13. This manuscript, dated 1477, is now Vienna, Österreichische Nationalbibliothek, MS 1857. See also Robert Koch, "Flower Symbolism in the Portinari Altarpiece," *Art Bulletin* 46 (1984): 70–77.

fifteenth century, as the fashion had peaked among the upper classes, Netherlandish ateliers learned the secrets of its manufacture in Italy and started to produce it locally at a price the emergent bourgeoisie would pay.[70]

The coral rosary overhanging the side of the coffer on the floor by the woman's feet is also an example of an imported Mediterranean material; it is similar to the one offered to the sleeping man in the tabletop's register of Sloth. Coral rosaries were often expensive jewelry. Probably a good indication of the value of the higher grades of red coral may be got from a branch of the material resting on a shelf amid a jeweler's stock of precious raw materials in an illusionistic painting by Petrus Christus of a goldsmith's shop in Bruges in 1449 (fig. 6.10).[71] This woman, apparently neglecting her rosary's primary use, seems to consider it as an ornament and, instead of having it within her immediate reach, keeps it in a chest as a possession rather than as a part of her devotional life.

The Tabletop Artist's treatment of Pride and that of the section depicting Lust (to be discussed below) rely heavily on contemporary literary and artistic sources relating to social status, in particular a woodcut (fig. 6.11) illustrating female vanity and its punishment in Marquart von Stein's translation of Geoffrey IV de la Tour Landry's conduct manual *Livre pour l'enseignement de ses filles*. Geoffrey wrote this manual in 1372 for the moral education of his daughters as they were about to experience court life. It appeared in Middle English in 1483, and in 1493 was first printed in German by Michael Furter in Basel as *Der Ritter vom Turn*.[72] Furter illustrated Von Stein's text

---

70 Richard A. Goldthwaite, "The Economic and Social World of Italian Renaissance Maiolica," *Renaissance Quarterly* 42, no. 1 (Spring 1989): 1–32. Janssen ("Everyday Objects," 174), notes that "among the proportionally correct pottery there is one unusual object, a two-handled majolica flower vase with blue decorations in the painting …. The vase, clearly part of the denounced ostentation of the patrician lady … is probably meant as a product of Italian majolica or the earliest imitations of it made in the Low Countries by Italian immigrants." For a good selection of late medieval majolica, see Zsombor Jékely, "Maiolica Jugs in Late Medieval Painting," in *The Dowry of Beatrice: Italian Maiolica Art and the Court of King Matthias*, exhibition catalog, ed. Gabriella Balla and Zsombor Jékely (Budapest: Museum of Applied Arts, 2008), 55–66.

71 *A Goldsmith in His Shop*, by Petrus Christus (New York, Metropolitan Museum of Art, acc. no. 1975.1.110), 1449. On coral, see J. Malcolm Shick, *Where Corals Lie: A Natural and Cultural History* (London: Reaktion, 2018), and Anne Margreet As-Vijvers, "Weaving Mary's Chaplet: The Representation of the Rosary in Late Medieval Flemish Manuscript Illumination," in *Weaving, Veiling, and Dressing: Textiles and Their Metaphors in the Late Middle Ages*, ed. Kathryn M. Rudy and Barbara Baert (Turnhout, Belgium: Brepols, 2007), 41–80. We are grateful to Larry Silver for bringing the Shick book to our attention.

72 See Ruth Harvey and Peter F. Ganz, eds., *Marquard vom Stein, Der Ritter vom Turn: Kommentar*, Texte des Späten Mittelalters und der Frühen Neuzeit 37 (Berlin: Erich Schmidt, 1996), 43–44 on this exemplum. See also Hans Joachim Kreutzer, "Marquart vom Stein," in *Die Deutsche Literatur des Mittelalters: Verfasserlexikon*, ed. Wolfgang Stammler, Karl Langosch, Kurt Ruh, Kurt Illing, and Christine Stöllinger-Löser (Berlin: de Gruyter, 1987), vol. 6, col. 133, 129–135. The woodcut in question is also reproduced in Joseph Leo Koerner, *The Moment of Self-Portraiture in German Renaissance Art* (Chicago: University of Chicago Press, 1993), 350, as plate 122. The entire text of *Der Ritter vom Turn* is available online at https://reader.digitale-sammlungen.de/de/fs1/object/display/bsb10990824_00206.html.

Fig. 6.10: Raw coral branch and a string of beads, some of which are coral, shown among other materials to be used for jewelry. Detail of *A Goldsmith in His Shop*, by Petrus Christus (New York, Metropolitan Museum of Art, acc. no. 1975.1.110), 1449. Photo: Courtesy Metropolitan Museum of Art.

with forty-six woodcuts now attributed to Albrecht Dürer and Urs Graf, and other publishers used the same woodcuts in later editions.[73] The book was extremely popular throughout Europe in both manuscript and print copies, and the Von Stein translation printed with the woodcuts was likely current in 's-Hertogenbosch.

One of the many stories offered in Geoffrey's advice manual warns readers against an excess pride in dress and preparation of appearance by telling of a woman who

73 On the matter of Dürer and these woodcuts, see Hans Koegler, "Die Basler Gebetholzschnitte vom Illustrator des Narrenschiffs und Ritters vom Turn," *Gutenberg-Jahrbuch* 1 (1926): 117–31.

Fig. 6.11: Woman, mirror, and devil. Woodcut attributed to Albrecht Dürer, in Marquart von Stein, *Der Ritter vom Turn* (1493; repr., Augsburg, Germany: Johann Schönsperger, 1498). Photo: Courtesy Library of Congress, Rare Book and Special Collections Division.

habitually took so long readying herself for church on Sunday that she angered her relations:

> sum of hem cursed her, and saide, "The deuell arraye her onis, and be her merour, for because she makithe us euery day in use and to abide after her." And … atte the same tyme and houre as she loked in a mirrour, in stede of the mirrour, the deuell turned to her his ars, the whiche was so foule and orible that for ferde she was wode and oute of her mynde.[74]

> [Some of them cursed her and said "may the devil dress her and be her mirror, for she makes us wait on her every day." And at the very time of the day when she looked in the

74 Thomas Wright, ed., *The Book of the Knight of La Tour-Landry*, trans. William Caxton (London: Kegan Paul, Trench, Trübner, 1906), chap. 31, 43–44. The story is closely related to the Netherlandish proverb "When you look in the mirror, you are looking up the devil's ass," quoted by Gelfand, "Social Status," 243. Hans Van Gangelen and Sebastiaan Ostcamp, "Parallels between Hieronymus Bosch Imagery and Decorated Material Culture from the Period Between circa 1450 and 1525," in Koldeweij, Vermet, and Van Kooij, *New Insights*, mention a lead-tin badge dug up at Reimerswaal that "shows a chaperon with a face in the form of a bare behind [that] might be meant to represent vanity."

mirror, instead of the mirror she saw the devil's ass, which was so foul and horrible that for fear she went altogether out of her mind.]

The illustration for this story in *Der Ritter* has the main outlines of the tabletop Pride scene: the interior of a stone house with a multi-paned window, an open coffer of finery on the floor, a convex mirror on a wall, a devil, and a woman fussing with her appearance. That this woodcut should be considered a primary source for the Tabletop Artist is suggested by the fact, as we shall see shortly, that two other woodcuts from the Furter version of Geoffrey's manual are used as iconographic models in the section depicting Lust, although the Tabletop Artist gives a somewhat less scatological treatment to the story. In Bosch's *Garden of Earthly Delights* in Madrid, a devil's rump presents an image of a face in a convex mirror to a naked woman encircled by tentacle-like limbs similar to those of the devil that we see in the Pride segment and suggests Bosch's awareness of the *Der Ritter* woodcut as well (fig. 6.12).

The Pride lady's square linen headdress is a variant of the *houve*,[75] a motif from Bosch's known work, where in the Vienna *Last Judgment* a demon in just such a flat-topped headdress cooks a body in a pan.[76] A *houve* very close to that worn by the woman in Pride appears in a French stone relief of 1448 (fig. 6.13), where the flattish top of the *houve* is just at the point of changing to the more fancifully horned styles which so drew the ire of moralists of the fifteenth century. For example, while the *houve* in Jan van Eyck's portrait of his wife, Margaret, painted in 1439 is still relatively flat-topped and square,[77] that of the wife in Petrus Christus' *Goldsmith's Shop*, painted just 10 years later, shows the newer horned style of the mid-fifteenth century.[78] Pride's flat-topped headdress must, then, have been of a shape quite unfashionable by the end of the fifteenth century. Quentin Massys used a similar style in his satirical image of an old woman clinging to the fashions of her youth (sometimes known as "The Ugly Duchess") in 1513.[79]

The Ugly Duchess also shares another very out-of-date detail with the Pride figure: Their veils have ruffled edges. Veils such as these were quite popular in the fourteenth century, and though headdresses with the squarish shape and ruffled edges seen on Pride's lady appear in portraits as late as 1439—Margaret van Eyck's being the latest—

---

75 A houve was a linen veil sometimes worn over hair dressed in a particular shape so that the veil took on a fashionable silhouette. See Van Buren and Wieck, *Illuminating Fashion*, 308. Gelfand ("Social Status," 243, 245) mischaracterizes this accessory, saying that Pride "wears a foolishly large hat," and that "the fancy hat worn by the woman in *Superbia* is also singled out for mockery by the devil who sports a similar one." Neither figure wears a hat. Silver ("God in the Details," 628) calls this accessory an "archaic and absurd linen cap."

76 See the bottom third of the center panel of Bosch's triptych *The Last Judgment* (Vienna, Academy of Fine Arts, 1504–8; online at https://commons.wikimedia.org/wiki/File:Last_judgement_Bosch.jpg, accessed Dec. 7, 2019).

77 Jan van Eyck, *Margaret van Eyck* (Bruges, Groeninge Museum, 1439). See Van Buren and Wieck, *Illuminating Fashion*, 163, B.47, for the image and 162 for a brief discussion.

78 See note 71 above.

79 Quentin Massys, *An Old Woman* (London, National Gallery, 1513; online at www.nationalgal-lery.org.uk/paintings/quinten-massys-an-old-woman-the-ugly-duchess).

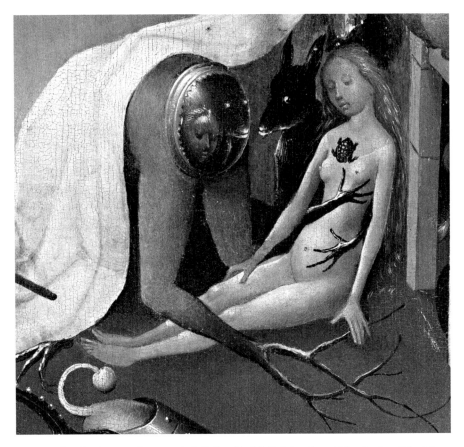

Fig. 6.12: Devil, mirror, and woman in hell. Detail of *Hell*, right wing of *The Garden of Earthly Delights* triptych, by Hieronymus Bosch (Madrid, Museo Nacional del Prado, inv. no. P002823), 1490–1510. Photo: Courtesy Museo Nacional del Prado.

they were rare even at that date.[80] They were notable for their expense, which probably stemmed from the difficulty of manufacturing them.[81]

Pride's fur-lined gown is flipped up in the back with the hem pinned to the bodice to display the lining.[82] A much more fashionable gown with the skirt pinned in

---

80 Carla Tilghman, "Giovanna Cenami's Veil: A Neglected Detail," *Medieval Clothing and Textiles* 1 (2005): 162–66.

81 Ibid., 167.

82 Another technique for showing off a fur lining, with folds of the skirt gathered and held at the waist, appears in a miniature painted in 1479 in a Valerius Maximus manuscript, *Les Fais et Dis des Romains* (London, British Library, MS Royal 18 E IV, 229r; online at www.bl.uk/catalogues/illuminatedmanuscripts/illumin.asp?illid=51523), and the *Wedding of Hercules and Alise*, note 35 above.

Fig. 6.13: Flat-topped *houve*. Limestone relief, Palais de Jacques Cour, Bourges, France, 1448. Photo: John Block Friedman.

the same manner appears in an illumination from around 1500.[83] What look to be the seams of individual skins sewn end to end are visible in the calculated display of the Pride lady's gown lining, which also shows what may be fur at collar and cuffs. The fur is probably miniver, which was relatively expensive, though its popularity was waning at the turn of the sixteenth century. Another, more realistic, depiction of this fur as a skirt lining (this one flipped up in front) can be seen on the leftmost figure in a painting of the birth of Mary from 1470–80.[84]

The sleeves of the Pride figure are bulky at the elbow but tapered to the wrist, a shape that had been popular decades previously. More fashionable sleeves were either narrow or widening at the wrist (see the seated lady of Lust below).[85] Pride shares

83 Master of the Prayer Books of ca. 1500, in *Poems*, Charles d'Orléans, "Castle of Love" (London, British Library, Royal 16 F II, 188r; online at www.bl.uk/catalogues/illuminatedmanuscripts/illumin.asp?illid=44743).

84 Master of the Life of the Virgin, *Birth of Mary* (Munich, Alte Pinakothek, 1470–80; online at https://www.sammlung.pinakothek.de/en/bookmark/artwork/5RGQezPpGz).

85 See the paintings cited in note 31 above for further examples.

these sleeves and the color of her gown with a woman involved in the fighting in the tabletop's section representing Wrath and with the innkeeper carrying a tray in the depiction of Gluttony. This suggests that the Tabletop Artist is making a connection between women of low status and the lady of Pride, who seems to be trying but failing to assert a high status.

Pride's skirt is pleated to a fitted bodice instead of the fullness coming from the torso area and being belted in as would have been popular in previous decades.[86] The waist seam is the most up-to-date feature of the gown, however. In other respects, her gown with its full sleeves of the earlier fifteenth century, V-shaped neckline, fur at the collar and cuffs, and girdle is quite similar to that worn in the portrait of Margaret van Eyck of 1439 and that of the woman distracted from her devotions by wealth in *The Moneylender and His Wife* of 1514.[87] The late date of this latter painting and the much earlier date of the fashion shown in it make it clear that Massys and the Tabletop Artist were both using the same technique to mock bourgeois sinners. In short, the Tabletop Artist seems here—as in the case of Envy—to have shown expensive bygone finery in an ironic manner, as a warning to the beholder not to emulate the unreflectively basking woman before the mirror.

LUST

As with the image of Pride, the material culture and clothing fashion of the figures convey much of the meaning in the tabletop's segment illustrating Lust (fig. 6.14), though the highly conventional bodily poses or postures in this segment take on greater significance than was the case in the other scenes discussed. In the immediate foreground is an ornate tent with a finial and cloth-of-gold patterning. In the late medieval and early modern periods moralists used the association of tents with sinister behavior and with exotic settings to symbolize the dangerous power of women. Negative associations of tents came in part from the Biblical story of Jael, who killed Sisera inside a tent with a tent peg driven into his temple (Judges 4:2), and from Psalm 83, where the speaker rejects dwelling "in tabernaculis peccatorum" [in the tents of the sinful]. Negative views of tents were also linked to the story of Judith, who, although presented as righteous, did, nonetheless, behead Holofernes in his own tent (Book of Judith 13:1–8).[88] From an iconographical perspective, most probably, the overall positioning

86 See for example *Margaret van Eyck* (see note 77) and Quentin Massys, *The Moneylender and His Wife* (Paris, Louvre, 1514; online at www.louvre.fr/en/oeuvre-notices/moneylender-and-his-wife).

87 Massys, *Moneylender and His Wife* (see note 86, above).

88 For the bad reputation of tents, see Michael Gnehm, "Orientalism in a Tent," in *Clothing the Sacred: Medieval Textiles as Fabric, Form, and Metaphor*, ed. Mateusz Kapustka and Warren T. Woodfin, Textile Studies 8 (Emsdetten, Germany: Imorde, 2015), 189–207, and for Jael and the tent in which she kills Sisera, see Peter Scott Brown, *The Riddle of Jael: The History of a Poxied Heroine in Medieval and Renaissance Art and Culture* (Leiden: Brill, 2018). Chaucer, in "The

Fig. 6.14: Lust scene, detail of fig. 6.1. Photo: Courtesy Museo Nacional del Prado.

of this tent and the couples in and beside it derives from the Master of the Gardens of Love's *Small Garden of Love*,[89] but the Tabletop Artist has reversed the positioning and made the sexuality slightly less apparent.

Wife of Bath's Prologue," line 770, places the murder of Sisera by Jael among the deeds in a long list of women who kill or damage their husbands, lovers, and so on.

89 Master of the Gardens of Love, single-leaf engraving, *The Small Garden of Love* (Boston, Museum of Fine Arts, acc. no. 65.594, 1440–50; online at https://collections.mfa.org/objects/155705/the-small-garden-of-love). Silver (*Hieronymus Bosch*, 28) mentions that this setting is "a more conventional Garden of Love." It is discussed by Favis, "Garden of Love," 70–71, 165–94. See more recently Holm Bevers, "Master of the Gardens of Love," Oxford Art Online (www.oxfordartonline.com).

Fig. 6.15: "Chin chucking" in Lust scene, detail of fig. 6.1. Photo: Courtesy Museo Nacional del Prado.

Within this tent are two couples, one in the rear where the man is "chin chucking" the woman (fig. 6.15), a widely represented erotic gesture from about the thirteenth century onwards, which can also be mutual or made by the woman to the man, as on an ivory comb from Paris made about 1320 (fig. 6.16).[90] Lust's chin-chucker bears an exotic[91] turban-like headdress of rounded strips somewhat similar to that worn by one

90 For this amorous gesture, see Malcolm Jones, *The Secret Middle Ages: Discovering the Real Medieval World* (Stroud, UK: Sutton, 2002), 53. On such decorated ivory combs and mirror backs, see Diane Wolfthal, "The Sexuality of the Medieval Comb," in *Thresholds of Medieval Visual Culture: Liminal Spaces*, ed. Elina Gertsman and Jill Stevens (Woodbridge, UK: Boydell, 2012), 176–94; and Katherine Elisabeth Staab, "Tactile Pleasures: Secular Gothic Ivory" (Ph.D. diss., University of Pennsylvania, 2014), esp. figures 11, 12, and 13, available online at https://etda.libraries.psu.edu/catalog/23514.

91 For the differing interpretations of turbans in the later Middle Ages, see John Block Friedman, "The Art of the Exotic: Robinet Testard's Turbans and Turban-like Coiffure," *Medieval Clothing and Textiles* 4 (2008): 173–91.

Fig. 6.16: Chin chucking by a man (at left) and by a woman (at right) with varying responses. Ivory comb (London, Victoria and Albert Museum, inv. A 560.1910), Paris, 1320–30. Photo: Courtesy Victoria and Albert Museum.

of the tormentors in Bosch's *Ecce Homo* (now in Frankfort; fig. 6.17), an out-of-date pleated knee-length houppelande with bag sleeves similar to that worn by the falcon holder in Envy, and the dubious pattens we saw in Envy. The woman appears to have no headcovering, which may indicate her availability for a liaison.

The man of the second couple reclines on the train of his lover's gold brocade gown[92] with fur lining at the collar and cuffs. His position, longish hair, and nearby food and drink suggest two iconographic poses that appear in the woodcuts for *Der Ritter vom Turn*. The first and more commonplace of these postures is that of the Biblical Samson, ruined by his passion for Delilah, which is the subject of an influential garden scene by the Master E. S.[93] Probably that version of the scene also influenced the artist of the *Ritter vom Turn* cycle of woodcuts, in which Samson reclines on Delilah's lap and two wiser citizens of a town observe them (fig. 6.18).[94]

Much more important and more specific to the tabletop's Lust is a complex figural arrangement that most likely comes from the woodcut for *Der Ritter*'s chapter

92 Long gown trains were frequent subjects for moralists. For example, Bernard of Siena likened them in a sermon to the coils of sinful serpents. For a discussion of the motif, see Thomas Izbicki, "Pyres of Vanities: Mendicant Preaching on the Vanity of Women and Its Lay Audience," in *De Ore Domini: Preacher and Word in the Middle Ages*, ed. Thomas Leslie Amos and Eugene Green (Kalamazoo MI: Medieval Institute, 1989), 211–34.

93 The Master E. S. engraving of Samson and Delilah is reproduced in Max Lehrs, *Late Gothic Engravings of Germany and the Netherlands: 682 Copper Plates from the "Kritischer Katalog"* (New York: Dover, 1969), fig. 194. See Favis, "The Garden of Love," 99, 203, and Madlyn Millner Kahr, "Delilah and Samson," *Art Bulletin* 54 (1972): 282–99, now conveniently reprinted in *Feminism and Art History: Questioning the Litany*, ed. Norma Broude and Mary D. Garrard (New York: Routledge, 2018), 118–45.

94 This is chapter 70 in *Der Ritter*. See on this exemplum Harvey and Ganz, *Marquard vom Stein*, 91–92. Kahr ("Delilah," 124–25) discusses this woodcut, which she publishes as fig. 5, and notes that it influenced similar scenes in Brant's *Ship of Fools* (her fig. 6) and in Andrea Mantegna's "Samson and Delilah," 1495, now in the National Gallery, London (her fig. 1). She also points to the connection between the Master of the Gardens of Love's *Small Garden of Love* and the Samson and Delilah motif, 141 n. 21.

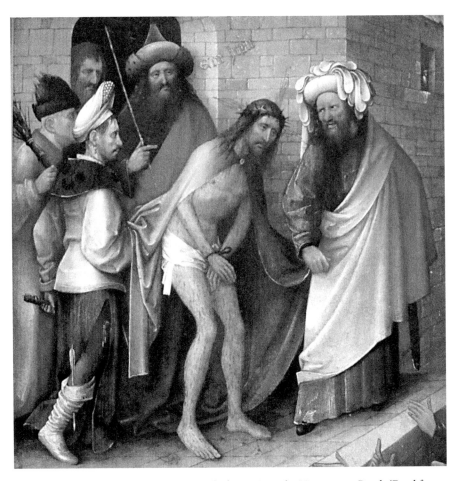

Fig. 6.17: Dagged "Eastern" headdress. Detail of *Ecce Homo*, by Hieronymus Bosch (Frankfurt, Städel Museum, inv. 1577), 1475–85. Courtesy Städel Museum. Photo: Public domain, via Wikimedia Commons.

60 (fig. 6.19).[95] The woodcut shows two lovers embracing in front of an open tent with an armored man moving in from the right to attack them with a sword.[96] The Tabletop Artist seems to have taken the positioning in front of the tent, the food and

---

95 See on this exemplum Harvey and Ganz, *Marquard vom Stein*, 77–78.

96 In brief, the story is that of how Phineas the Israelite kills his fellow Israelite Simri for consorting with a Midianite princess, Cozbi, as the story is told in Numbers 25:1–9. In the scriptural account Simri seems eager to integrate his new love with his own tribe not as a paramour but as his wife, but the woodcut artist heightens the elements of illicitness, lust, and drunkenness implied in the lovers' posture and by the cooling wine jug common in such pictures, as for example that in Sebastian Brant's *Das Narrenschyff* (Basel: Johann Bergmann von Olpe, 1494), which was modeled on the *Der Ritter* Samson and Delilah woodcut.

Fig. 6.18: Samson and Delilah. Woodcut attributed to Albrecht Dürer, in Marquart von Stein, *Der Ritter vom Turn* (1493; repr., Augsburg, Germany: Johann Schönsperger, 1498). Photo: Courtesy Library of Congress, Rare Book and Special Collections Division.

drink, and the lovemaking from the woodcut, and the man with upraised sword at the couple's right is ingeniously transmuted into the tabletop's irate man beating the fool with an upraised ladle.

The Tabletop Artist's reclining lover holds a wine bowl upwards towards his part-ner, a gesture associated with betrothals and the sealing of engagements.[97] At left is a table with the Biblical apple of temptation and cherries, which were, as Bax points out, a symbol of female genitalia and lust generally.[98] The presence of a high-status,

97 Favis, "Garden of Love," 93.
98 Bax, *Picture-Writing*, 251–52.

Fig. 6.19: Phineas, Simri and Cozbi. Woodcut attributed to Albrecht Dürer, in Marquart von Stein, *Der Ritter vom Turn* (1493; repr., Augsburg, Germany: Johann Schönsperger, 1498). Photo: Courtesy Library of Congress, Rare Book and Special Collections Division.

costly Venetian *cristallo* cup, as in the Pride segment, helps to establish the scene's social milieu. In the foreground—paralleling the cooling wine jug in a tub in the tent of the *Der Ritter* woodcut—a pewter wine jug with a coat of arms rests next to the word *Luxuria*; its heraldic chevron is the same one seen in the windowpanes of the Envy register, again tying the scene to the upper levels of society.

As with the young woman in Envy, the seated lady holds a carnation, indicating betrothal or courtship,[99] yet ironically, her hair is covered, suggesting perhaps an adulterous relationship with the man. Her gown is the most fashionable of any depicted

99 Stewart, *Unequal Lovers*, 93.

on the tabletop and seems designed to portray excess—flecks of gold scattered across the fabric probably indicate that the gown was made of cloth of tissue, which would have had precious-metal thread woven into the pattern. Its voluminous sweep, long enough for her lover to lounge upon, also points to extravagant indulgence of the sort criticized by Chaucer. The sumptuous and extremely expensive fabric makes up a gown with a fashionably pointed neckline filled in with a layer of black beneath, but curiously modest sleeves and the linen veil popular among the bourgeoisie of the late fifteenth and early sixteenth century in the Low Countries.[100] Most gowns of this type were painted in plain solid colors with contrasting edging, especially when paired with the white veil.[101] The tabletop's presentation of fabric patterned with precious metal and extra length juxtaposed with the modest style and accessories of the Tabletop Artist's contemporaries suggests once more his moralizing scheme of mocking their sins by combining material realism with symbolic exaggeration.

The reclining lover is also well dressed, though his lack of a gown, which would have been worn in a more public or formal venue, speaks to the intimacy of the situation. There was also a class differential between men at the upper end of the social scale who wore gowns and those lower down who did not, but in this image, the implication is that the lovers in front enjoy a fairly high status, so the lack of gown would have been a choice.[102] Instead he wears a well-fitted coat with matching hose, very current round-toed shoes,[103] and green velvet cap with matching sash. The cap is quite fashionable as well. It is probably one of the high-sided variants of the *carmignolle*

100 The next rung of fashionability included flared sleeves and one of the variants of the French hood that were worn by ladies of high status, for example, the three ladies standing before the Castle of Love in London, British Library, Royal 16 F II, 188r (see note 83 above). These wider sleeves are depicted on women of high status in the 1490s in the Low Countries and came into more general fashion there at the turn of the sixteenth century. See for example *Wedding of Hercules and Alise*, note 35 above; *Wedding of Jupiter and Juno* (Raoul Lefèvre, *Recueil des Histoires de Troie*; Paris, Bibliothèque Nationale de France, MS fr. 22552, 33r) in Van Buren and Wieck, *Illuminating Fashion*, 265, fig. B.92; and *André de la Coste and His Wife, Agnes Adornes, in Prayer* (*Triptych of St. Andrew and the Miracles of Christ*, central panel; Santa Margherita Ligure, Italy, Church of San Lorenzo della Costa, 1499) in Van Buren and Wieck, *Illuminating Fashion*, 269, fig. B.95.

101 See, for example, the two images cited in note 31 above, as well as *The Virgin and Child Between Two Donors* by the Master of 1499 (Paris, Louvre, ca. 1490; online at http://cartelen.louvre.fr/cartelen/visite?srv=car_not_frame&idNotice=24153), in which the gown unusually has buttons down the center front; and several ladies in the Frankfurt Master of ca. 1490–1500's *Festival of Archers* (see note 58 above).

102 The practice of wearing a gown in formal situations can be seen in portraits of donors (who would presumably wish to present themselves in the most formal and respectable way possible) such as the man in the upper left corner of Gérard David's *Virgin Among the Virgins* (see note 31 above)—the edge of his gown lapel is just visible. See also the Walters Art Museum's *Triptych with Lamentation over Christ with Donors and Saints* (also at note 31 above) and *The Virgin and Child Between Two Donors* by the Master of 1499 (note 101 above).

103 See, for example, a page from the *Roman de la Rose* from ca. 1490 (cited in note 36 above), which shows a deliberately historicized character at left in *poulaines* or long-toed shoes observing very fashionable courtiers in round-toed shoes.

that became popular around the turn of the century and was favored by the French king Louis XII.[104] His shoulder-length, wavy hair, while it may have been a reference to Samson, also happened to be at the height of fashion at the time.[105]

Particularly dramatic and puzzling in this depiction of leisured upper-class people is the untoward presence of a fool and his chastiser in front of the scene of lovers as if to comment on it (fig. 6.20). This chastiser is apparently inspired, as noted, by the armor-wearing Phineas with upraised sword in the *Der Ritter* woodcut. Fools were quite common in late medieval art, particularly in scenes of lust involving lewd gestures, often wearing attire of a traditional, yet coded sort. Malcolm Jones has pointed out that "nothing in the costume of the fool—including the various accessories—is accidental,"[106] and certainly that is true in the Tabletop Artist's depiction. He notes further that

> if the central image in a scene designed to convey folly in some fashion is not itself
> given any standard attributes such as the fool stick or marrote, asses' ears, and so on,
> often a fool will be present somewhere in the scene to connect folly with the action
> being depicted.[107]

The Tabletop Artist's fool, then, is the sort that Jones called the "commentary" type. An excellent example of such a fool appears as an illustration for Psalm 52, the "Dixit insipiens" Psalm, from an English Psalter now in Turin. As here, a fool watches a

---

104 See for example *Dialogue Between Louis XII and Reason* (Petrarch, *Des Remedes de Fortune*; Paris: Bibliothèque Nationale de France, MS fr. 225, 55r, ca. 1503; online at https://gallica. bnf.fr/ark:/12148/btv1b60007782/f121) and Pierre Gringore, *Abuses of the World* (New York: Morgan Library and Museum, MS M.42, 1v, ca. 1510; online at www.themorgan.org/collection/ Illuminating-Fashion/45#). An even more similar style appears on the central figure in the *Time* panel of the Château de Chaumont Set of tapestries (Cleveland Museum of Art, ca. 1512–15; online at www.clevelandart.org/art/1960.176.3).

105 Van Buren and Wieck's *Illuminating Fashion* includes numerous images illustrating this fashion in the late fifteenth and early sixteenth centuries in the Low Countries; 257–69, figs. B.89, B.90, B.91, B.92, B.93, B.94, B.95. The first of these (see note 34, above) shows a nice contrast between a man in a fashionable gown and shoulder-length hair and the other male figures (who represent a range from burghers to laborers), all of whom have a bowl cut.

106 Jones, *Secret Middle Ages*, 101. The literature on fools in the Middle Ages is extensive. Some studies with an iconographic focus are Marco Assirelli, "L'Immagine dello 'Stolto' nel Salmo 52," in *Il Codice Miniato: Rapporti tra Codice, Testo e Figurazione: Atti del III Congresso di Storia della Miniatura*, ed. Melania Ceccanti and Maria Cristina Castelli (Florence: Olschki, 1992), 19–34; François Garnier, "Les Conceptions de la Folie d'après l'Iconographie Médiévale du Psaume 52 'dixit insipiens,'" in *Actes du 102e Congrès National des Sociétés Savantes, Limoges, 1977: Section de Philologie et d'Histoire jusqu'à 1610*, vol. 2, *Etudes sur la Sensibilité* (Paris: Bibliothèque Nationale de France, 1979), 215–22; D. J. Gifford, "Iconographical Notes Toward a Definition of the Medieval Fool," in *The Fool and the Trickster: Studies in Honour of Enid Welsford*, ed. Paul V. A. Williams (Cambridge: D.S. Brewer, 1979), 18–35; Maurice Lever, *Le Sceptre et la Marotte: Histoire des Fous de Cour* (Paris: Fayard, 1983); and Philippe Ménard, "Les Emblèmes de la Folie dans la Littérature et dans l'Art (XIIe–XIIIe Siècles)," in *Hommage à Jean-Charles Payen: Farai Chansoneta Novele: Essais sur la Liberté Créatrice au Moyen Age*, ed. Hugette Legros (Caen, France: Université de Caen, 1989), 253–65.

107 Jones, *Secret Middle Ages*, 119.

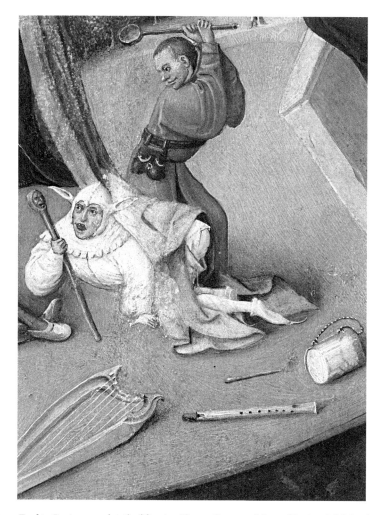

Fig. 6.20: Fool in Lust scene, detail of fig. 6.1. Photo: Courtesy Museo Nacional del Prado.

riotous group, one of whose members inserts his hand directly into the placket of a woman's skirt. God looks down from above.[108]

If medieval fools typically wear a variety of apparel, some garment is almost always dagged, as the fool's hood is on the tabletop.[109] Their shoes are, as here, typically

108 This miniature from Turin, Italy, Biblioteca Nazionale Universitaria, MS I.1.9, 46r is reproduced and discussed in Kathleen Scott, *Later Gothic Manuscripts 1390–1490*, A Survey of Manuscripts Illuminated in the British Isles 6 (London: Harvey Miller, 1995), no. 17, vol. 1, fig. 118, and 2:106–9.

109 Dagging, or decoratively cut edges, appeared on many types of garments in the later Middle Ages but survived longest on fools' clothing. For more on dagging, see John Block Friedman, "The Iconography of Dagged Clothing and its Reception by Moralist Writers," in *Medieval Clothing and Textiles* 9 (2013): 121–38.

the long pointed types with stuffed toes called *poulaines* that were long obsolete by the late fifteenth century. They often hold a "fool stick" or *marrote* (here with a carved face). On occasion they moon the audience, again as happens in the Lust segment. Some of the features of the Tabletop Artist's fool appear in a nearly contemporary "Allegory of Folly" by Quentin Massys (1515)[110] where the figure carved on the *marrote* moons the beholder.

The tabletop fool's bare rump protrudes from his unlaced hose and doublet, suggesting a connection with two of the other sections. Although sometimes unlaced points merely represent physical labor in art of this period, those of the fighter in Anger, those on the bag-carrying man in Envy, and here in Lust all seem to point to the base or uncivilized nature of the wearer.[111] The fool, moreover, is probably the owner of the three musical instruments—wind, percussion, and strings—in the foreground of the scene, signifying the human soul in its responsiveness to the passion of lust. The fool gazes fixedly at the woman's lower abdomen—perhaps implying her concealed genitalia—while the woman looks down at the lover. The Tabletop Artist could have gotten this fool motif from its first introduction into love garden scenes,[112] and after him fools frequently appear in the erotic garden scenes of manuscript painting and graphic media as actors in and commentators on lust's folly.

There is, as well, an underside to the elegant upper-class tent-lovers-fool ensemble. An erotic Dutch lead-tin badge-like lid from a small box made about 1475 to 1525 shows a similar amorous scene of a "Venus" tent with conical roof and finial (fig. 6.21). Inside are naked lovers copulating. A fool in a full dagged *chaperon* watches them from the sidewall.[113] The lid is probably intended to depict a small traveling brothel (not uncommonly housed in tents)[114] and its similarity to Bosch's *Allegory of Intemperance*

110 See Larry Silver, *The Paintings of Quinten Massys, with Catalogue Raisonné* (Montclair, NJ: Allanheid and Schram, 1984), 146–47, 227–28 n. 44.

111 See, for example, the *Banner of Mère Folle with Mooning Figures* now in Dijon, France, Musée Archéologique, ca. 1490–1510, and Christ's tormentor with unlaced points in a scene of Christ carrying the cross by the Master of the Worcester Panel, where unlaced points are associated with folly and violence. Both images are published in John Block Friedman, *Brueghel's Heavy Dancers: Transgressive Clothing, Class, & Culture in the Late Middle Ages* (Syracuse, NY: Syracuse University Press, 2010), figs. 11 and 12.

112 Favis ("Garden of Love," 195–99) discusses how Master E. S. introduced the fool into his love gardens and was followed by other artists of his time.

113 This lid is in Köthen, Germany, in the H. J. E. van Beuningen collection of lead-tin badges (inv. no. 1235). See items 270 and 280 in Han Bos and Gerrit Groeneweg, eds., *Schatten uit de Schelde: Gebruiks-en Siervoorwerpen uit de Verdronken Plaatsen in de Oosterschelde* (Bergen op Zoom, Netherlands: Gemeentemuseum Bergen op Zoom, 1987), an exhibition catalog from the East Schelde River region where the lid was found. Louis Hopstaken has also discussed it in his "Erotische Symboliek op Veertiende Eeuwse Profane Insignes," *De Waterschans* 15, no. 4 (1985): 2–7.

114 The miniaturist Jean Pucelle, in the Belleville Breviary of 1323–1326, depicts such a tent brothel to which Saint Agnes was consigned, as Alexa Sand notes, speaking of "the opened flap of the tent-bordello waiting to engulf Agnes." Alexa Sand, "Religion and Ritualized Belief, 800–1500," in Milliken, *Cultural History of Hair*, 19–35. The quotation is from 27 and the miniature is published as figure 1.5, 38.

Fig. 6.21: Brothel scene. Lead-tin box lid (Köthen, Germany, H. J. E. van Beuningen Collection, inv. no. 1235), 1425–1500. Photo: Courtesy H. J. E. van Beuningen Collection.

painting fragment in the Yale Art Gallery and the Master of the Gardens of Love engraving as well as to the tabletop's Lust section with its tent and fool is unlikely to be coincidental. Possibly the fact that the tabletop's fool is partly draped with the tent wall fabric suggests that his punishment may reflect an attempt to enter the tent or some other form of voyeurism such as that reflected on the box lid. Thus, the conventional use of morally ambivalent tent settings in mid-fifteenth-century engravings of love gardens certainly feeds into the interpretation of the Tabletop Artist's presentation of Lust. That such scenes had moved downward in social class and were connected with *parvenu* social behavior and intended to comment upon it is suggested by Larry Silver, who says of the Bosch *Intemperance* fragment—which has close ties to the scene of Lust in the tabletop—that the "image offers revelry that is usually associated with noble privileges, but now has been appropriated by middle-class imitators."[115] The image on the quite un-aristocratic lead-tin box lid certainly reinforces this sense of the trajectory of class descent.

The three scenes of Envy, Pride, and Lust present a complex interplay of factors to create meaning. The Tabletop Artist drew on previous and contemporary images and beliefs about fashion, such as the Boethian *varietas vestium* topos and those of Samson and Delilah and the motif of the seduction in a tent, to create a recognizable moral context for his viewers. At the same time, he realistically depicted settings and fashions from a bourgeois milieu as well as using cultural cues such as varying styles of clothing and hair, both of which localized the sins in a familiar context to make it clear that such failings were personally relevant to his own social group. He also pointedly included objects, clothing, and accessories that were obviously expensive but in some way undesirable to mock those who would fall prey to these sins. And finally, the links between his depictions of various sins ensured that his intentions would be clear to his viewers. With all of these interlocking strategies, the Tabletop Artist sought to communicate effectively with his audience by building layers of meaning that relied heavily on material culture and the inherent fallibility of fashion. To fully recover his meaning requires modern viewers to understand cultural cues that were particular to the tabletop's time and place.

115 Silver, *Hieronymus Bosch*, 245.

The Broderers' Crown: The Examination and Reconstruction of a Sixteenth-Century City of London Livery Company Election Garland

Cynthia Jackson

It has been a longstanding custom for many London livery companies to inaugurate the newly chosen master and wardens with a crown or garland during an election ceremony.[1] The tradition may have derived from the Puy of Arras, an extravagant medieval festival of community and music dedicated to the Virgin, originating in the textile manufacturing city in northern France.[2] A fraternity of the Puy was established in London and the membership was diverse, admitting merchants trading in a variety of commodities. The first set of statutes was in existence as early as 1280, and a revised set dates from the early fourteenth century. The statutes are transcribed in the *Liber Custumarum*,[3] a collection of medieval manuscripts pertaining to the laws and history of London preserved in the London Guildhall and compiled by city chamberlain Andrew Horn in the 1320s. Written in French, they describe the election process and official ceremony for crowning the selected *prince* with the *coroune dou Puy* in detail. The popularity of the London Puy was short-lived, however, and appears to have declined with the adversities brought on by economic and social hardships in the early decades of the fourteenth century.[4]

This research was made possible by grants from the Textile Society UK and the Society of Antiquaries of London. The author is grateful to Jessica Burgess, Kate Heard, Gale Owen-Crocker, Mike Parr, Jane Ruddell, the Broderers' Company, and the clerks and archivists who generously provided access to examine and photograph their embroidered treasures. Special thanks are due to Monica Wright and the anonymous reviewers for helpful comments and suggestions.

1 Throughout the body of this article the words garland and crown are used interchangeably except where they have been transcribed or quoted from referenced documents.
2 Anne F. Sutton, "Merchants, Music, and Social Harmony: The London Puy and Its French and London Contexts, Circa 1300," *London Journal* 17, no. 1 (1992): 1–17. For an explanation of the use of the word "Puy," see p. 1.
3 Henry T. Riley, ed., *Munimenta Gildhallæ Londoniensis: Liber Albus, Liber Custumarum, et Liber Horn*, Rolls Series 12 (London: Longman, 1860), 2:xlviii–liv, 2:216–28.
4 Anne Lancashire, *London Civic Theatre: City Drama and Pageantry from Roman Times to 1558* (Cambridge: Cambridge University Press, 2002), 40.

In 1345, the first documented statutes for a London guild were recorded by the fraternity of the Peppers in Soper Lane.[5] Similar to those of the Puy but wholly unrelated, these ordinances were also written in French and included a schedule of events defining the election procedure and investment ceremony of the two wardens (*deux gardiens*) who wore crowns (*chapletz*). A description of the *chapletz* is not provided in these first ordinances but, in 1405, the accounts of the Grocers' Company[6] show the chaplets are included with an entry for bread, wine, cheese, apples, and beer, so we may logically assume that they were made of an organic substance, such as rosemary or perhaps roses.[7] The next recorded entry is in 1408 when, having been struck from an entry including bread, wine, and apples, they appear as the single item on the next line at a cost of 20d. for three.[8]

A review of documentary and material evidence of the city livery company crown from the fifteenth to the early seventeenth centuries, focusing on the materials and techniques used, illustrates how the crown developed from a transitory wreath of fresh leaves or herbs to a more permanent textile object. Each garland, crown, chaplet, or hat was designed to uniquely represent the particular company by displaying the coat of arms, devices, and emblems of the company. Some were simple bands of velvet with appropriate gold or silver badges sewn on. Some, such as that of the Barber Surgeons' Company, were circlets of silver-gilt (that is, gilded silver).[9] Still others were sumptuously embroidered with gold and silver wire and silk threads. Research conducted by John L. Nevinson provided this author with the starting point for further investigation into the history of this tradition.[10] A review of additional city livery company archives proved how widespread the practice was.[11] Today many of the livery companies continue the tradition of crowning the elected officials, and several use crowns or garlands dating from the sixteenth century.[12]

A list of extant embroidered livery company crowns with photographs and further details regarding the design, materials, and techniques follows in Appendix 7.1, which illustrates the variety of work produced in embroidery. Unusual in the study of embroidered textiles is the fact that we know the provenance of these objects and that we can definitively date some of them. We can also compare the materials and

---

5 John Abernethy Kingdon, *Facsimile of First Volume of Ms. Archives of the Worshipful Company of Grocers of the City of London, A.D. 1345–1463* (London: Richard Clay, 1886), 9–10, 18, 91, 98, 104.

6 "A Short History of the Grocers' Company," Grocers' Hall, https://grocershall.co.uk/the-company/history, accessed Dec. 11, 2019. The pepperers and spicers became known collectively as the Company of Grocers in 1376.

7 Lisa Jefferson, *The Medieval Account Books of the Mercers of London: An Edition and Translation*, 2 vols. (Farnham, UK: Ashgate, 2009), 1:409. The Mercers' Company records the expense "for 4 garlands of roses at the election of the new wardens, total—6d" in 1428.

8 These entries appear in Kingdon, *Archives*, 98 and 104.

9 Anne Wickham, "The Garlands of the Barbers' Company," *Barbers' Historical Group*, fol. 3 (2002), 51–57, here 52.

10 John L. Nevinson, "Crowns and Garlands of the Livery Companies," *Guildhall Studies in London History* 1 (1974): 68–81.

11 Companies not mentioned in Nevinson's study that also record the use of embroidered garlands in their history include the Clothworkers, Tallow Chandlers, and Goldsmiths.

12 Among the companies known to be continuing the custom are the Barber Surgeons, Carpenters, Cooks, Drapers, Girdlers, and Leathersellers.

techniques used in these objects with other extant textiles, making it possible for us to determine more precise dates of construction.

THE BRODERERS' CROWNS

Of these extant garlands, the most elaborate are the two still in possession of the Broderers' Company. These are also the only ones to emulate closely the original fresh floral garlands: Rose, larkspur, and lily are among the flowers represented, along with fruits such as grapes, strawberries, pomegranates, and cherries.[13] A casual observer in the sixteenth century would have seen the surface beauty of the crown: the floral design, the colour, and the sparkle of the gold and silver threads. However, these were special ceremonial objects to be used in the annual celebration of the duly elected masters of the Broderers' Company and illustrate the highest level of skill practiced by the professional Tudor embroiderer. Members of the company would have appreciated the skill and creativity required to produce these quality products and would have taken much pride in the work of their professional peers.[14]

Both crowns are outstanding examples of the embroiderer's art: bands of silk velvet exquisitely embroidered around the circumference with fruits, flowers, and the dove badge of the Broderers' Company. They are approximately 7.6 centimetres (3 inches) high and have a circumference of approximately 71 centimetres (28 inches). They are embellished on the upper and lower edges with a fringe made from a combination of silk and gold filé.[15] The inner surface of each crown is embroidered with the Latin motto of the Broderers' Company, *omnia de super*, in opulent, large uppercase lettering, the words separated by small embroidered decorations. On the outer surface, the same fruits and flowers are for the most part depicted on both crowns, but the embroiderer employed different materials and techniques to construct each of them. The motifs on one crown are small and have not been padded, so that the decoration, once placed onto the surface of the velvet, appears to be flat. The motifs on the other crown appear to be padded and overlap one another, giving the embroidery a densely covered and "raised" surface. Therefore, for identification purposes throughout this article, the crowns are designated "flat" and "raised" accordingly.

On a purely aesthetic level, the raised crown (fig. 7.1) is the more appealing of the two.[16] There is a fine band of lace woven from filé and narrow plate running along the inside edge of both top and bottom fringes. The floral design (fig. 7.2) is repeated

---

13 Nevinson, "Crowns," 72. Nevinson suggested that the embroidery on the crowns indicates a later date of perhaps the mid-seventeenth century.
14 Jasmine Kilburn-Toppin, "Gifting Cultures and Artisanal Guilds in Sixteenth- and Early Seventeenth-Century London," *Historical Journal* 60, no. 4 (2017): 865–87; see 883: "[T]he objects presented for use at election ceremonies were highly valuable, both in their use of precious natural and manufactured materials, such as gold, silver, rock crystal, pearl, and velvet, and through exquisite craftsmanship."
15 See explanation of terms starting on page 177.
16 The raised crown appears in several publications as a black-and-white photograph or drawing.

Cynthia Jackson

Fig. 7.1: Broderers' crown with "raised" embroidery. Photo: Cynthia Jackson, courtesy of the Broderers' Company.

166

Fig. 7.2: Line drawing of section D of the raised crown. Drawing: Cynthia Jackson.

four times around the circumference, separated by the larger badges. The design is very uniform in layout, material, technique, and execution, and the very consistent quality of stitch and technique distinguishes it as a superlative example of the skill of the professional embroiderer. It has survived remarkably intact: The original colour of the silk thread is recognizable, the stitches are well executed overall, and the uniformity of the twist and use of the metal thread is notable, although the metal itself is tarnished. There are three missing appliqués along the top edge, and letters or initials—an F, a C, and an S—appear to have been sewn on the velvet before these motifs were stitched in place. The outlines of the missing leaves are clearly visible as imprints on the velvet, and one can speculate that there may be another initial under the fourth leaf, which remains in place. On other livery crowns such as those of the Carpenters and Brewers, the initials of the wardens at the time of presentation were prominently displayed.[17] The fact that these very small letters were covered may indicate that they belonged to the embroiderers who created the garland, serving as a maker's mark[18] rather than a perpetual acknowledgment of the donor or warden at the time of the garland's creation.

At first glance, the flat crown (fig. 7.3) is much less visually appealing: It is in very fragile condition and has not survived the accumulation of centuries of dust and grime as well as the raised crown has. Its design, although similar, is more formal. The flowers and fruits are arranged on a trellis in a similar pattern in all four sections (fig. 7.4). The colours of the silk are much less vivid, and much of the stitching has been worn away. Moreover, the techniques and materials used differ greatly from those of the raised crown.[19] The flat crown's design is more traditional; the buds, leaves, and stems meander gracefully through the trellis to give it a more delicate appearance. A detailed examination reveals a more improvised or creative approach to the selection of materials and techniques used to embroider the motifs. Each fruit and flower consists of several layers of stitching using coloured silks and a wide variety of metal threads; the twist of the metal thread is inconsistent throughout; and, in contrast to the raised crown, each motif possesses its own unique combination of materials. It is this varied and complicated layering of colourful silk and shiny metal that achieves what must have been a remarkable scintillating effect while preserving a uniformly realistic appearance.

BACKGROUND

The crowns came to this author's attention while she was researching the history of the professional Tudor embroiderer. Both crowns have been in storage—unused—at

---

17 Kilburn-Toppin, "Gifting Cultures," 883.
18 Ibid., 877.
19 Although the embroidery techniques and materials used on the flat crown are unusual, other sixteenth-century objects using similar attributes exist; see notes 70 and 74 below.

the Mercers' Hall for many years. In 1910, Past Master Christopher Holford described them in his published general history of the company:

> They consist of broad bands of brocade, very much the worse for wear, but most elegantly worked; the silk stuff being woven with raised figures and gold and silver threads; the subjects being flowers and leaves, with a centre garter containing the Company's emblem of the Holy Dove.[20]

Attempts have been made to determine the origins and history of the crowns before 1910 but to date, there has been no documentary evidence found. All of the day-to-day records of the company were destroyed during the Fire of London in 1666. The surviving documents, mainly consisting of the company's royal charters, conveyances and ordinance books, and the Court Minute Books beginning in 1679, are held by the Guildhall Library. The first mention of the crowns as individual objects does not appear in the extant records until 1926, when a representative of the Victoria and Albert Museum (henceforth V&A) included "the old embroidered crowns" in a review of the company's "plate and other works of art" conducted for the purposes of a potential loan for an upcoming exhibition. The V&A subsequently offered to "have them cleaned and repaired by their own experts at no charge to the Company."[21] This generous offer was accepted, and the crowns appeared in the accompanying catalog described as "519. TWO MASTERS' CROWNS, embroidered. Late sixteenth century" along with a black-and-white photograph of the raised crown, numbered plate 70.[22]

The crowns were included in a valuation required for insurance purposes when a loan of the embroidered crowns and banners was requested for the "Exhibition of English Decorative Art at Lansdowne House" in 1929. The valuation indicates that the crowns were included in the company policy, and the value was to be "left in the general sum of £500."[23] They appear in the catalogue as a pair of masters' crowns of crimson velvet with "a rich design of flowers and fruits, embroidered mainly in button-holing."[24] It is worth noting that neither of the crowns is embroidered using the referenced technique.

---

20 Christopher Holford, *A Chat About the Broderers' Company* (London: George Allen and Sons, 1910), 24.

21 Court Minute Book (1909–33), London, Metropolitan Archives, CLC/L/BG/B/001/MS14657/008, 352–53, letter of Jan. 6, 1926.

22 William W. Watts, *An Exhibition of Works of Art Belonging to the Livery Companies of the City of London* (London: Victoria and Albert Museum, 1927). This image was later requested by Leigh Ashton of the V&A for publication in an article for *International Studio* magazine (see note 25 below); Court Minute Book (1909–33), 421–22, letter of Nov. 23, 1929. No reference to any repair work done on the objects included this exhibition was found in the V&A archives. The only remaining documented evidence of the exhibition is a black-and-white photograph, "View of the North Court Victoria and Albert Museum during the City Companies Exhibition"; V&A Archive, MA/32/198 (1927), no. 58790.

23 Court Minute Book (1909–33), 404 (Dec. 1928).

24 A. J. B. Wace and Helen Wace, *Illustrated Catalogue of the Loan Exhibition of English Decorative Art at Lansdowne House* (London: The Collector, 1929), 13.

Fig. 7.3: Broderers' crown with "flat" embroidery. Photo: Cynthia Jackson, courtesy of the Broderers' Company.

Fig. 7.4: Line drawing of section C of the flat crown. Drawing: Cynthia Jackson.

The raised crown was pictured with two other embroidered livery crowns in a 1931 article by Leigh Ashton.[25] In comparison with the Girdlers' and Carpenters' crowns that were also illustrated, Ashton writes: "The Broderers' is the most interesting as here is an early example of a floral design such as was to become the most popular of all Elizabethan patterns. In this example it has still the stiff formality of the border of a Flemish illuminated manuscript …."[26]

George Wingfield Digby presents the crowns in his *Elizabethan Embroidery* and includes a plate with the same photograph and this description:

> It is a crown of tawny-orange velvet and is embroidered with a rich floral pattern in which silver and gold in a great variety of threads and strips have been used, together with coloured silks, also with seed pearls, though these have now almost entirely disappeared; the use of silver strips in place of sequins is noteworthy. The method of embroidery is principally couched work, with a certain amount of raised work.[27]

It is an accurate description, and he further declares that they "show a cosmopolitan sense of style, and the rich but not heavy or gaudy effects which the best professional embroiderers in Queen Elizabeth's reign could achieve."

The latest publication of an image of the raised crown was in Percy Levy's *Plain Dealing Fellows*, in which he mentions both crowns only briefly in connection with their loan to the 1926 V&A exhibition.[28]

RATIONALE FOR RECONSTRUCTION OF THE FLAT CROWN

Until recently, the crowns were stored in a specially constructed wooden box. Although very sturdy, lined with velvet, and fitted with forms to secure the crowns, it was not an ideal situation. Both crowns were removed to separate conservation-grade textile storage boxes with unbuffered acid-free padding in 2016. At that time, neither crown had been subject to any conservation treatment. Due to its unusual use of technique,[29] variety of materials, and extremely damaged condition, this author determined that a preliminary visual assessment of the flat crown by qualified conservators would be

---

25 Leigh Ashton, "Elizabethan and Jacobean Secular Embroidery," *International Studio*, Aug. 1931, 40–43.
26 Ibid., 40.
27 George Wingfield Digby, *Elizabethan Embroidery* (New York: Thomas Yoseloff, 1963), 75–76.
28 Percy R. Levy, *Plain Dealing Fellows: A Second Chat About the Broderers' Company* (London: Worshipful Company of Broderers, 1986), 33: "The Museum offered to clean and repair free of charge the Company's two ancient embroidered crowns." See also the plate on 34, captioned as follows: "One of two Masters embroidered crowns (late sixteenth century). Its diameter of nine inches was presumably to accommodate a full bottomed wig, or a swollen head!" The crowns are included in a list of plate and treasures on 87, "TWO MASTER'S CROWNS. Late sixteenth century."
29 The stitches commonly used in this period are generally referred to as "Elizabethan" and include looped, knotted, buttonhole, and a variety of chained or laddered stitches; see Jacqui Carey, *Elizabethan Stitches: A Guide to Historic English Needlework* (Ottery St. Mary, UK: Carey Co., 2012).

a practical course of action. In their report, the conservators recommended adopting only measures to prevent further damage, such as correct storage with respect to light, temperature, and humidity, and a policy of minimal handling only with nitrile gloves.[30] Any attempt to restore the flat crown's original magnificence could damage its significance as a historical artefact, and its current condition would suggest that public display or exhibition would be unlikely. In consideration of the flat crown's importance as an extremely rare and exceptional example of a highly valued sixteenth-century art[31] and because of the restrictions imposed by conservation recommendations, the author determined that it would be desirable to reproduce the flat crown as accurately as possible[32] so that an accessible illustration of this extraordinary specimen could be made available for exhibition and to other institutions for educational purposes.

The author identified several potential learning outcomes from such an undertaking. Research into the traditional use of the object and its origin of design and choice of motifs would be possible from social, civic, and art historical perspectives. However, the primary goal of a detailed examination and reconstruction of the flat crown was to identify and document the materials and techniques employed by professional Tudor embroiderers. Subsequently, the reconstruction was supported both by the 2016 Professional Development Award from the Textile Society and by the 2017 Janet Arnold Award from the Society of Antiquaries of London. This article presents the reconstruction methodology employed, the challenges encountered, and the outcomes of the study.

INITIAL OBSERVATIONS

The outer design of the flat crown consists of four sections separated by four large badges (none of which is intact). Originally, the outer design consisted of eighty motifs (fig. 7.5 and table 7.1). Ten are now missing, leaving impressions in the velvet that help to identify the shapes of the lost pieces. Many of the remaining seventy motifs are in poor condition: Except for the gold filé, which retains its original colour, the metal

---

30 Jessica Burgess, unpublished condition report, Oct. 2017. The author is grateful to Janie Lightfoot Textiles, which generously sent two conservators, Jessica Burgess and Jenny Beasley, to examine the crown at Mercers' Hall early in October 2017.

31 Eleri Lynn, *Tudor Fashion* (New Haven, CT: Yale University Press, 2017), 33; Charles Germain de Saint-Aubin, *Art of the Embroiderer*, trans. Nikke Scheuer (Los Angeles: Los Angeles County Museum of Art, 1983), 145; Maria Hayward, *Dress at the Court of King Henry VIII: The Wardrobe Book of the Wardrobe of the Robes prepared by James Worsley in December 1516, edited from Harley MS 2284, and His Inventory Prepared on 17 January 1521, edited from Harley MS 4217, both in the British Library* (Leeds: Maney, 2007), 187 and 360. Guild inventories indicated the crowns were valuable enough to keep them in the treasury with the plate. Further research is necessary to quantify the use of embroidery during the Tudor era; to date research on textile items has primarily focused on specific textile type and colour and cut of fashion, not the embellishment.

32 Because the raised crown was almost entirely intact and in a considerably less fragile state, the author decided against recreating it and chose instead to focus on the reconstruction of the flat crown.

Fig. 7.5: Diagram of the motifs on the flat Broderer's crown. Drawing: Cynthia Jackson.

Table 7.1: Motifs and their locations on the diagram of the flat crown (fig. 7.5)

Motif	Section and location			
	A	B	C	D
Half roses	A1	B20	C41	D56
Cherries	A2, A4	B22, B24	C38, C40	D57, D59
Cherry leaves	A3	B23	C39	D58
Larkspur	A5	—	C43	D60
Rose buds	A6	B25	—	D61
Open roses	A7	B26	C42	—
Closed lilies	A8	B28	C44	—
Pomegranates	A9	B32	C46	D65
Lily leaves	A10, A11	B30, B31	C47	D63, D64
Grapes	A12	B29	C48	—
Strawberry flower	A13			
Strawberries	A14, A19	B33, B37	C51	D70
Strawberry leaves	A15, A16, A17, A18	B34, B35, B36	C52, C53, C54, C55	D66, D67, D68, D69
Rose leaves	—	B21	—	—
Open lilies	—	B27	C45	D62
Grape leaves	—	—	C49, C50	—

Notes: Dove badges are located between sections B and A (BA) and sections D and C (DC); the scrollwork frame is on the border between sections C and B (CB). A fourth badge is missing but would be at DA. Other possible missing motifs are (by section): (A) an open lily at the bottom of the trellis oval; (B) a larkspur and a strawberry flower; (C) a strawberry, a strawberry flower, and a rose bud; (D) a strawberry, a strawberry flower, an open rose, grapes, and a closed lily.

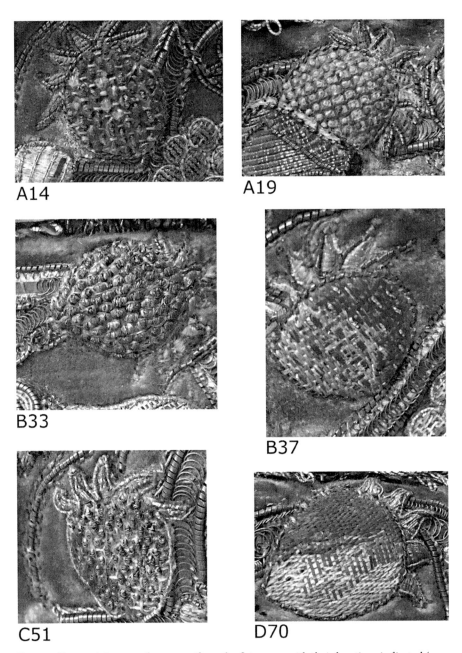

Fig. 7.6: Six remaining strawberry motifs on the flat crown with their locations indicated (see fig. 7.5). Photos: Cynthia Jackson, courtesy of the Broderers' Company.

threads have tarnished, and many are broken and distorted, whether bent or out of alignment. There may have been dozens of seed pearls highlighting specific areas of the design, but only one, in a sheltered location, remains securely attached.

Between each section of fruit and flowers are embroidered badges similar to those sewn onto livery gowns and which identified the wearer as a member of specific company or guild in sixteenth-century London.[33] The Broderers' badge, which depicts the dove as the Holy Ghost on a blue ground surrounded by rays and set within a scroll-work frame, appears twice.[34] All that remains of a third badge is an empty scrollwork frame which may have surrounded an oval enameled badge depicting the Broderers' arms.[35] The fourth badge is missing entirely.[36]

All the motifs and badges were embroidered separately on a ground fabric of fine linen, and each motif was uniquely stitched. For example, there were originally eight strawberry motifs, two located in each of the four sections. Two have been either removed or lost, and each of the remaining six (fig. 7.6) was embroidered using a unique combination of separate layers worked with silk thread and very fine strips of metal and coiled wire (fig. 7.7). This suggests that the missing strawberries were also unique.

The flowers, fruits, and leaves were cut from the linen ground and appliquéd in four sections on the velvet ground which had been previously prepared with the four embroidered trellises. The four sections are almost identical, but each is unique in the level of skill and the choice of technique, suggesting that perhaps it was the work of more than one embroiderer.

EMBROIDERY MATERIALS

The silk threads used for adding texture and colour were likely purchased dyed and ready to work when obtained from a silkwoman.[37] They appear to have no discernible twist. The motifs missing from the crown have been lost and therefore could not be examined for technical details. The remaining motifs are still securely attached, so there was no opportunity to examine them from the underside, making it impossible

33 "Report of the Commissioners: Part 2," in *City of London Livery Companies Commission: Report and Appendix* (London: Eyre and Spottiswoode, 1884), 1:21 n. 1.

34 Grant of arms to the Company by William Hervy (Clarenceux), Aug. 17, 1558; London, Metropolitan Archives, CLC/L/BG/A/011/MS31365. The dove appears on the crest on the Broderers' Company arms.

35 Similar to the company arms badges attached to the Leathersellers' crowns; or there might have been a City of London badge similar to that on the Carpenters' Company crown. See Appendix 7.1.

36 This may have been an embroidered shield of the Broderers' Company arms similar to company arms on the Parish Clerks', Brewers', and Carpenters' crowns. See Appendix 7.1.

37 References to purchasing silk threads for embroidery directly from silkwomen (and to a lesser extent silkmen) are abundant in wardrobe accounts and household accounts throughout the century. See Janet Arnold, *Queen Elizabeth's Wardrobe Unlock'd* (Leeds, UK: Maney, 1988), 219–27.

Fig. 7.7: Embroidery layers for the reconstruction of the strawberry motifs. Darker lines indicate the stitching added in each of the numbered steps. See article text for definitions of material terms. All silk threads are 6-fold (120 denier) silk loose twist. Regarding colour names for the selected silk threads, see note 50. (1) Satin stitch berry with two strands of Carnation. (2) Stitch sixteen vertical rows of fine plate across berry. (3) Couch gilt filé in each section of the calyx. Twist three strands of Basil together and place fifteen horizontal stitches across plate. (4) Stitch across the filé with one strand of Basil, bunching and bending the filé to fit the shape of the calyx. Do not completely cover the filé. Stitch small pieces of check thread over the long rows of Basil in between the plate. (5) Stitch around the check pieces with two strands of Roseate and Glace in the areas indicated to effect shading. Stitch around the remaining check pieces with two strands of Linden. Couch heavier filé around the perimeter of the strawberry and calyx. Drawing: Cynthia Jackson.

to determine the sequence of stitching and type of thread, as well as the colour prior to any damage caused by exposure to light or the accumulation of dust.

Crimson silk velvet was a popular ground fabric for embroidered garlands as it was used by other guilds at the time, but extant examples of crimson appear to have retained much of their original colour and thus suggest a different choice of colour for the Broderers' crowns, since they are a lighter or more faded colour.

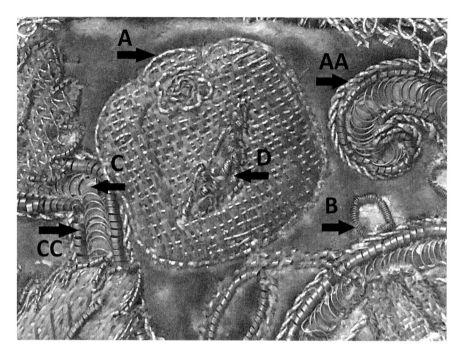

Fig. 7.8: Part of section C, motif 46, of the flat crown, indicating the different types of metal. Labeled here: (A) filé; (AA) two-ply filé; (B) round wire; (C) flattened wire, or plate; (CC) coiled plate; (D) wire with rectangular cross-section. Photo: Cynthia Jackson.

The metal threads used on the flat crown can be put into two categories: all metal and metal with a silk core. The latter type is sometimes called filé or passing. To produce a filé thread (fig. 7.8, at A), a fine metal strip is wound around a core of yellow silk. Documents from the early sixteenth century refer to this type of thread as venice (*venyce*) gold.[38] Several different thicknesses of filé are used in different areas of the crown, and in some cases two threads are twisted together to make a two-ply cord (fig. 7.8, at AA). Filé was also couched with silk thread on the ground singly or in pairs. A different colour of silk thread could have been used to add shape or shading: for example, in a regular upright brick pattern or tapestry stitch, or by placing stitches at varying distances from one another, concentrating the colour, and obscuring the gold to an extent as is the case for *or nué*.[39]

The all-metal threads are not really threads at all: They are varying shapes and thickness of wire, manipulated, twisted, or cut to provide an almost limitless range of sizes and textures. Gold, silver, and silver-gilt were all used during the sixteenth

38 Santina Levey, "The Art of the Broderers," in *The Inventory of King Henry VIII*, vol. 2, *Textiles and Dress*, ed. Maria Hayward and Philip Ward (London: Harvey Miller, 2012), 145–86, here 154.
39 *Or nué* (shaded gold) is a type of goldwork embroidery produced with a couching technique.

century,[40] when all-metal wire thread was referred to as "gold of damask."[41] There are three shapes of wire used on the crown: round wire, flattened wire, and wire that is rectangular in cross-section. Many different sizes of each are used for different effects. Different gauges of wire are used on the crown to achieve different textures. For example, a very fine wire is sewn vertically around the dove to add dimension, while a heavier gauge is used to embroider the centre of the trellis.

The round wire (fig. 7.8, at B) is wound onto a long needle to produce a coil. Then the needle is removed, and the spring is pulled to separate the coils to the desired distance depending on the amount of flexibility needed in the design. The coil is then flattened—likely with the fingers or by putting it through a roll(er)ing mill—and couched onto the surface of the fabric.[42] A very fine round wire is also used to wind around a core of coloured silk to make a composite thread.[43]

The flattened wire is referred to as plate, and a very narrow plate sewn down in rows or grid patterns provides the base for many of the shaded motifs. A plate of medium width (fig. 7.8, at C) is threaded through the coiled round wire before flattening the spring. A marginally thicker plate is wound on a very fine round needle to produce a smooth, dense coil that modern manufacturers call lizerine or lizerdine. The sixteenth-century lizerine plate was produced in many different widths and wound on several sizes of needle producing coils of different diameters. The length of coiled plate is used mainly for outlining and is secured on the surface with couching stitches that are placed between the individual coils (fig. 7.8, at CC).[44] Coloured silk is also stitched between the individual coils or sometimes threaded through the centre of the coiled length. Wide plate is cut to form the triangular-shaped rays on the badges.

The rectangular wire (fig. 7.8, at D) is twisted onto an irregular-shaped needle, which provides the bends in what is called now called check thread; when the needle is removed and the tension on the coiled wire is released, the coil unwinds a little, misaligning the bends. This adds texture and allows the light to reflect off the different flat areas, thereby increasing the sparkle.[45]

40 Christine Balloffet Carr, "Materials and Techniques of Secular Embroidery," in *English Embroidery from the Metropolitan Museum of Art, 1580–1700: 'Twixt Art and Nature*, ed. Andrew Morrall and Melinda Watt (New Haven: Yale University Press, 2008), 99–106, here 99–100.

41 Levey, "Art of the Broderers," 154.

42 Both the technique and materials used here are unusual. The thread is not lizerine nor pearl purl (see Appendix, note 2), although there is an undescribed example in Carey, *Elizabethan Stitches*, 53, fig. 58.

43 We can find a similar thread illustrated in Carey, *Elizabethan Stitches*, 12, fig. 9, but the wire used in the crown is coiled more uniformly around the silk core, and the resulting thread is couched in rows similar to couching rows of filé.

44 There is a brief reference to this in Carey, *Elizabethan Stitches*, 13, fig. 10.

45 Elizabeth Glover, *The Gold and Silver Wyre-Drawers* (London: Phillimore, 1979), 4. The check used in the crown is neither bright nor dull but of a single type that does not fit into either modern category, as it is made with a thicker, rectangular-shaped wire.

The process used to spin the different shapes of wire used by the embroiderer is now referred to as purling, and the resulting length of coiled wire is cut into shorter lengths as required, to stitch onto the design. These individual shorter pieces are referred to as purls. It is not clear who spun the wire into the variety of forms used on the crown. The wire-drawing process had been employed in London since the fifteenth century.[46] It is possible that the purling process was done by the wire drawer and that the embroiderer purchased it ready for use. An example of this is found in the wardrobe accounts of 1536–37, which records that a gold-drawer was paid for "pypes and pyrles for a gowne for my ladys grace."[47] It is also possible that the silkwomen who spun silk threads spun wire as well.[48] However, the range of sizes, diameters, and shapes and, importantly, the lack of consistency in the coiled wires in the flat crown may also indicate that the embroiderer, an apprentice, or someone close at hand created bespoke metal threads as they were needed from wire or plate that had been purchased from a wire drawer.[49]

RECONSTRUCTION

The initial step was to photograph the crown in detail. As every one of the seventy remaining floral elements is different and there was no opportunity to deconstruct the artefact to investigate methods from the underside, the author photographed each motif in detail. Each section was labeled, moving from right to left, with a letter, and the badges were identified with two letters locating them between sections (for example, "BA" is between sections A and B). A number was assigned to each fruit, flower, and trellis and was added to the letter of the section to which it belonged (e.g., B26).

Measurements were required to determine the size of each element and to place each element in its correct relative position. To avoid handling the artefact, the author used dividers to take measurements, which were then used to create scale drawings of the motifs to be compiled into a pattern for the crown.

Because of the accumulation of dust, the likelihood of fading, and the inability to examine the underside for original colour, determining the colour of the silk threads was challenging. In some cases the thread had disintegrated entirely, leaving only holes to indicate where stitches had been. The author used commercially available sample

---

46 Ibid., 6.
47 Fredrick Madden, *Privy Purse Expenses of the Princess Mary* (London: William Pickering, 1831), 12. See also Glover, *Wyre-Drawers*, 6 n. 20.
48 Glover, *Wyre-Drawers*, 16. Women and children were employed as outworkers to spin gold and silver thread in the seventeenth century.
49 The original will of John Farnham, "imbrotherer," included a device called a "twistinge wheele" in the list of embroidery tools he bequeathed to his servant. London, Metropolitan Archives, DL/AL/C/003/MS09052, Archdeaconry Court of London, Feb. 22, 1612.

swatches of silk to tentatively identify the colours in each motif on the flat crown.[50] A review of the underside of a selection of other extant sixteenth-century embroidered artefacts at the V&A confirmed that the colours were likely to have been vivid.[51]

All of the appliquéd motifs were stitched individually on a fine ground fabric. Upon close examination of the original, it was possible to see the linen ground material where stitches were worn, where the appliqués had fallen off, or where they had been previously removed. There is no evidence of how the original embroiderer transferred the design to the linen; it may have been by a prick-and-pounce method, or the design may have been drawn or traced directly on the linen using ink, charcoal, or lead. The author could however see the pattern shape through the very fine linen and thus traced each motif individually using a pencil.

The metal threads had tarnished, and it was impossible to determine the original colour (silver or silver-gilt) of the metal without chemical analysis or microphotography, both of which were outside the scope of the project. Moreover, many of the different types and sizes of required metal threads are not currently commercially available. Metal threads manufactured today are uniform in shape and size, making it impossible to recreate the inconsistencies in the sixteenth-century threads. The author produced some through experimentation, but others could not be reconstructed, and therefore substitutions were required. An example of the former is the combination thread used in one of the dove badges which consists of a fine gold wire wrapped around a silk core.[52] The author found a commercial version of this thread, but experimental stitching indicated that it was far too small in diameter, and the shade required for the crown was not in the available colour range. The author arrived at a close approximation of the original thread by making a tight coil of commercially available 34-gauge gold-filled wire on a narrow needle, removing the needle, carefully threading the core silk through the coil, and then gently pulling the coil open as evenly as possible.[53] A substitution also had to be found for the check thread: The diameter and shape of the gold wire used in the sixteenth century and the irregular-shaped needle required to produce an angular twist proved elusive. Although not ideal, a commercially available modern thread was used in place of the original.

High-resolution photography was helpful in determining stitch sequence and technique. The four trellises and large badges were closely examined. Although all were similar, there was a marked difference in sequence of stitch and materials: For example, the two doves on the badges were of the same size and outline, but each had been intricately stitched by combining very different techniques. The author kept a photographic record of each embroidered element as she progressed and followed

---

50 A sample card of available colours and weights from Devere Yarns in Halsted, England (www.devereyarns.co.uk), was used to select appropriate silks.
51 Author's visual survey of sixteenth-century objects conducted with the assistance of Susan North, Curator of Fashion, 1550–1800, V&A, Oct. 2017.
52 See the description of round wire threads on page 180.
53 See note 43 above.

them carefully when embroidering the motifs for the final reconstruction. Sketches of each layer and suggestions for colour and metal thread were made for every motif. The author stitched a sample of each fruit and flower completely using available materials and then updated the sketches and recorded any adjustments necessary for the final series of motifs.

After all the embroidered elements were complete, the underside of each needed to be coated with a stabilizer to reduce the risk of fraying. Rabbit glue was likely used on the original and is still available. However, it dries to a very stiff consistency and is difficult to stitch through, making appliquéing the motifs on the original embroidery much harder on the hands, almost certainly requiring the use of thimbles.[54] The author found a more conservation-friendly solution in the form of a commercially available adhesive which dries with a greater degree of flexibility. It is stable and is completely removable if necessary. Each element was painted on the underside with a fine brush, allowed to dry completely, and then trimmed as close as possible to the edge of the embroidery to reduce the visibility of the linen ground.

The original colour of the silk velvet used for the background was difficult to determine. It has been described as a variety of colours in different publications.[55] Consultation with professional conservators confirmed that results of recent studies on the use of safflower dyes on sixteenth-century silk fabrics were consistent with the characteristics displayed in the velvet of the crown. The consultations confirmed that "the fading is consistent with other objects that are confirmed to be dyed with Safflower"[56] and that the original colour may have been a "deep orange red" rather than crimson.[57]

It is possible that the Broderers deliberately chose a slightly different shade of red, scarlet being the colour occasionally used to distinguish officials of the artisan community in official ceremonies.[58] Since scarlet is the liturgical colour closely associated with Pentecost, it is also a likely choice in view of the Broderers' association with that celebration. The Broderers were also known as "the Brotherhood of the Holy Ghost," which provides an explanation for the dove symbol of the Holy Spirit as depicted on the two identifiable badges on the crown. The election of officers traditionally took place on the day following Whitsunday, the beginning of Pentecost and the day marking the manifestation of the Holy Spirit to the Apostles.[59]

54 An assortment of late medieval thimbles and needles were on exhibit at the Museum of London as of April 2019.

55 For "brownish-red," see Nevinson, "Crowns," 76; for "tawny-orange," see Digby, *Elizabethan Embroidery*, 75; for "crimson," see Barbara Snook, *English Embroidery* (London: Mills & Boon, 1970), 37.

56 Burgess, condition report.

57 Email correspondence with Jessica Burgess, Janie Lightfoot Textiles, Oct. 15, 2017.

58 Maria Hayward, "Luxury or Magnificence?" *Costume* 30, no. 1 (1996): 37–46, here 42.

59 Broderers Ordinances, 1528, London, Metropolitan Archives, COL/AD/01/014, letter book O, 100v.

A base of medium-weight cotton[60] was mounted in a slate frame,[61] and two long rectangles of silk velvet were stitched onto the surface. The author determined how to position the four sections of trellis—all made with different combinations and sizes of flattened round wire coils, plate, lizerine, and cord—and stitched each in place on one of the rectangles of velvet. After having been basted in place, the individual fruit and flower motifs were also stitched in place, with the author facing challenges in maintaining the correct positioning due to the pile of the velvet. Even with the motif basted in place, the pile would shift as the motif was being stitched around its edge, altering the angle of placement.[62] Before starting to stitch around, the author had to place tacking stitches at strategic locations—several points around the edge or through the motif itself depending on the shape—before stitching the motif securely to the velvet. Motifs and stems stitched over the trellis were also a challenge owing to the density of the metal thread: Very fine needles were required to find small gaps between the layers of metal thread—especially when the close rows of plate within the motif coincided with the plate in the trellis—through which to sew. Stems and veins were worked directly on the velvet, connecting and completing the design (fig. 7.9).

On the second rectangle, the borders of flattened coils of gold wire threaded with medium-width plate, alternating with spangles and gold filé, were embroidered along the top and bottom edges. The letters of the motto, which had been stitched individually in rows of plate, overstitched with brick stitch in yellow silk, and outlined in lizerine, were placed and stitched between the borders, and additional motifs were stitched directly onto the velvet.

With all the embroidery complete, the underside of the embroidered rectangles was painted with a thin layer of adhesive to reduce the risk of fraying. When it was completely dry, the embroidery was removed from the frame, and the two pieces of velvet trimmed to the correct size.

The supporting inner core on the original crown can only be seen through a small gap in the stitching between the velvet and the fringe, and the content was unidentifiable without further, more invasive analysis. It was possibly made of wood or of layers of linen rag paper compressed into a firm form. The latter seems more likely, as this method has been attested in the stiffening of collars in extant garments from the

---

60 There was no visible evidence of a backing fabric on the original, and there was no opportunity to examine the underside of the embroidery. Some contemporary examples of metal-thread embroidery are stitched directly on the velvet, for example, Museum of London, no. C2116 (a short cloak of crimson velvet with gold embroidery worked directly on the velvet with no linen backing). However, because of the weight and large number of motifs being stitched through the modern silk velvet, which was less closely woven than the original, the author chose to add the extra security of the cotton layer.

61 A slate frame is the device used to hold the fabric taut while working. It is very similar to the apparatus used in the sixteenth century. See Arnold, *Queen Elizabeth's Wardrobe*, 219 and fig. 273.

62 The original embroiderers working on the denser, shorter pile on the original velvet might not have had the same issues with the pile shifting as the author did.

Fig. 7.9: Reconstruction embroidery in progress on a slate frame. Photo: Cynthia Jackson.

sixteenth century.[63] The core for the reconstruction was made of two layers of heavy interfacing,[64] cut to the exact size required and glued together in a complete circle to provide a substantial foundation. The construction method used on the original crown could not be determined without deconstruction, but on close inspection the velvet appeared to be glued into place on the core.

As the making of silk fringe is outside the purview of an embroiderer, it was necessary to find a specialist in handmade passementerie.[65] Initial experimentation indicated that weaving two separate fringes—a gold one and a silk one—would be the most effective process to recreate the combined fringe, particularly as the gold filé had to be hand-twisted as it was woven. Then, the silk and gold fringes were basted together to make a single combined fringe.

The inner layer of velvet, embroidered with the letters of the Broderers' motto, was basted onto the core first, and then the fringe was pinned along the top and bottom edges of the outside of the core. The outer layer of embroidered velvet was placed over the fringe and pinned carefully to the core. The two layers of velvet were carefully stitched together through the fringe to complete the reconstruction (fig. 7.10).

The only remaining issue was how the crown was actually used: Its circumference made it too large to rest comfortably on an average-sized head. Careful examination did not reveal any visible remnants of attachments as were common for other extant examples of sixteenth-century livery crowns. It may be that they were worn over the crown of a hat, resting on the brim. There are several examples of large brimmed hats worn during the last half of the sixteenth century; however, the style known today as a Tudor bonnet seems a likely candidate. Several livery companies still employ hats of this style on official occasions,[66] and they are also used in formal graduation ceremonies.[67] Alternatively, the garland may simply have been carried by the new warden and placed on the table before him, as is currently the case in the Barber Surgeons' ceremony.[68] The fact that there are no visible wear marks or any other evidence that would indicate that the crown was worn may suggest that it was simply presented and not worn.[69]

---

63 Susan North, in conversation with author, Oct. 9, 2017.

64 For historical accuracy, the author might have used either compressed linen rags or wood pulp as stiffening instead of heavy interfacing.

65 The fringe was created by Gina Barrett, Gina-B Silkworks, Grantham, Lincolnshire (www.ginab-silkworks.co.uk).

66 See, for example, a photograph showing members of the Worshipful Company of Painter-Stainers; Linda Fasteson, "Imperial London," Notable Travels: Inspiration for Exceptional Journeys, www.notabletravels.com/imperial-london, accessed March 11, 2019.

67 The Tudor bonnet is part of the regalia currently used in the University of East Anglia Ph.D. ceremony.

68 Victoria West, archivist, Barber Surgeons' Company, email correspondence with author, Oct. 31, 2018.

69 This was the case for the cap of maintenance presented to the city of Waterford by Henry VIII with the instructions for it to be carried in the procession and not worn. Hayward, *Dress at the Court*, 286.

Fig. 7.10: Reproduction of flat crown. Photo: Bronwyn Jackson, courtesy of the Broderers' Company, used by permission.

CONCLUSION

The Broderers' flat crown is a rare example of the important and intricate work of the professional embroiderer of the sixteenth century.[70] Research into the traditional use of the livery crown or garland has established the significance of embroidered livery crowns as visual reminders of the important role embroidery played in the material culture of the City of London livery companies of the sixteenth century. The unique

---

70 Further investigation is required to locate other extant embroidered artefacts of the period that compare in technique and materials. On display at Petworth House in West Sussex (National Trust Collections no. 486522, viewable online at http://www.nationaltrustcollections.org.uk) is an embroidered panel believed to be the work of Lady Jane Grey. As she was executed in 1554, the panel would have been completed well before the crown's estimated date. It is a finely embroidered scrolling design of fruits, flowers, birds, and heraldic motifs on a white linen or silk ground. It is worked in silk and metal threads both filé and coiled metal and plate. Another comparable object is the mariner's cap (see note 76 below) on loan to the V&A, traditionally thought to have been presented to Sir Francis Drake by Queen Elizabeth I after his successful circumnavigation of the globe in 1580, thus dating it closer to the crown.

floral designs, the intricacy of the techniques, and the quality of the materials all in-dicate that the Broderers' Company was committed to maintaining a high level of workmanship while encouraging the continued development of their craft. The of-fice of Warden of the Broderers' Company held significant responsibilities, and the wearing of the embroidered garland was designed to encourage respect for the office and pride in the profession.

The marked difference in several aspects of the four embroidered sections of the flat crown suggests that the crown was the work of several embroiderers. The purpose of this is subject for speculation. The symbolic importance of a livery crown suggests that it may have been an exercise set by the wardens to determine the best, most ap-propriate application of materials and technique for the purpose at hand: a task set to the most prominent workshops to showcase their individual skills and styles on the same design, making this crown the result of a search for design, materials, and work-manship that constitute the most timely representation of the craft of the embroiderer.

Another possible theory is that the embroidery was the result of a set assignment to determine the skill level of an embroiderer. The third known set of ordinances was approved in 1562 with the Broderers' Company royal charter.[71] These were the first to include the requirement of the completion of a master piece. Ordinance 28 states: "No p[er]son to make woᵗke or sett upp any woᵗkhouse or shoppe before his masters peece be allowed" specifying that the "Keap[er]s or Wardens have appointed hym one pece of woᵗke to be made and wrought for example." The embroiderer was set this task to complete in one of the workrooms of the Hall of Brodery within a set period of time, and "no other p[er]son or p[er]sons shall come into the saied woᵗkehouse withoute licence of the Keap[er]s or Wardens or their Deputies duringe the tyme whilest the saied woᵗke is a woᵗking."[72] Upon completion, the sample was to be presented to the wardens and assistants for examination. It is possible that the individual motifs or sections were the result of this task.[73]

Reconstructing this significant artefact has reaffirmed the high level of technical skill and creativity required for the vast quantities of embroidery demanded by an ev-er-increasing clientele, due in part to the significant rise in population over the century. The process has subsequently identified a variety of materials and complex layering techniques used in sixteenth-century embroidery but which are virtually unknown to practitioners and historians today. The resulting documentation of the techniques and materials will provide additional information to aid in the identification of em-broidery work of the Tudor period.

71 London, Metropolitan Archives, CLC/L/BG/A/006/MS14789, Dec. 4, 1562.
72 Ibid., fol. 10.
73 In any of these suppositions, although the pattern or design may have been provided on paper, instruction with respect to material and technique was most likely delivered verbally. Individual interpretation of verbal directions, possibly given by different instructors, may also explain the diversity in the motifs.

The Broderers' flat crown is only one of several recent rediscoveries of extant six-teenth-century professional embroideries. The Elizabethan burse now in the British Museum,[74] the Bacton altar cloth currently on display at Hampton Court,[75] and the mariner's cap and scarf on loan to the V&A from a private collection[76] are indications that there may be many embroideries dating from the sixteenth century in museums, country houses, and private collections all over the world. In the conclusion of her recent book *Tudor Fashion*, Eleri Lynn, collections curator at Historic Royal Palaces, writes: "There are Tudor fragments distributed in museums and homes across the country. Some are recognized and some are not. The prospect of discovering one of them is more than enough reason for the modern historian to keep looking."[77] The search for forgotten or overlooked extant examples of sixteenth-century embroidery in any condition is crucial because if they are not identified as such, they could instead be considered an insignificant fragment of embroidered textile and lost through ig-norance or neglect. Detailed examination of extant objects using high-resolution and extensive photography, ideally with a compositional analysis of the many styles of met-al threads[78] and use of different techniques, is indispensable. Whichever technique is used on an embroidered textile under study could, in concert with further targeted re-search, provide crucial evidence from which to construct a practical timeline of Tudor embroidery that would prove invaluable to future studies in textile and dress history.

74 London, British Museum, no. 1997,0301.1.
75 Eleri Lynn, "The Bacton Altar Cloth: Elizabeth I's 'long-lost skirt'?" *Costume* 52, no. 1 (2018): 3–25.
76 Angus Patterson, *Fashion and Armour in Renaissance Europe: Proud Looks and Brave Attire* (London: V&A Publishing, 2009), 50–51.
77 Lynn, *Tudor Fashion*, 171.
78 Carr, "Materials and Techniques," 100.

Appendix 7.1

Surviving Sixteenth- and Seventeenth-Century Embroidered Crowns of the City of London Livery Companies

The following embroidered garlands have remained as treasured possessions of their respective companies.[1] Their frequent inclusion in exhibitions and publications highlights their respected status as works of art. Their survival provides a unique opportunity to study the development of professional embroidery, to note the changes in threads and progression of techniques over a century, and, potentially, to stimulate discussion and generate hypotheses.

For example, the metal thread known as pearl purl was used sparingly in this period, with many crowns using only the smoother lizerine.[2] This may suggest that cost was a factor in the choice of thread; it may indicate a development in the production of drawn wire for embroidery; or perhaps the availability of metal thread was restricted during the seventeenth century. The presence of pearl purl also may indicate that a repair or replacement has been made to the original object, the original thread type (likely lizerine) not being available. Comparison with other extant embroideries may help to identify further details with regard to the date of production of other items of embroidery: A close examination of the damaged Girdlers' Company crown (see section IV below) indicates that lizerine was used for the most part, pearl purl being used only for emphasis, while the reproduction, made in the twentieth century, does not use any lizerine at all, pearl purl being used throughout. Further examination and documentation over a larger body of embroidered artefacts employing a prescribed methodology will help to develop a more accurate timeline of materials, design, technique, and perhaps even makers.

---

1   All the crowns in this list are catalogued in John L. Nevinson, "Crowns and Garlands of the Livery Companies," *Guildhall Studies in London History* 1 (1974): 68–81; hereafter cited as Nevinson. Nevinson's thorough study of the ceremonies included a catalogue of forty-eight extant crowns and garlands and provides a physical description of each, indicating that 19 were embroidered. However, there are few details with respect to threads or techniques used.
2   Lizerine is made with a length of flat plate with a rectangular cross-section which results in a coil with a smooth surface. Pearl purl is made with a wire with a C-shaped cross-section which results in a bumpy surface similar to a string of pearls. There is no pearl purl used on either of the Broderers' crowns.

I. THREE CROWNS OF THE BREWERS' COMPANY

Date: 1629.

Approximate dimensions: Height 8 centimetres, diameter 20 centimetres.

Description: All three crowns are identical on the outside and have two appliquéd motifs of a maiden holding grain—thought to be Thomas Becket's stepmother (fig. 7.11), eight appliquéd heads of grain (fig. 7.12), two appliqued shields of the company arms (fig. 7.13), and embroidered borders at top and bottom of purl and couched cord, on a crimson velvet ground. Garnished at upper and lower edges with applied filé lace. The dates "1628 : 1629" are embroidered on the inside of every one with the initials HL (Henry Leake), IH (John Heylin), or HB (Henry Bridges).

Materials: Filé, check purls of varying sizes, lizerine, coloured silks, composite silk and metal twisted cord.

Techniques: Appliquéd motifs consisting of silver filé grid, silk, gold filé hair, silk split stitch face and hands, silk and purl over linen padding. Couched cord, filé, and check purl details sewn directly on velvet. Red area of shield consists of filé made with silver strip loosely wound around a core of red silk couched in pairs with red silk. Initials and dates are appliqued gold-coloured satin outlined with two-ply filé cord. Circle motifs are twisted silk satin stitch surrounded by stitched knots.

Display and publication: On loan to the Guildhall Museum from 1949 to 1970. On exhibit at "Treasures of the City of London" during British Week in Vienna, October 1969. Nevinson, 72, plate 6, nos. 5, 6, 7.

Current location: On display in Brewers' Hall.

Current use: Not in use.

Figs. 7.11–7.13: Brewers' Company crown. Fig. 7.11 (opposite top): Figure of a maiden from the Brewers' Company arms. Fig. 7.12 (opposite middle): Barley motifs from the Brewers' Company arms. Fig. 7.13 (opposite bottom): Shield from the Brewers' Company coat of arms. Photos: Cynthia Jackson, courtesy of the Brewers' Company.

II. TWO CROWNS OF THE BRODERERS' COMPANY

Date: Late sixteenth century.

Approximate dimensions: Height 7.6 centimetres, diameter 23 centimetres.

Description: Both crowns (distinguished here based on "raised" and "flat" embroidery styles) have a ground of faded red silk velvet and are garnished on the upper and lower edges with a combination of silk and gold filé fringe. The Latin motto of the Broderers' Company, *omnia de super*, is embroidered inside both, with a border above and below (fig. 7.14). The raised crown has four sections of overlapping appliquéd larkspur, rose, pansy, pomegranate, cherry, strawberry, and leaf motifs (fig. 7.15) separated by two dove crests, one empty frame, and a large area where the appliqué is missing (fig. 7.16). The letters F, C, and S are embroidered near the top. For description of the flat crown, see the accompanying article.

Materials: Both crowns use twisted cords in various ply of filé; purl and lizerine in a variety of sizes; plate in various widths and shapes; coloured silks; spangles; pearls (only one left on each); and composite threads of silk and metal twisted cord, and coiled wire around a coloured silk thread. The letters of the motto are appliqués of silk and plate.

Techniques: For the raised crown: Roses in upright brick stitch in shaded silk over rows of plate, with the centre of lengths of raised purl enclosed in an upright looped wire; larkspur, pomegranates, leaves, cherries, pansies are also in upright brick stitch in shaded silk but over rows of filé with added details in filé and purl; strawberries are similar to the roses but have chips of purl oversewn with silk for shading. All are outlined with lizerine or filé and attached to the velvet, overlapping to give a raised appearance. Dove badges use couched filé, upright coiled wire, lizerine, plate, and twisted silk and filé cord. The empty frame is made of individual sections of silver filé couched with coloured silk for shading, outlined with lizerine and appliquéd separately to build the dimension required. Stems and letters are embroidered directly on the velvet. For the flat crown: See pages 173–81 of the accompanying article.

Display and publication: On exhibit at "Works of Art Belonging to the Livery Companies of the City of London," V&A, 1926, no. 519, and at "Exhibition of English Decorative Art at Lansdowne House," Feb. 17–28, 1929, no. 61. For publications, including those associated with these exhibitions, see accompanying article, pages 168–72. Nevinson, 72, plate 5, nos. 8 and 9.

Current location: In storage at Mercers' Hall.

Current use: Not in use.

Figs. 7.14–7.16: Details from Broderers' Company raised crown. Fig. 7.14 (top): Inner border. Fig. 7.15 (middle): Rose, pomegranate, and letter F. Fig. 7.16 (bottom): Empty frame showing areas of missing appliqué. Photos: Cynthia Jackson, courtesy of the Broderers' Company.

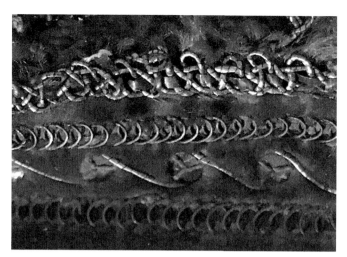

III. FOUR CROWNS OF THE CARPENTERS' COMPANY

A. John Tryll Crown, 1561 (fig. 7.17).
Approximate dimensions: Height 7.75 centimetres, diameter 24 centimetres.
Description: On the outer circumference are two enameled shields of the company arms marked with 1561, two etched gold plates (merchant's mark) flanked by two embroidered flowers (added in the seventeenth century), two enamelled shields of the City of London, two sets of etched gold initials I and T (John Tyrell) separated by a flourish. Bordered top and bottom with two rows of couched loosely twisted filé. Trimmed at the top with red silk and filé fringe. Crimson velvet ground. Cap of red silk (recent addition) with wide silk ribbons attached to the main band at four points, meeting at the top center, with a ribbon rosette at the intersection.
Materials: Pearl purl, lizerine, coloured silks (S-twist), spangles, purls, composite silk and metal twisted cord.
Techniques: Enamelled shields and gold plates are sewn on, flowers and leaves in long and short stitch, outlined with lizerine and stems of pearl purl. Spangles secured with purls. The date 1561 is sewn in pearl purl below the City arms.

B. John Ansell Crown, ca. 1601–6 (fig. 7.18); William Wheatley Crown, ca. 1609–19 (fig. 7.19); Peter Thornton Crown, ca. 1610 (fig. 7.20).
Approximate dimensions: Height 7.5 centimetres, diameter 25 centimetres.
Description: All three are similar, with subtle differences as indicated. Initials (IA, WW, PT) interlaced, vases and foliage, embroidered motifs of the company arms and the City arms (one is marked with 1561 in pearl purl below the City arms) and a maker's mark. Bordered at top and bottom with couched four-ply filé. Crimson velvet ground. Cap of red silk with silk ribbon attached at four points with a ribbon rosette at the intersection.
Materials: Pearl purl, lizerine (there is no lizerine on the Ansell crown), red and black silk, spangles, purls in varying sizes, filé, filé/silk twist.
Techniques: Appliquéd City arms is of filé couched in pairs; sword is of red silk padded satin stitch; cross is of red filé/silk twist outlined in filé cord. Company arms is similar, with chevron in black filé/silk twist and dividers in black silk (fig. 7.21). Appliqués are outlined in pearl purl. Vases worked in pairs or fours of filé in basket stitch (over string) on JA and in pairs on WW (fig. 7.19) and PT (fig. 7.20). Initials are purl over padding. Foliage stems are worked directly on velvet in lizerine outlined in four strands of loosely twisted filé cord. Purls in round, flat wire and check to effect shading on foliage and acorns. Spangles are attached singly and embellished with purl.
Display and publication: On exhibit at "Antiquities and Works of Art" at Ironmongers' Hall, May 1861, and subsequently published in George Russell French, *A Catalogue of the Antiquities and Works of Art Exhibited at Ironmongers' Hall* (London: Harrison and Sons, 1869), 427. On exhibit at "Special Exhibition of Works of Art of the Medieval, Renaissance and More Recent Periods" at the South Kensington Museum, June 1862, no. 5408. On exhibit at "Works of Art Belonging to the Livery Companies of the City of London," V&A, 1926, nos. 415 and 416. Published in Leigh Ashton, "Elizabethan and Jacobean Secular Embroidery," *International Studio* (Aug. 1931): 40. Nevinson, 70, 72, 74, plates 3 and 4, nos. 10, 11, 12, 13.

Current location: In storage at Carpenters' Hall.
Current use: In the yearly ceremony.

Figs. 7.17–7.21: Four crowns of the Carpenters' Company. Fig. 7.17 (top left): The John Tryll Crown. Fig. 7.18 (top right): The John Ansell Crown. Fig. 7.19 (middle left): The William Wheatley Crown. Fig. 7.20 (middle right): The Peter Thornton Crown. Fig. 7.21 (bottom): Detail of embroidered shield of Carpenters' Company arms. Photos: Cynthia Jackson, courtesy of the Carpenters' Company.

IV. GIRDLERS' COMPANY CROWN

Date: 1575.

Approximate dimensions: Height 20 centimetres, diameter 20 centimetres.

Description: "Mr Cuthbert Beeston Master of the said Company of Girdlers the said yere, of his owne free will gave unto the use of the Mr of the said Companye yerely to be elected and chosen forever, one crowne Garlande of blacke velvett imbrodered wth the Ires of his name, a Tonne, and a gridyron of golde, and the girdle wth the buckles of brodered golde lace compassinge the crowne of the said garland" (London, Metropolitan Archives, CLC/L/GB/G/001/MS05817, Aug. 15, 1575, Register of Benefactors, at 20). The Girdlers' Hall was destroyed during the Second World War but the master's crown was rescued and remodelled by Past Master Lionel Straker and has been preserved as a relic of the company.

Materials and techniques: A detailed examination has not yet been performed. However, a close study of the damaged crown in conjunction with earlier photographs should enable the identification of several techniques and types of metal threads.

Display and publication: On exhibit at "Works of Art Belonging to the Livery Companies of the City of London," V&A, 1926, nos. 377, 378, and 379, and subsequently published in William W. Watts, *An Exhibition of Works of Art Belonging to the Livery Companies of the City of London* (London: Victoria and Albert Museum, 1927), plate 70. On exhibit at "Exhibition of English Decorative Art at Lansdowne House," Feb. 17–28, 1929, no. 62. Published in Leigh Ashton, "Elizabethan and Jacobean Secular Embroidery," *International Studio* (Aug. 1931): 40. Published in H. G. Smith, "Emblems of English Tradesmen and Merchants," *CIBA Review 13* (1938): 455. Nevinson, 70, 74, nos. 24, 25, 26, 27.

Current location: In storage at Girdler's Hall.

Current use: The original, damaged master's crown (fig. 7.22) is displayed in a glass case at the yearly ceremony and a replica made in 1941 (fig. 7.23) is used to crown the master.

Figs. 7.22–7.23: Girdlers' Company crown. Fig. 7.22 (opposite top): Original master's crown of the Girdlers' Company, ca. 1575, damaged in 1940. Fig. 7.23 (opposite bottom): Replica of the Girdlers' Company crown, made in 1941. Photos: Cynthia Jackson, courtesy of the Girdlers' Company.

V. FOUR CROWNS OF THE LEATHERSELLERS' COMPANY

Date: 1638.

Approximate dimensions: Height 7.75 centimetres, diameter 24 centimetres.

Description: All four are identical. Dark blue ribbed silk ground. Badge of the company arms in silver-gilt with traces of enamel, embroidered flourishes in silver lizerine, and purl on either side (fig. 7.24). Several silver-gilt badges (fig. 7.25) sewn on including silver rams and goats with gilt horns and hooves, gilt bucks with black horns, silver buck heads with gilt horns, and a badge of the crest. Embroidered borders at top and bottom featuring a central coil of heavy silver wire embellished above and below with finer lizerine and a design of purl outlined in check purl. Powdered amongst the badges with small flowers in purl and lizerine. Dark blue velvet gathered for cao and padded inside for lining. Two embossed black leather cases were made at the same time, each holding two crowns (fig. 7.26).

Materials: Varying sizes of smooth and check purl in silver, lizerine.

Techniques: Enamelled badges are sewn on, lizerine coils and purls embroidered directly on the ground.

Display and publication: On exhibit at "Antiquities and Works of Art" at Ironmongers' Hall, May 1861, and subsequently published in George Russell French, *A Catalogue of the Antiquities and Works of Art Exhibited at Ironmongers' Hall* (London: Harrison and Sons, 1869), 426. On exhibit at "Special Exhibition of Works of Art of the Medieval, Renaissance, and More Recent Periods" at the South Kensington Museum, June 1862, no. 5451. Nevinson, 70, nos. 36, 37, 38, 39.

Current location: Stored in leather cases at Leathersellers' Hall.

Current use: In the yearly ceremony.

Figs. 7.24–7.26: Leathersellers' Company crown. Fig. 7.24 (top): Leathersellers' Company arms. Fig. 7.25 (middle): Silver-gilt badges. Fig. 7.26 (bottom): Leather case for storing two crowns. Photos: Cynthia Jackson, courtesy of the Leathersellers' Company.

VI. PARISH CLERKS' COMPANY CROWN

Date: 1601.

Approximate dimensions: Height 12 centimetres, diameter 18 centimetres.

Description: Velvet ground, original colour undetermined, currently a red/brown. Two appliquéd motifs of the crest from the company arms, a hand holding a song book (fig. 7.27); two appliquéd shields of the company arms (fig. 7.28); stylized sprig design between motifs; narrow border top and bottom. Inside, the date 1601 and the initials HW (approximately 1 centimetre in height) have been embroidered in purl on a ground of the same velvet (fig. 7.29). Silk ribbons (5 centimetres wide) currently a dull pink, are attached approximately 5 centimetres from the top edge at four points, and gathered into a bow at the top center.

Materials: Spangles, purl, plate, lizerine, coloured silks, black (possibly glass) beads; composite threads: coiled wire and coloured silk thread, twisted filé cord.

Techniques: Appliquéd motif of hand consists of laid silk secured with a silk grid for large areas, split stitch for flesh; sleeve area is a combination of coiled wire shaded with coloured silk, outlined with lizerine and twisted filé cord, satin stitch over padding at base of sleeve (fig. 7.30). Appliquéd motif of shield consists of laid silk with grid, folded plate, purl over linen padding on a satin stitch with securing grid, crimped plate, threaded lizerine. Sprig design is embroidered on the velvet ground with purl and cord. Borders are of couched cord and spangles.

Display and publication: On exhibit at "Works of Art Belonging to the Livery Companies of the City of London," V&A, 1926, no. 675. On exhibit at "Exhibition of English Decorative Art at Lansdowne House," Feb. 17–28, 1929, no. 63. On loan to V&A from 1921 and featured prominently on exhibit in the main gallery of Elizabethan and Jacobean embroidery; one was removed to the Museum of London in 1976, and the other remained on exhibit in V&A gallery 53 until 1998 when it was returned to the Parish Clerks' Company. Figures 7.27–7.30 show the crown in the Museum of London. Nevinson, 72, plate 2, nos. 40 and 41.

Current location: On loan (in storage) at the Museum of London with the hearse-cloth of an earlier date. One other identical garland is thought to be in the possession of the Parish Clerks but this has not been confirmed.

Current use: Two replicas were made in 1991 and are used in the yearly ceremony.

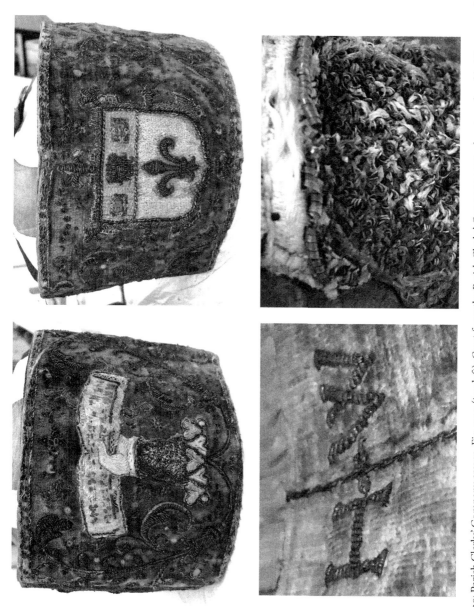

Figs. 7.27–7.30: Parish Clerks' Company crown. Fig. 7.27 (top left): Crest from the Parish Clerks' Company arms, showing a hand holding a song book. Fig. 7.28 (top right): Shield from the Parish Clerks' Company arms. Fig. 7.29 (bottom left): Detail of letters inside the crown. Fig. 7.30 (bottom right): Detail of embroidered sleeve from the hand motif in figure 7.27. Photos: Cynthia Jackson, by kind permission of the Worshipful Company of Parish Clerks.

Recent Books of Interest

Arrayed in Splendour: Art, Fashion, and Textiles in Medieval and Early Modern Europe, edited by Christoph Brachmann (Turnhout, Belgium: Brepols, 2019). ISBN 978-2503579658. 264 pages, 119 illustrations (111 in color).

This collection, based on a series of lectures at the University of North Carolina at Chapel Hill from 2011 to 2013, seeks to elevate the status of historical textiles in the art world to the way they were perceived at their creation—as very expensive, meaningful, and luxurious pieces of art—compared to their typical current ranking as a secondary or low form of art. There is a good deal of research presented in these essays to support this position and hopefully convince nonbelievers to reconsider their outlook. Herein lies the rub. No one needs to convince me that textile art is high art. Whether the arguments would convince a skeptic is not a question I can answer.

The volume consists of an introduction, eight papers, a useful glossary, biographies of the authors, a comprehensive bibliography divided into primary and secondary sources, and an index. The editor's introduction lays out the argument for elevating historical textiles to a higher level of art, describes the recent work being done on the topic, and summarizes each essay.

Six of the papers address periods covered by this journal. Evelin Wetter assesses the significance and use of textiles in ecclesiastical consecration rites from the twelfth through fourteenth centuries, highlighting an extant "nun's crown." Christoph Bachmann covers the funeral garments of Holy Roman Emperor Charles IV (d. 1378) and family members, with particular emphasis on the iconography of the textiles. Lisa Monnas traces the evolution of cloth of gold in England and Italy from 1300 to 1550. Ulinka Rublack explores the use of fashion and color as the language of power and political symbolism at the 1530 Imperial Diet in Augsburg. Roberta Orsi Landini considers Cosimo I de' Medici's use of textiles adorning both person and place in sixteenth-century Florence as a method to balance tradition with wealth and status while underscoring the ruler's power. Katja Schmitz-von Ledebur looks at the role of textiles, specifically tapestries, as exemplars of royal wealth and power, beginning with the Duke of Burgundy and continuing into the nineteenth century.

One should take care to handle this volume carefully if one places a value on one's toes. It is printed on glossy paper in a large format, making it a bit unwieldy as well as unexpectedly heavy. The page size does allow for wonderful color illustrations, many of extant textiles, that are large enough to show detail without the need for a magnifying glass and complement the text well. — *Gina Frasson-Hudson, Kalamazoo, Michigan*

Bonds of Wool: The Pallium and Papal Power in the Middle Ages, by Steven A. Schoenig (Washington, DC: Catholic University of America Press, 2016. ISBN 978-0813229225. 545 pages, 6 black-and-white illustrations.

The pallium is a simple, white, wool stole, worn by popes since antiquity (and up to the present), which, from the sixth century, came to be granted, as a personal gift, to other bishops. Pope Gregory the Great made the pallium the insignia of archbishops in the Church he established in England in 597, and this custom was taken to the Continent by English missionary bishops.

This fascinating book—thoroughly scholarly, yet written in a clear, accessible style, with Latin quotations translated into easily comprehensible English, and chapters divided into bite-size subsections—traces, in three chronological chapters and an epilogue, the development of pallium use into a tool with which the papacy established authority over the Western Church.

In the Carolingian period the act of gift-giving incurred obligation from the recipient; thus a pope's personal gift of a pallium conveyed both prestige and subordination. There developed the custom that the recipient must petition for it within three months of his appointment, and he could not ordain other bishops until the pallium was received. It became the norm for an applicant to submit a profession of faith as well as a "pallium fee," and for the gift to be accompanied by "admonitions," papal advice on the behaviour expected of the recipient. Since each pallium was laid on St. Peter's tomb in Rome before it was conferred, it became a contact relic, and the wearer became holy by association. Various symbolic interpretations arose, ranging from St. Peter's chains, to Christ's yoke, to preaching, with the hanging ends representing the Old and New Testaments. Gradually the pallium transformed from a mark of distinction to a badge of office.

The period 882–1046 saw pallium-granting become more routine, with some popes neglecting the matter and rarely using their right to withdraw the gift. Others, however, developed its use, encouraging personal reception of it, and increasing the occasions on which it might be worn. Occasionally popes gave away their personal pallium as a mark of special favour.

The Reform era of 1046–1119 brought new requirements of recipients as the pallium was used to target specific issues and increase papal influence. Steven Schoenig writes, "The pallium deserved to be recognized alongside the rest of the machinery of Roman centralization, such as legates, synods, canon law, *ad limina* visits, and curial bureaucracy." The epilogue (covering ca. 1140–ca. 1271) traces the systematization of ecclesiastical law on the pallium and its use and meaning, from what had been individual papal pronouncements over the centuries.

Very few medieval pallia survive, because they were buried with their owners. Schoenig works from documentary evidence, imaginatively bringing alive the personalities of the medieval men involved in pallium transactions: Hincmar of Rhiems, constantly pushing for greater authority but professing humility when challenged by a pope; Argrim, deprived of an archbishopric but granted a bishopric and the consolation of a pallium; the wretched Aelfsige of Canterbury, who died of cold crossing the Alps on his journey to collect his pallium; and many more.

It was inspirational to approach the history of the medieval Western Church through this simple wool vestment, and Schoenig succeeds magnificently. — *Gale R. Owen-Crocker, University of Manchester*

The Burial Dress of the Rus' in the Upper Volga Region (Late 10th–13th Centuries), by Iuliia Stepanova (Leiden, Netherlands: Brill, 2017). ISBN 978-9004314658. 393 pages, 205 illustrations (11 in color).

Stepanova's comprehensive study is based on collections of archaeological textiles, jewellery, and adornment artefacts for men and women in the Tver State Historical Museum and the Archaeological Museum of Tver State University. Roughly half the book comprises the introduction, text catalogue, and interpretation; a quarter is images; and the last quarter is appendices of tabulated finds information, bibliography, and geographical and subject indices. Stepanova provides a clear introduction to the geographical and cultural background of the Upper Volga region, and a useful methodological outline of the issues around non-survival of early dress and textiles and the conditions of archaeological textiles. The information is organised and accessible, and carefully documents the parameters and limitations of the research project.

Most of the textile finds are decayed and fragmentary and listed in the tables along with remains of leather, birch bark, and felt. Dye analysis has been undertaken where possible. The book's primary focus is therefore on more durable headdress ornaments and jewellery, including rings, bracelets, neck rings, pendants, buckles, knives, brooches and fasteners, chains, and diverse sewn-on metal ornamentation. Other finds include many beads of glass, amber, precious stones, and metals. One of the book's strengths is its depiction of these finds' positions on 185 individual drawn figures, allowing quick visual understanding, plus an idea of how the vanished clothing may have appeared. This is based on comparative research into depictions of dress and clothing types surviving in Russian ethnographic dress, such as the sarafan. Stepanova also outlines the influence on Upper Volga dress from neighbouring ethnic groups, including the Balts, Eastern Slavs, and Finno-Ugrics, giving scope for more comparative work.

Other strengths are the history of Russian archaeological approaches outlined in the introduction, valuable as a case study of how the field developed. The survey also aids an understanding of the specific nature of the partiality of each find, and how the frequently patchy contextual information was recorded. For anyone interested in medieval Eastern European dress, the book is a valuable introduction in English to the Russian secondary literature on many related areas. Other details are of relevance to larger European studies of burial, archaeological and ethnographic dress, and cultural practices around garment construction. The idea of "reconstructing" dress is used throughout: as the conceptual process of recording an ensemble in drawings, and the physical process of sewing garments after study of the originals. The visual depiction of the material is uneven, however, and the few photographs of the actual artefacts very small, and printed in grainy black and white. — *Hilary Davidson, La Trobe University, Melbourne*

The Corporeality of Clothing in Medieval Literature: Cognition, Kinesis, and the Sacred, by Sarah Brazil (Kalamazoo, MI: Medieval Institute Publications: 2018). ISBN 978-1580443579. 174 pages, 7 illustrations (5 in color).

Sarah Brazil's goal is to use body-related theoretical underpinnings to "interrogat[e] Christian identity" in medieval literature and drama. Unfortunately, this goal is only one of far too many, and her explanations of her theoretical tools are obscure at best, resulting in a book which is deeply flawed.

In addition to exploring medieval Christian identity, another aim of the book is to provide "new ways of thinking" about objects in narrative, finding "new ways of answering the questions" which other scholars have asked. She is particularly concerned that the body in medieval literature has not been adequately studied—a position with which not everyone would agree—and wants to reconsider "how cloth and body relate to each other in narrative," using the concepts of "embodied cognition" and "kinetic knowledge," i.e., the sense memories which we as readers bring to a work. Her analytic work with these tools is effective; her theoretical explanation is not. (For readers interested in these ideas, the article by Guillemette Bolens and Brazil in *A Cultural History of Dress and Fashion in the Medieval Age* expresses them more clearly, and Monica Wright's article in the same volume gives a cogent and succinct summary of similar theories.)

Brazil also aims "to provide a perspective on the study of clothing as a literary affordance," but her theoretical explanation of this is murky. "Affordances," a term which is popular in industrial design, are opportunities for action, the potential uses and functions an object can provide; how clothing can be seen as an affordance—one "that can move up to the level of concept"—remains unexplained.

Once past the introduction, Brazil is more successful. Three of the four chapters are devoted to specifically religious narrative, including literary works, theological exegeses, and drama. They cover the uses of clothing to symbolize the Fall in medieval Genesis retellings; graveclothes, particularly in Resurrection narratives; and performances of the raising of Lazarus, including the problem of getting him out of his graveclothes on stage. The final chapter is on the use of shoes as metaphor, particularly in a religious context. Here again, the author has widened her scope to the point of confusion: The various types of literature don't necessarily fit together very well, and the attempt to include the physical logistics of dramatic performance is particularly jarring. Nonetheless, by exploring these works through the prism of the bodily experience of clothing, Brazil does supply new and interesting insights into meaning and belief. — *Laurel Wilson, Fordham University*

Decoding the Bayeux Tapestry: The Secrets of History's Most Famous Embroidery Hidden in Plain Sight, by Arthur C. Wright (Barnsley, UK: Frontline, 2019). ISBN 978-1526741103. 175 pages, 53 illustrations (most in colour).

The first part of this book, colloquially written, peppered with rhetorical questions, claims to reinterpret the Bayeux Tapestry through the commentary of its borders. There are reputable scholars who claim the borders are mere decoration. I am not one of them, and had hopes that this book might indeed unravel some mysteries. However, the author rather explains the borders in relation to his interpretation of the story; is inconsistent, identifying birds as "ill-omened" because they are black (actually dark blue), while identifying others as the caladrius, despite the fact that the latter were white and the birds on the Tapestry are not; and ignored existing scholarship on the fables, reidentifying the wolf-and-lamb and pregnant bitch scenes as a fox-and-lion and animals hiding in a cave. Ignorance is betrayed on the first page, when the Tapestry is said to consist of eight pieces; the fact that there are nine was published in 2004. The author does not know about, or dismisses, the extensive evidence for the Tapestry's borrowing from Anglo-Saxon manuscripts, misspelling the Cædmon manuscript when he does mention it, and asserting "No one in 1066 could imagine or draw an outline of the British Isles" when they are depicted on the earlier world map in the British Library's MS Cotton Tiberius B.v. He introduces new animals into the Tapestry's bestiary—flamingos, parandrus, and pard—and, on the grounds that it is "striped and not plain or spotted," a tiger, even though the creature is not striped, but embroidered in triangles. The image of Mont Saint-Michel, which other writers have found effective, if not architecturally accurate, is curiously dismissed as "an arcaded and turreted charpoy on a molehill Ararat," while the Tapestry's castles are considered authentic, but English, rather than continental. He relocates the Battle of Hastings to Calbec Hill, relating the details of the battle to the geography.

The second part of the book is different in content and style. "The Landscape of Invasion" gives an account of the area round Pevensey Lagoon, where the Normans landed. The assertion that a duck in the Tapestry's border "tells us of the general diversity of fish and fowl to be found in such an ecosphere—a gastronomic paradise" surely overstates the case. "The Accuracy of Weapons and Armour" is interesting (the author is a military historian), though the passage on crossbows is incongruous in a book about the Bayeux Tapestry, which does not depict them.

The author throws out some interesting ideas. They include the possibility that rivals for the throne may have been concerned about Queen Edith inheriting and remarrying; but to suggest that this is indicated by "plotting vultures at Bosham" is absurd. The thought that Harold might have set out to visit Eustace of Boulogne (rather than William of Normandy) is also intriguing, but again, not supported in any way by the Tapestry. I welcome the identification of Guy's costume as "squamatid armour," though the author identifies the wearer, first, as possibly "one of Odo's bodyguards" and later as "one of Guy's men" when the inscription indicates that it is Guy himself. Odo's armour, twice, is identified as lamellar, with which I agree, but the possibility that this might be copied from a model is not considered.

The final chapter "Who Embroidered the Tapestry and How" is the least convincing. The author assumes the relatively simple stitch was embroidered by secular men, who had previously experienced warfare, navigation, building, and other practical matters, and that they embroidered authentic images of these things directly onto the cloth without any underdrawing. When he suggests the colour choices are the result of colour blindness due to head injury in battle, the argument reaches the point of absurdity.

The plates in the book do not bear the authorisation of the city of Bayeux (the source is not given), and most of them have been garishly retouched. Like the whole book, this is a very individual "take" on the Bayeux Tapestry. — *Gale R. Owen-Crocker, University of Manchester*

The English Woollen Industry, c. 1200–c. 1560, by John Oldland (London: Routledge, 2019). ISBN 9780367179748. 357 pages.

Oldland's purpose in writing this book is to, as he puts it, "explain [the] remarkable ascent in the importance of cloth to the English economy." Beginning with what he describes as its "uncertain beginnings" in the thirteenth century, when England was primarily an exporter of wool rather than cloth, he traces the rise of the English cloth industry all the way to its sixteenth-century domination of the European cloth markets. He is particularly interested in what he sees as a period of rapid growth from 1450 to 1550. In opposition to the many historians who believe that the English economy declined during exactly that period, Oldland argues that the economy was growing, in part because of a dramatic rise in both sheep numbers and cloth production.

Oldland was a student of the late John Munro, and, as might be expected, he has included a great deal of data, some of it firm and some of it speculative; as he nicely puts it, some of it had to be "tickled from the records," particularly his projections of the number of sheep. But economic historians are not the only ones who will be interested in this book. Anyone interested in any aspect of cloth and clothing of this period will find something engaging, whether it be a chronological history of the cloth trade in England and its geographical distribution from the thirteenth century on, a detailed examination of changes in attitudes toward dress and its effect on cloth, or a discussion of the social place of clothiers in the fifteenth and sixteenth centuries.

Most compelling to me were the detailed technical data about different types of cloth and how they changed over time. Oldland is very conscious, as someone who formerly owned a cloth business, of the need to keep changing and adapting as tastes change. He sees the ability to adapt as particularly important in an industry in which "product and market are always in flux," as he says—in other words, an industry governed by fashion—and makes a compelling case for the idea that this is one of the factors which accounts for the overwhelming success of the English cloth industry. — *Laurel Wilson, Fordham University*

Grandes Cornes et Hauts Atours: Le Hennin et la Mode au Moyen Âge, by Alix Durantou (Paris: École du Louvre, 2019). ISBN 978-2711863334. 168 pages, 182 illustrations (27 in color).

The headdress known as the *hennin*—or, more accurately, *atour*—is the most emblematic female accessory of the late medieval period. The conical and horned headdresses popularized in fifteenth-century Flemish paintings are now the subject of a comprehensive book based on an École du Louvre dissertation. The volume is richly illustrated, mainly with paintings and illuminations, and contains a glossary and an index. It appears to be a highly useful text when it comes to the headdress itself. It is interesting that the author goes back to the origins of the much misused term *hennin* and studies the history of this terminology.

She also mentions the possible origins of the headdress, some of her hypotheses being rather surprising. As with some French studies about medieval textiles, Durantou's statements about costume from before the mid-fourteenth century seem very questionable. The same is true when it comes to medieval iconography. And it seems obvious that some aspects she points out as she looks at the origins of the *atour* would have deserved better comparisons, in quantity and quality, with thirteenth-century fashion. The book unfortunately conveys the idea, often found in French publications, that there was no fashion before the fourteenth century, despite the inclusion of Sarah-Grace Heller's *Fashion in Medieval France* (which argues otherwise) in the bibliography. Moreover, this bibliography leaves out some major publications in English which were written before 2012, the year Durantou presented her dissertation.

Apart from these disputable angles, the analysis of the *atour* in the fifteenth century is quite complete, and fascinating. The iconographical approach is cautious and avoids dangerous literal readings of medieval images. Durantou quotes a lot of medieval texts, some of them famous, others less so, but always in a very accurate way. She presents the social, economic, cultural, artistic, and religious contexts of the *atours* and the horned headdresses, leading to other reflections on the meanings of head ornamentation in the Middle Ages.

Durantou's book provides a comprehensive analysis of a fashion phenomenon and definitely will be a useful resource for scholars of medieval French as well as people interested in Burgundian fashion. (Readers should be aware not only that the book is written in French, but also that quotations from French medieval texts are not translated into contemporary French.) — *Tina Anderlini, Centre d'Etudes Supérieures de Civilisation Médiévale de Poitiers*

The Lost Art of the Anglo-Saxon World: The Sacred and Secular Power of Embroidery, by Alexandra Lester-Makin (Oxford: Oxbow, 2019). ISBN 978-1789251449. 243 pages, 126 illustrations (32 in color).

As the title says, the subject of this book is largely "lost." Organic materials survive only in limited archaeological contexts, textile remains are rare, and since embroidery would have been applied to a minority of textiles it is not surprising we have so few surviving examples from the Anglo-Saxon world. Lester-Makin has assembled the known fragments and the few larger pieces and has produced a fascinating study. The great strength of the book is her practical experience and knowledge of embroidery. Her previous studies have shown how close attention to the details of stitches can help unravel the process of production and demonstrate the skills of early medieval needlewomen. Their stitches were so small and so well worked it is difficult to imagine how they managed it without good lights and magnifying glasses.

Some of the fragments yield new information; for example, the pieces from Kempston from a possibly Christian relic box in a seventh-century grave have a zoomorphic design, which is less surprising than it might seem, given the appearance of such images on a gold cross from the Staffordshire hoard. The few larger pieces also yield new information. The Bayeux tapestry—actually an embroidery—will be known to most readers, but Makin's analysis tells us things we did not know about the organisation of its manufacture. The account of the problems of accessing the finds is a case study in modern obstacles to study of museum items: "closed for reconstruction"; restoration obscuring detail; worst of all, "lost."

The catalogue, with associated tables, is clear and useful, as are the diagrams of embroidery stitches.

There are weaknesses. The book shows traces of its origin as a thesis in the pie charts in chapter 2, which (as the author admits) are not as informative as they appear, given the limited number of works to be analysed. Her knowledge of archaeological and historical contexts is less extensive than of embroidery, and some of her summary statements could be queried. Comparative discussion of other early medieval embroidery is lacking. For example, there is no mention of the embroidered tunic attributed to Balthild. This was presumably made at Chelles in France, where it still is, but some of the nuns, including Balthild herself, came from England, so there was likely to have been interchange of ideas in embroidery as in other things. There is no reference to the work of Anna Muthesius on Byzantine silk, which includes papers specifically on the textiles from Cuthbert's tomb, not only the stole and maniple which are part of Lester-Makin's data, but also other pieces of silk of different dates and origins.

But overall this is a welcome account of a little-studied subject, based on the author's firsthand practical knowledge and providing an excellent basis for future research. — *Catherine Hills, University of Cambridge*

The Oseberg Tapestries, by Marianne Vedeler (Oslo: Scandinavian Academic Press, 2019). ISBN 978-8230402436. 144 pages, 78 illustrations (50 in color).

Marianne Vedeler presents fifteen short chapters providing an accessible introduction to the Oseberg tapestries and their context. The grave of two women from about 834, including many textile fragments, was excavated in 1904, but the official report on the textiles was not published until 2006. Vedeler's analysis focuses on the narrative function of the tapestry fragments, and discussion of their structure and production is limited. The English-language edition is generally clean, but the text includes occasional errors and ambiguities where specificity was lost in translation from the original Norwegian.

Chapters in the book are very short, which limits the depth provided on any given topic. "Women's and Men's Clothing in the Tapestries" assesses the depiction of clothing, particularly its prominent role in denoting the gender of the humanoid images, even when other attributes, such as weaponry, are present. In "The Beast Man," the many images of human-animal hybrids are related to figures in Norse legends, including berserkers, Valkyries, and magical practitioners. In "The Hanged Men's Tree," Vedeler provides a helpful analysis of the narrowest and least well-known tapestry, which retains tablet weaving on both edges and apparently survives at its full width of only 16 centimeters. This fragment depicts a large central tree filled with the bodies of hanged men and surrounded by female figures (many carrying crossed rods), horses, and other beasts, which she suggests could be related to reports of human sacrifice and the practice of *seiðr*, a Norse form of shamanism.

In addition to some of the familiar illustrations by Sofie Krafft, the book includes many new or previously difficult-to-obtain photos and illustrations. The photos and schematics of the 1904 dig provide information about the placement of the tapestries in the grave. While the original colors have almost entirely disappeared from the textiles, new detailed color photos of the tapestries provide a clear view of their motifs and techniques. Digital reconstructions of tapestry segments by Stig Saxegaard are striking to look at, but required some speculation to produce. Further, it is disappointing that the colors chosen are all invented; the illustrator has made no attempt to recreate the original colors, even where reliable evidence of them exists.

Despite referencing unpublished dig diaries and original reports that are not generally available, the book does not contain much original textual content for readers already familiar with the previously published literature on the Oseberg textiles and Norse legends. However, the inclusion of rare historical images and especially the new photographs of the tapestries are extremely useful to any study of these artifacts. — *Jean Kveberg, Madison, Wisconsin*

The Right to Dress: Sumptuary Laws in a Global Perspective, c. 1200–1800, edited by Giorgio Riello and Ulinka Rublack (Cambridge: Cambridge University Press, 2019). ISBN 978-1108469272. 523 pages, 53 black-and-white illustrations.

Sumptuary laws are a tantalizing source for the social context of dress and lexicon of luxury products. Arching histories of the legislation have been written, but have often failed to account for the variability of the laws, which defy organization into a precise chronological pattern, as the editors note. Questions inevitably persist. What implicit purposes did these laws serve? Were they enforced? What real impact did they have? While laws of England, France, and Italy have received attention, for other polities little has been published or made available in English. This volume is tremendously exciting because it makes a wealth of comparative information accessible. Diachronic descriptive essays are offered by historians specializing in the cultures of Germany, the Low Countries, Scotland and England, Sweden, the Swiss Confederation, Italian cities such as Padova and Milan, Castile, Russia, China, Japan, the West African kingdoms of Benin and Dahomey, the Ottoman empire, Portugal and its colonies, colonial Spanish America, North America and the Caribbean, and the Dutch East India Company's Indonesian capital of Batavia. Rather than composing a metanarrative of the evolution of global sumptuary legislation themselves, the editors chose to ask specialists to present overviews grounded in thoroughgoing knowledge of each culture, thus inviting a nuanced picture. It is remarkable that such significant amounts of dress regulation were produced in all these societies in this period, and moreover that it all diminished by around 1793, when French revolutionaries decreed all citizens should have "the right to dress" freely, to which the title alludes. Riello and Rublack call the sumptuary law project utopic, relying on an idea of "past times when hierarchies had existed untouched and unchallenged."

The volume will most interest scholars of the Early Modern period, when regulations multiplied a hundredfold and enumerated offending accessories. While the collection purportedly ranges from 1200 to 1800, discussions prior to the fifteenth century are scant. Amanda Wunder's chapter on Spain examines Alfonso X of Castile's decrees of 1258 that limited cloth colors by courtly vocation, and then later garments self-imposed or forced as penitence during the Inquisition. BuYen Chen's fascinating chapter on Ming China opens with the conqueror Zhu Yuanzhang's outlawing of Mongol dress in favor of a radical shift to the scholarly reconstruction of ancient Chinese attire. Nonetheless, medievalist readers will find this an essential tool for understanding the longer global history of fashion. — *Sarah-Grace Heller, Ohio State University*

The Treasure of Münster: Precious Reliquaries and Works of Art from the Domkammer (Der Schatz von Münster: Wertvolle Reliquiare und Kunstwerke aus der Domkammer), edited by Udo Grote (Münster, Germany: Aschendorff, 2019). ISBN 978-3402133996. 280 pages, numerous illustrations (nearly all in colour).

The collection of treasures in the Cathedral of St. Paul in Münster is one of the most important in Germany. This volume opens with a series of introductory essays on the nature of a cathedral treasure, treasuries as representations of power, treasure of the region, the history of the Münster Cathedral treasure, and the textiles. The catalogue itself is divided into reliquaries (which were eventually displayed on the High Altar installed in 1662); textiles; sculptures from the rood screen; and "uniques"—individual items which include a rare and beautiful gaming table dating to ca. 1500–30, and some pieces of ecclesiastical jewellery: a silver morse (a brooch for securing a cope), dated to 1556, and a gold and silver pectoral cross and an episcopal ring, both dating to the mid-seventeenth century.

The textiles—here called "Paraments," which word is defined as "all textile objects that are part of the furnishings of the church space, the decoration of the reliquaries, and the shaping/design of the liturgy"—are introduced in an essay by Gudrun Stracke-Sporbeck and described by the same author, accompanied by striking colour photographs.

The first two items are very unusual. A large fragment (15 by 57 centimetres) of tapestry-woven textile, employing silk and gilded leather thread, is dated to the late eleventh or early twelfth century and attributed to either the royal workshops of Palermo or a Spanish-Moorish workshop. The textile, which bears a striking pattern of confronted monsters (here identified as chimeras), flanked by human-like figures, in one case a human-bird hybrid, enclosed by snakes and bordered by birds, has been compared to the internal border of the mantle of Roger II of Sicily (ca. 1130). The cloth had been cut and used as the lining of a relic casket, and was recovered in the nineteenth century. The casket is now lost.

The second item is a pannisellus, an umbrella-like appendage to an episcopal crosier of painted, partly gilded ivory. The whole ensemble is attributed to Perugia and dated ca. 1260–80. The pannisellus is said to be of linen cambric, with red silk embroidery, overlaid with a lattice of braided cords knotted round "formerly gold pearls" [beads?] and finished with green silk tassels. Pannisella are said to have been employed from the eleventh to the seventeenth centuries, becoming widespread from the late thirteenth.

The other textiles catalogued, all sumptuous, consist of eight chasubles ranging in date from the fourteenth to the eighteenth centuries, an early-sixteenth-century cope, two sixteenth-century dalmatics (with orphreys that include male saints "in contemporary imaginative headgear"), and an embroidered altar frontal, Italian, of the late seventeenth to early eighteenth century.

The whole book is bilingual, German/English. It includes a glossary of terms and a bibliography. — *Gale R. Owen-Crocker, University of Manchester*

ALSO PUBLISHED

Refashioning Medieval and Early Modern Dress: A Tribute to Robin Netherton, edited by Gale R. Owen-Crocker and Maren Clegg Hyer (Woodbridge, UK: Boydell, 2019). ISBN 978-1783274741. 293 pages, 46 illustrations (32 in color).

Author Index, Volumes 1–15

Ward, Susan Leibacher. "Saints in Split Stitch: Representations of Saints in *Opus Anglicanum* Vestments," vol. 3 (2007).

Warr, Cordelia. "The Devil on My Tail: Clothing and Visual Culture in the Camposanto *Last Judgment*," vol. 11 (2015).

Wendelken, Rebecca Woodward. "Wefts and Worms: The Spread of Sericulture and Silk Weaving in the West before 1300," vol. 10 (2014).

Whitfield, Niamh. "Dress and Accessories in the Early Irish Tale 'The Wooing Of Becfhola,'" vol. 2 (2006).

Wild, Benjamin L. "The Empress's New Clothes: A *Rotulus Pannorum* of Isabella, Sister of King Henry III, Bride of Emperor Frederick II," vol. 7 (2011).

Williams, Patricia. "Dress and Dignity in the *Mabinogion*," vol. 8 (2012).

Wright, Monica L. "'De Fil d'Or et de Soie': Making Textiles in Twelfth-Century French Romance," vol. 2 (2006); "The *Bliaut*: An Examination of the Evidence in French Literary Sources," vol. 14 (2018).

Zanchi, Anna. "'Melius Abundare Quam Deficere': Scarlet Clothing in *Laxdœla Saga* and *Njáls Saga*," vol. 4 (2008).

Zumbuhl, Mark. "Clothing as Currency in Pre-Norman Ireland?" vol. 9 (2013).